Killing Crazy Horse

Killing Crazy Horse

THE MERCILESS INDIAN WARS IN AMERICA

BILL O'REILLY

AND

MARTIN DUGARD

ST. MARTIN'S
GRIFFIN
NEW YORK

Published in the United States by St. Martin's Griffin, an imprint of
St. Martin's Publishing Group

KILLING CRAZY HORSE. Copyright © 2020 by Bill O'Reilly and Martin Dugard.
All rights reserved. Printed in the United States of America. For information,
address St. Martin's Publishing Group, 120 Broadway, New York, NY 10271.

www.stmartins.com

Designed by Meryl Sussman Levavi

Library of Congress Control Number: 2020931465

ISBN 978-1-627-79704-7 (hardcover)
ISBN 978-1-627-79703-0 (ebook)
ISBN 978-1-250-78221-2 (trade paperback)

Our books may be purchased in bulk for promotional, educational, or business
use. Please contact your local bookseller or the Macmillan Corporate and
Premium Sales Department at 1-800-221-7945, extension 5442, or by email
at MacmillanSpecialMarkets@macmillan.com.

First published in the United States by Henry Holt and Company

First St. Martin's Griffin Edition: 2022

10 9 8 7 6 5 4 3 2 1

This book is dedicated to Makeda Wubneh—
my assistant for twenty-seven years.
There is no finer human being around.

AUTHORS' NOTE

Writing a book of history about Native Americans is an arduous task. There were literally thousands of tribes throughout North America, more than five hundred of which still exist. In this book, we use the terms *Indians* and *Native Americans* interchangeably, as has been done historically. We realize each tribe is unique and has its own culture. We are respectful of that and have tried to deal with it accurately.

KILLING CRAZY HORSE

Legend

UNITED STATES		INDIANS
	Movement	
	Highlighted movement	
	Retreat	
	Cavalry/ horsemen warriors	
	Infantry/ foot warriors	
	Artillery	
	Wagons	
	Encampment/ village	

MILITARY FEATURES

 Clash/event

✕ Previous engagement

PHYSICAL FEATURES

○ City/town

□ Feature

⊐⊏ Bridge

⌣ Pass

⊨ Fort

✗ Mines

⛰ Mountain

〰 Road

╱ River

▦ Forest

⌁ Terrain

⣿ Wetlands

▢ Water

Prologue

AUGUST 30, 1813
FORT MIMS, ALABAMA
11:00 A.M.

The Creek nation is out for blood.

The red-painted bodies of hundreds of warriors are pressed into the earth, awaiting the signal to attack. These men have hidden since sunrise, intending to kill every person they can. They conceal themselves in a valley four hundred yards outside the new log walls surrounding the sprawling plantation of Samuel Mims. More than six hundred men, women, and children live inside the month-old fort located thirty-five miles north of Mobile. They are comprised of white settlers, Negro slaves, and mixed-race Indians who have adopted white ways. Almost all of them have just hours to live.

The Indian force numbers somewhere between seven hundred and a thousand. Some are not Native American at all but African slaves who have escaped and joined the Creek nation. The warriors are naked, save for a loincloth, to which a red-painted cow's tail has been tied at the back.* Some wear an owl feather, believing it will

---

* The cow tail symbolized the Creek rebellion against the ways of the white settlers. Prior to the conflict, raids to steal cattle were considered a method of training young warriors for actual warfare. Cutting off a stolen cow's tail was the same as taking a scalp. In prior centuries it was customary to wear a buffalo tail, but that animal was hunted to extinction in the Southeast by the end of the eighteenth century, leading to the adoption of the cow's tail.

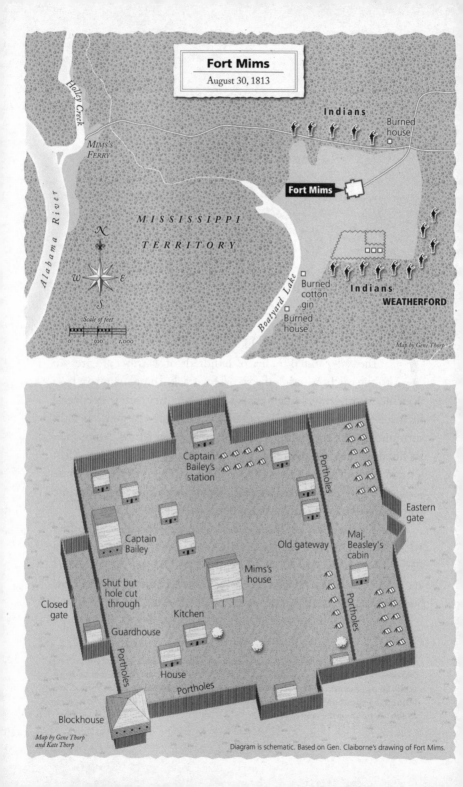

Fort Mims
August 30, 1813

Holley Creek

MIMS'S FERRY

Alabama River

MISSISSIPPI TERRITORY

N W E S

Scale of feet
0   500   1,000

Indians

Burned house

Fort Mims

Boatyard Lake

Burned cotton gin

Burned house

Indians

WEATHERFORD

Map by Gene Thorp

Captain Bailey's station

Portholes

Eastern gate

Captain Bailey

Old gateway

Maj. Beasley's cabin

Mims's house

Shut but hole cut through

Closed gate

Kitchen

Portholes

Guardhouse

Portholes

House

Portholes

Blockhouse

Map by Gene Thorp and Kate Thorp

Diagram is schematic. Based on Gen. Claiborne's drawing of Fort Mims.

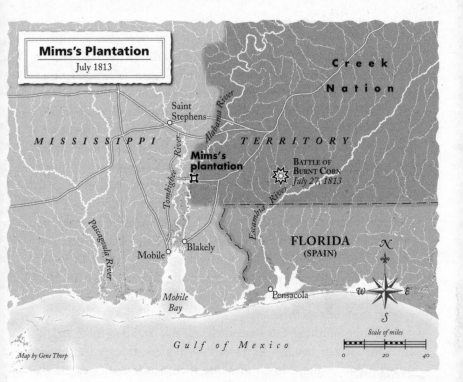

Mims's Plantation
July 1813

C r e e k   N a t i o n

Saint Stephens

MISSISSIPPI   *T E R R I T O R Y*

Mims's plantation

BATTLE OF
BURNT CORN
July 27, 1813

Alabama River

Tombigbee River

Escambia River

Pascagoula River

FLORIDA
(SPAIN)

N

Mobile   ○ Blakely

W   E

S

Mobile Bay

Pensacola

Gulf of Mexico

Scale of miles

0   20   40

Map by Gene Thorp

House

House

Mims's house

Kitchen

House

Map by Gene Thorp and Kate Thorp

Diagram is schematic. Based on Gen. Claiborne's drawing of Fort Mims.

give them improved vision. Each warrior has forced himself to drink a strong emetic that has made him vomit—again, in the belief that this will prevent infection if he is stabbed or shot.

Every fighter is armed with a flintlock rifle, as well as a bow and iron-tipped arrows. Their most lethal killing weapon is a two-foot-long war stick carved from dense wood. Almost every man carries one. They have trained countless hours with these war clubs and wield their cudgels with the same finesse shown by master swordsmen. Like the Indians' torsos, each club is painted red.

The Creek warriors have waited days and marched in complete stealth for miles, determined to remain unseen and attack with complete surprise. They know the precise moment at which they will attack. They have studied the routines of the fort and are aware that the settlers gather each day for a noon meal. A dinner bell is the signal to come together.

On this morning, the dinner bell will also be the signal to attack.

The Creeks struggle to remain motionless. Insects crawl over their prone bodies. Mosquitoes bite their hands and faces. Beads of sweat sting their eyes as the day grows warmer and the air more humid. The Creeks' intent is murder. However, their ultimate goal is survival—for they believe that only a mass slaughter will prevent intruders from stealing the Creek ancestral homeland.

Just one more hour until the lunch bell clangs.

Inside Fort Mims, a slave belonging to Josiah Fletcher is being tied to the whipping post. He is stripped to the waist. There is no shade here in the center of the fort, and sweat runs down the man's bare flesh. He hears the murmurs of the crowd gathering in a circle around the pole, eager to witness his suffering. The slave presses his body into the rough wood, his torso tensed to absorb one hundred lashes.

Incredibly, the slave's only crime is telling the truth. Yesterday, while working outside the walls, he saw some Creek warriors gathering in the forest. But when he raced back inside to sound a warning, the slave was accused of lying and spreading fear. In the eyes of Fort Mims's military leadership, this is a crime that must be punished.

Few men can survive a hundred lashes. The slave is sure he will die on this spot, bound helplessly to this pole.

The Creek Indians massacring the inhabitants of Fort Mims, Alabama, 1813

Major Daniel Beasley of the Mississippi Volunteers holds the whip, eager to administer the lash. Beasley is forty-five and just shy of six feet tall. Women normally consider him attractive, but this morning Beasley's face is red and puffy, his eyes bloodshot. Even after a stiff drink of whiskey to start the day, Beasley's head throbs from a long night of sucking down alcohol from the fresh barrel that arrived yesterday. It is the job of the major and his 170 militiamen to protect those seeking refuge in Fort Mims. There have been rumors of Indian sightings for more than two weeks. Major Beasley and his men responded immediately in the beginning, but as day after day passed without an attack, he came to no longer consider those warnings credible. The major is so sure the slave is lying about the Indians that he has not even bothered to send his men out into the forest to investigate.

Yet even as the young black man is bound to the post, there is evidence he *is* telling the truth.

Just an hour ago, a local farmer galloped his horse into the fort, also warning that Creek warriors were nearby. Jim Cornells specifically asked to speak with Major Beasley, then informed him that he had personally seen Indians in the forest.

The twenty-five-year-old Cornells is himself of mixed race, the son of a young Indian woman and a British father. His farm was recently burned to the ground by a group of Creek warriors nicknamed the "Red Sticks"—so called for the brightly painted color of their war weapons. Cornells suffers from a disfigurement known as yaws, common to this humid climate. His condition leaves his face covered with lesions and the skin stretched back on his head, making it difficult for him to speak clearly. This combination of heritage and horrible disfigurement makes Cornells's very presence a source of discomfort to Beasley.

"You've only seen a gang of red cattle," the major insists, his speech so thick that Cornells will later insist Beasley is drunk.

"Those red cattle will give you one hell of a kick before night," Cornells responds, still astride his horse.

An enraged Beasley orders his men to arrest the farmer, but Cornells is too fast. He quickly gallops from the fort, straight into the waiting Creek army.

Watching from a hiding place in the woods, the Creek leader, William Weatherford, sees Cornells race away from the fort. Weatherford is in his mid-thirties. He is six foot two and known for his handsome looks, extreme bravery, and dark black eyes. Killing the farmer would spoil the element of surprise, so the warrior leader lets him pass. Yet as the rider goes by, Weatherford notices that no one has bothered to close the east gate to Fort Mims. He is stunned at this incredible lapse in security.

William Weatherford's mother is from a prominent branch of the Creek nation known as the Wind Clan, while his father was a Scottish plantation owner named Charles Weatherford who had a reputation for debauchery. However, the Creeks believe that the line of descent goes through the maternal side. Thus, Weatherford's loyalty belongs not to his European ancestors but to his Native American brothers and sisters. This devotion is so strong that the fair-skinned Weatherford, who is just one-eighth Creek, with light

General Andrew Jackson and Creek chief Red Eagle
after the Battle of Horseshoe Bend, March 27, 1814

brown hair, likes to proclaim that he has no white blood at all in his veins.

Inside the fort, another mixed-blood Creek named Richard Dixon Bailey is actually in charge of security. Like Weatherford's, Bailey's mother also hails from the Wind Clan. Just a few weeks ago, at a conflict known as the Battle of Burnt Corn, a group of warriors smuggling arms north from Florida was ambushed by a contingent of Mississippi Militia. The Creek rallied after the initial surprise and the battle ended in a draw. But spotted among the militia was Dixon Bailey, leading the attack against his own flesh and blood. In his youth, the squat and thickset Bailey was sent off to Philadelphia to be educated and has completely absorbed the life of the white man.

The United States of America
1813

Lake Superior

CANADA
(U.K.)

Quebec

NORTHWEST
TERRITORY

Lake Huron

Montreal

MAINE
(MASS.)

Lake Michigan

MICHIGAN
TERRITORY

**BATTLE OF
THE THAMES**
Oct. 5, 1813

Lake Ontario

NEW
YORK

VT.

Portland

N.H.

Detroit

Lake Erie

BOSTON

MASS.

ILLINOIS
TERRITORY

**BATTLE OF
TIPPECANOE**
Nov. 7, 1811

INDIANA
TERRITORY

Pittsburgh

PENNSYLVANIA

New Haven

CT.

R.I.

Newport

MISSOURI
TERRITORY

OHIO

New York

**MASSACRE OF
PEQUOT TRIBE**
May 26, 1637

Missouri River

Ohio River

Philadelphia

N.J.

Baltimore

DEL.

Washington

MD.

KENTUCKY

VIRGINIA

**VIRGINIA
COLONY
MASSACRE**
Mar. 22, 1622

Norfolk

Mississippi R.

Nashville

TENNESSEE

NORTH
CAROLINA

Jacksonville

Atlantic Ocean

SOUTH
CAROLINA

Wilmington

MISSISSIPPI
TERRITORY

Alabama R.

GEORGIA

**Creek
Nation**

Charleston

N

LOUISIANA

Fort Mims

Savannah

W   E

Mobile

S

New
Orleans

Pensacola

St. Augustine

Scale of miles

0   100   200

FLORIDA
(SPAIN)

Gulf of
Mexico

BAHAMAS
(U.K.)

CUBA
(SPAIN)

Map by Gene Thorp

He now owns a prospering plantation a few miles from the Mims property, where he lives with his wife and many children. Unlike Weatherford, who can pass for white, Bailey is dark-skinned but considers the whites to be his true people.

In the mind of William Weatherford, the betrayal by Bailey—who now wears the U.S. military rank of captain—is just another reason for attacking Fort Mims. If Weatherford is sure of anything on this day, it is that Captain Richard Dixon Bailey will pay a dear price for his lack of loyalty to his Indian heritage.

❖

William Weatherford and Dixon Bailey exemplify all that is wrong in the Creek nation right now. For three centuries, the Creek have endured the advance of white settlers onto their lands. It was in 1536 when Spanish explorer Hernando de Soto led his army north from the Gulf of Mexico, systematically looting villages and enslaving the Native American population in his relentless search for gold. At the time, there was no such thing as the Creek nation. Tribes in the areas that would come to be known as Alabama, Mississippi, and Georgia were separate and independent but bonded by a complex political alliance that prevented warfare with one another. It was only when the British arrived in the region in the early 1700s that the name "Creek" was given to the population of ten thousand Indians living in the Deep South. The name is a shortened version of "the Indians living on Ochese Creek" and soon caught on.

At the time, the bond between the British settlers and the Creek was economic. In exchange for goods such as cloth and guns, the Indians provided deerskins that were shipped to England for the manufacture of gloves and riding breeches.

The Creek coexisted peacefully with the British, but they regularly raided other Indian tribes in Florida to capture slaves. Most were women and children, who were then sold to the French, Dutch, and British for use on the sugar plantations of the West Indies and the coastal tobacco farms of Virginia and South Carolina. But just as the sale of deer hides came to an end when the forests were depleted from overhunting, so the Indian slave trade ended as tribes either moved to distant locations or were simply wiped out.

In the southern part of North America, it was the Spanish who came first to steal the land from Indigenous peoples. In the east, the British and French did it. It was soldiers of those nations who first navigated the new territories. Fur traders then opened up commerce. Farmers came last, with their hoes and cattle, felling trees to open up acreage for planting and grazing. For the last two hundred and more years, this desire for land has created unabated conflict between white European settlers and Native American tribes—and with every clash have come massacres and atrocities. In 1622, the Powhatan tribe murdered 347 settlers in the colony of Virginia. Fifteen years later, on the shores of what is now Long Island Sound, British loyalists surrounded a village of the Pequot tribe and murdered seven hundred men, women, and children with muskets, swords, and flames.

At the end of the War of Independence, a new people simply known as "Americans" continued to push westward, not caring that the land they required for farms and homes was not their own. American expansion was a result of either making peace or subduing Indian tribes through armed conflict. The process was often decades in the making, but the Native Americans almost always lost. In this way, the Americans advanced slowly westward across the continent, building cities, roads, and military outposts, even as the Indians retreated.

One Indian chief, Tecumseh, whose headquarters were located in a small northern border town known as Detroit, tried to halt the white man's intrusion. He attempted to organize all of the Indian nations from the Great Lakes to the Gulf of Mexico, traveling thousands of miles on horseback to forge alliances. The attack on Fort Mims is taking place in 1813, but its genesis was two years before, in the summer of 1811, when the charismatic Shawnee chief traveled south from Detroit to meet with the Creek leadership—among them William Weatherford.

Lending a celestial aura to Tecumseh's arrival was a mighty comet that shone in the nighttime sky. The chief preached that the Indians should turn their backs on farming and return to hunting

*Tecumseh rebukes General Henry Procter for retreating during
the Battle of the Thames, also known as
the Battle of Moraviantown.*

and other traditional ways of life. His primary goal, however, was to
form an Indian alliance that would stem the westward advance of
whites.*

True to his word, Tecumseh soon returned to a place known as

---

* The forty-five-year-old Tecumseh allied himself with the British during the War
of 1812, seeking to defeat American military forces and establish an independent
Indian nation west of the Mississippi River. He would be killed one month after the
attack on Fort Mims, at the Battle of the Thames on the shores of Lake Erie.

the Indiana Territory to wage war on the United States. Utilizing an alliance of tribes from the Great Lakes region, he battled to stop the whites' migration. But inevitably, the growing power of the new nation overwhelmed the Indian chief.

Under President James Madison, General William Henry Harrison was ordered to destroy Tecumseh's forces in Indiana. Harrison was successful, defeating Tecumseh at the Battle of Tippecanoe in 1811.

Yet Tecumseh's dream of stopping the whites' westward advance lives on. William Weatherford and the fierce warriors surrounding Fort Mims are vivid proof.

✵

In the Deep South, white settlers and some blacks who had successfully fled slavery actually began living among the Creeks. Some even intermarried with the Indians. This diluted not just the bloodline but also such simple traditions as personal identity. This is why the Creek attack on this sweltering August morning is led by a warrior with the given name William Weatherford, who not only speaks fluent English but has also been a regular visitor to the house of Samuel Mims—the same plantation home that will burn to the ground in just a few short hours.

To Weatherford's dismay, a segment of the tribe known as the Lower Creek is in favor of continued assimilation with the whites. They want to be farmers, speaking English, living in towns similar to the Americans', and wearing the same clothing. One prime example of this group is the mixed-race militia captain Dixon Bailey.

The Upper Creek, of which Weatherford is a member, seek a return to traditional ways and actively attempt to expel whites from their lands. Their strategy is simple: kill any Creek who is friendly to the Americans and follow up that violence by slaughtering all the white people they can. Rather than the ungainly term "Upper Creek," they prefer to be known as "Red Stick."

The result is civil war within the Creek nation.

Caught in the conflict are all nearby inhabitants. In the summer of 1813, it becomes necessary to build a series of forts in which settlers can shelter until the Creek War ends. American soldiers are also ordered into southern Mississippi and Alabama. Rather than the regular army, which is currently busy fighting the British in what will become known as the War of 1812, a volunteer force is assembled. Each man signs a twelve-month commitment before marching off to stop the Red Stick aggression.

Construction of Fort Mims, as the protective barrier around the plantation is now known, began one month ago, in July 1813. From all around the region, scores of families fled their farms and homes and traveled to the fort in search of protection. Five acres in size, it is situated on a high plain overlooking the Alabama River. Those sheltered are hard people. Driven by poverty and ambition, they have chosen to make their living in an unremitting land full of poisonous snakes, where the rivers are filled with alligators and the distinction between friend and foe has grown vague. All of this, so that they can live on a plot of land they can call their own.

So as they come together at Fort Mims in an attempt to preserve their way of life, these families work as a team to chop down acres of longleaf pine trees, erect walls, and construct their new homes within the fort. All labor side by side. It is hard work by day but dancing, drinking, and merriment by night. They have brought with them their cows, pigs, and sheep, which are left to roam free in the pines and canebrake beyond the walls. Dozens of small children play in the midst of the construction. A well within the fort provides fresh water, though, unlike the Creek Indians, who bathe each morning in the local streams and rivers, these settlers do not practice daily hygiene and are largely unwashed. So many hundreds of people have come to Fort Mims seeking refuge that there is little room for personal space. This claustrophobia is made worse by the shortage of outhouses for private routines and a growing rate of disease borne by the thick clouds of mosquitoes. In this way, the fortress has the feel of a small, doomed city.

Now, as the hoofbeats of Jim Cornells's galloping horse fade into the distance, William Weatherford and his warriors lie in wait. Though his bravery is undisputed, Weatherford's fair skin and close ties with the whites have some doubting whether or not he truly believes in the Red Stick cause. Weatherford is charismatic and courageous, and possesses a deep knowledge of the terrain around Fort Mims. But the doubts about his true loyalties still bring forth suspicion. Thus, he is allowed to lead men into battle but has not yet been named a chief. The coming attack, however, offers Weatherford the perfect opportunity to prove his allegiance. He continues staring at the gate to Fort Mims, which still remains open.

From somewhere inside the fort, Weatherford hears a fiddle playing. But that is not the signal to attack. The Red Stick must wait for the lunch bell. With the east gate propped open and the noon meal drawing near, William Weatherford and his warriors grasp their war clubs tighter, eager to swing the blows that will cave in the skulls of their enemy.

※

Major Beasley and the Mississippi Militia arrive at Fort Mims on August 2. Beasley's men immediately go to work, fortifying the simple wall built by the settlers. A stockade of inner defensive walls is added, as well as a new addition to the fort built specifically to house the military. Gun ports are cut into the perimeter fencing, allowing Beasley's men to shoot without exposing themselves to danger. Within weeks, what was once a collection of homes and stables is completely fenced in by logs placed in the ground vertically, the tops sharpened to a point. In the event of an attack, a blockhouse allows a stout enclosure into which the defenders can retreat and open fire.

The fort was built in a hurry, with an undercurrent of fear permeating every moment of construction. But now that the walls are complete, a calm settles over Fort Mims. Where once there was just open space, there is now protection. The walls and the substantial military presence make the fort's inhabitants feel safe for the first time in months.

To keep his men happy, Major Beasley recently sent a letter by courier, requesting that his militia superiors send whiskey with which to reward them—the very whiskey that many of them drank to excess last night.

Beasley also requested a drum.

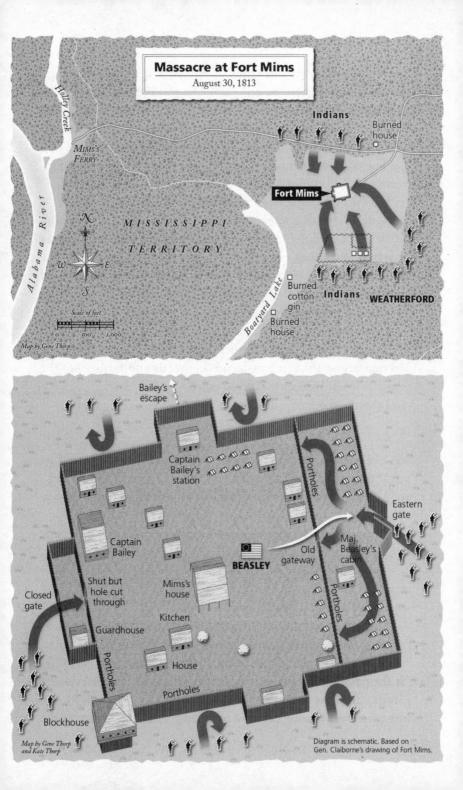

Massacre at Fort Mims
August 30, 1813

Holley Creek

Alabama River

Mims's Ferry

MISSISSIPPI TERRITORY

Indians

Burned house

Fort Mims

Indians

WEATHERFORD

Burned cotton gin

Burned house

Boatyard Lake

N
W E
S

Scale of feet
0   500   1,000

Map by Gene Thorp

Bailey's escape

Captain Bailey's station

Captain Bailey

Shut but hole cut through

Closed gate

Guardhouse

Portholes

Blockhouse

Mims's house

Kitchen

House

BEASLEY

Old gateway

Eastern gate

Maj. Beasley's cabin

Portholes

Portholes

Portholes

Map by Gene Thorp and Kate Thorp

Diagram is schematic. Based on Gen. Claiborne's drawing of Fort Mims.

To Major Beasley's delight, Martin Rigdon, a seventeen-year-old who has served in the army since he was nine, turns out to be an excellent drummer. Beasley himself is a lawyer by trade. He only became a professional soldier to advance his standing in society and has no formal military training. But the major believes that the regular beating of a drum will bring a stronger military bearing to Fort Mims.

Like the whiskey, the drum arrived yesterday.

Now, Martin Rigdon and his drum stand just a few feet from Beasley, who will not commence the whipping without a proper drumbeat. The major clutches the lash in his fist. The slave tenses. The circle of witnesses presses in closer. The soldiers standing guard are playing cards and telling stories.

The east gate remains wide open.

Beasley nods.

The rat-a-tat drumroll echoes through the thick morning air, carrying across the fort's manicured grounds and far beyond the brand-new walls smelling of fresh pine.

Into the woods.

※

The Creek decide to wait no longer. The drumroll now marks their signal to attack. The Red Stick rise from their hiding places without a war cry, sprinting toward the fort's two entrances in complete silence.

By the hundreds, they race across open ground from the south, east, and west. Now it is time to kill.

Two hundred warriors led by William Weatherford focus their attack on the east gate. It is vital that they get there before being spotted, before the gate can be closed.

Suddenly, a sentry cries: "Indians!" He immediately fires a warning, then runs for his life, making no attempt to shut the east gate.

Major Beasley drops his whip. Drawing his sword, he rushes for the outer walls, hoping to beat the Indians to the open eastern gateway. But just as he reaches the gate, Beasley is shot dead. The Indians swarm, beating his head repeatedly with clubs—leaving the major's corpse bloody and unrecognizable. The Creek pour through the open eastern entrance. One woman will remember seeing "Billy Weatherford as he came in the gate at a full run, at the head of his warriors."

To this she would add: "As he sprang over the logs he saw Dixon Bailey, who was a bitter enemy, to who he shouted, 'Dixon Bailey, today one or both of us must die.'"*

At the same time, a second body of warriors race toward the western entrance of the fort. "With few exceptions, they were naked," one survivor of the attack will remember. "Around the waist was drawn a girdle with a cow tail running down the back and almost dragging on the ground. It is impossible to imagine people so horribly painted."

Settlers are scalped, dead or alive. But many blacks are not killed—instead, they are captured, soon to become Indian slaves. The man tied to the whipping post is not so lucky.

The massacre is intense and unrelenting. In an act of desperation, a young scout named Cornet Rankin marches toward the Indians carrying a white flag of surrender.

He is shot dead.

Through the screaming of terrified women and children, and the hail of bullets, the Mississippi Volunteers somehow manage to regroup. The Red Stick attack stalls just inside the east gate, the newly built inner wall preventing them from penetrating into the center of the fort. On the south wall, soldiers fire through specially designed portholes with deadly accuracy, causing the Indian attack to fall back. On the north wall, Captain Dixon Bailey's men turn back the Creek advance, firing their single-shot muskets with deadly accuracy.

During construction of the fort, brush and trees were cleared for a hundred yards in every direction, allowing an unbroken field

---

* The quote comes from an 1890 letter William Weatherford's grandson, Charles Weatherford, wrote about the massacre. In this letter, later published by the Mississippi Historical Society, Charles claims that the unnamed woman to whom the quote is attributed is his aunt, Mrs. Susan Hatterway, who was living as a refugee inside Fort Mims in 1813.

of fire for the Americans. Indian bodies now lie across the plain, including those of several shamans who chose to wear "bulletproof" deerskin. Many Creeks, however, survive this barrage and reach the fort's walls. With Indians on one side of the portholes and militia on the other, the two sides literally take turns firing at one another through the same openings from just inches away.

Slowly, however, the Americans fall back into the center of the fort. Panicked women and children are ordered to find a building and go inside, away from the fight. Many women refuse, preferring to remain with their men, loading guns, drawing water from the well to put out fires, and bandaging the wounded.

"Help or hope there was none," one account written shortly after the battle will read. "Soldiers, women, children, Spaniards, friendly Indians fell together in heaps, the dying and the dead, scalped, mutilated, wounded, bloody, to be consumed [here] long by fire or to become food for hungry dogs and buzzards."

So it is that the dead and dying cover the ground inside and outside Fort Mims.

As the second hour of fighting comes to an end, many small buildings within the fort are ablaze. But the fight remains at a standstill. The Creek cannot penetrate the fort's inner walls and thus content themselves with looting the outer buildings, even as the defenders hunker down inside the blockhouse and small homes at the center of the fort.

The battle appears to be a stalemate.

For two hours, the Creek tend to their wounded, unsure of whether to leave with their captured slaves or to once more risk their lives in battle.

But there is one act that must be avenged: Dixon Bailey's betrayal against his people at the Battle of Burnt Corn. Until Bailey is dead, the fight cannot end.

William Weatherford longs to see Dixon Bailey killed for his treachery, but he is also friends with many whites still trapped inside and cannot bear to witness what will come next. So he departs the battlefield. He will later tell his sister-in-law "he rode off, for he had not the heart to witness what he knew would follow, to wit, the indiscriminate slaughter of the inmates of the fort."

※

The final confrontation begins with the launching of a single flaming arrow. The heartwood of the longleaf pine, from which every building is constructed, is known to burn at a tremendously high heat. First to blaze is the kitchen, a stand-alone structure. The fire quickly spreads to the compound of stables and workshops surrounding the Mims home. More fire arrows follow, and soon the Indians are penetrating the fort's inner defenses and setting every structure ablaze.

Frantic settlers seek to chop holes in the outer fences, hoping to escape the deadly chaos. Those trapped inside the burning structures face the agonizing decision between being burned alive or being scalped. Captain Dixon Bailey and his men still control the north wall, even as his brother James and sister Elizabeth have made the fatal decision to retreat to the Mims house. There, the root cellar is packed with children. As Indians enter the blazing home, James Bailey is shot dead while Elizabeth looks on. She could save her own life by feigning loyalty to the Creek, but instead Elizabeth points to her brother's corpse and proclaims, "I am sister to that man you have murdered there."

Benjamin Hawkins, a black slave who witnessed the incident before being led away as a Creek hostage, recounts what happens next: "Upon which they knocked her down, cut her open, strewed her entrails around. They threw several dead bodies into the fire and some that were wounded."

Settlers fleeing the flames are clubbed, shot, stabbed, sliced open with tomahawks, and scalped with special long knives carried for that specific purpose. This includes not just the men and women fighting so desperately to save Fort Mims but their infants and young children as well.

The last holdout is the north wall, where Dixon Bailey still fights. When they can take it no more, Bailey flees out of a hole hacked into the base of the north wall. His wife and four children escape with him. Bailey's son Ralph, unable to walk because he is wounded, is carried by a black slave named Tom. Despite a hail of bullets and arrows, the group makes it into the nearby woods before Bailey is shot down. He dies in a small grove of trees and is later buried in a mass grave, along with his wife, his children, and the hundreds of other victims of the Creek massacre.

It seems, however, that at least one of Dixon Bailey's offspring will survive. The slave Tom attempts to negotiate for the life of fourteen-year-old Ralph Bailey, hoping to offer both of them up as prisoners. But when Tom hands the boy over, the Creek immediately smash in his skull and take his scalp. Tom, meanwhile, is directed to join the group of slaves who have been taken captive.

William Weatherford, who could not even bear to witness the final carnage, has had his revenge—but at a great cost.

※

By evening the battle is done. Two hundred and forty-seven bodies are counted when a relief party finally arrives ten days later. One eyewitness put it this way: "At the East Gate of the stockade lay Indians, Negroes, men, women, and children in one promiscuous ruin. Within the gate lay the brave unfortunate Beasley. He was behind the same and was killed, as was said, in attempting to shut it. On the left within the stockade we found forty-five men, women, and children in one heap. They were stripped of their clothes without distinction of age or sex. All were scalped, and the females of every age were most barbarously and savage-like butchered, in a manner in which decency nor language can convey. Women pregnant were cut open and their children's heads tomahawked."

The victims are unrecognizable from heat, decomposition, and the ravages of wild dogs, insects, crows, and buzzards. In addition to those bodies littering this plain overlooking the Alabama River, many more dead have been incinerated inside the burning buildings, the flames so hot that nothing more than ashes is left of these men, women, and children. The exact toll is impossible to count, but it is estimated that almost five hundred settlers have been killed by the Creeks at Fort Mims. Adding to the carnage, the Indians continue their rampage in the days and weeks that follow, riding through the countryside to burn homes and slaughter thousands of cattle.

Both sides suffered in the Battle of Fort Mims. More than one hundred Creek also lie dead. But to this day, the fight marks the greatest Indian victory over Americans in U.S. history.[*]

The night after the massacre, a lone rider gallops away from St. Stephens, a trading post seven miles west of Fort Mims. Nineteen-year-old Samuel Edmondson is bound for the city of Nashville, 450 miles north. He carries news of the slaughter and two letters requesting immediate military assistance. One is addressed to Tennessee governor Willie Blount. The other is destined for a forty-six-year-old major general in the Tennessee militia named Andrew Jackson, a volatile plantation owner whose renown for personal toughness has led his troops to give him the nickname Old Hickory. Edmondson will ride night and day, changing horses as needed, in order to deliver these letters as quickly as possible. The Creeks must be stopped.

Thus begins a new chapter of warfare between Indians and settlers. No longer will hostile tribes face isolated enemies—now, they will be challenging the vast and growing power of the United States of America.

It is a challenge they will soon regret.

---

[*] Though the lives of many slaves were spared by the Creek, that of the young man tied to the whipping post was not among them. However, drummer Martin Rigdon managed to escape during a lull in the fighting. His parents and sisters, who had accompanied him to Fort Mims, were not as fortunate.

Chapter One

SEPTEMBER 3, 1813
NASHVILLE, TENNESSEE
9:00 A.M.

Andrew Jackson has vengeance on his mind.

The white-haired general with the soft southern accent is armed with a riding whip and a sword, which he carries every day. This morning the six-foot-one former senator is also carrying a loaded pistol in his back pocket. An up-and-coming politician named Thomas Hart Benton, a former friend and confidant, has publicly slandered Jackson, claiming he conspired to make a fool of Benton's brother in a recent duel.

But the fact is that young Jesse Benton has made a fool of himself. Instead of standing completely still after turning to fire his pistol, per protocol, he squatted down to avoid getting shot—only to end up with a lead musket ball in his ample backside. When Jesse relayed the news to his brother, who was visiting Washington, D.C., at the time, the young man wove a tale of deceit that blamed Andrew Jackson. After that, Thomas Hart Benton began making public assertions that the legendary general is a cheat and a liar.

Uncharacteristically, Jackson has held his temper for weeks. But as Benton journeys home to Nashville and is overheard repeating the slander in many a barroom along the way, Tennessee's "first citizen" can

Andrew Jackson in a painting by Thomas Sully, 1845

take no more. Andrew Jackson publicly pronounces he will horse-whip the thirty-five-year-old Benton "on sight."

That moment has come.

Thomas Hart Benton stands in the doorway of Clayton Tal-bert's Tavern. In time, he will become a formidable political figure, instrumental in America's westward expansion. But at present, he is struggling to find his way. Benton was born into wealth but was expelled from the University of North Carolina for stealing from his fellow students, an embarrassment he still carries.

His brother, the heavyset Jesse, stands a few steps back inside the barroom. He is six years younger than Thomas, with a reputation for being arrogant and impulsive.

Both Benton brothers are armed.

Andrew Jackson has spent the night at the luxurious Nashville Inn, one hundred diagonal yards across the town square. The three-story establishment is the general's favorite lodging and will remain so for decades. He enjoys gambling on the cockfights in the vacant lot next door. Wine and games of billiards flow freely in the ground-floor tavern, and the general stables his horses around back. The Bentons also normally stay at the Nashville Inn, but this is not a normal day. For their own safety, they selected Talbert's Tavern—for they know a battle is brewing. Word of the pending confrontation between Jackson and the Benton brothers has spread quickly. Local citizens fill the square at a discreet distance, keeping out of pistol range as they await the action to come.

Jackson ignores the bystanders. His close friend, Colonel John Coffee, walks at his side. Together, the two men follow the wooden sidewalk leading around the square to Talbert's. They stroll slowly, feigning deep conversation. Jackson is a rail-thin 145 pounds and prefers to wear his overcoats baggy, to give the appearance of being larger. Colonel Coffee is an enormous man, with a booming voice and an even temper that balances out Jackson's explosive personality. Both are in their forties, although the general's gray hair contrasts with Coffee's dark locks. Their friendship is so profound that Colonel Coffee once fought a duel to defend Jackson's honor, during which the military officer took a ball in the thigh.

"Do you see that fellow?" Coffee asks quietly, glancing at Thomas Hart Benton, who is still standing in the tavern doorway.

"Oh, yes," Jackson replies. "I have my eye on him."

Andrew Jackson feels the weight of the whip in his right hand, his sword in its scabbard, and the heft of the pistol against his back hip. The weapon weighs more than three pounds and features a barrel almost eight inches long. A scar creases Jackson's left arm, the result of a British sword three decades ago in the Revolutionary War. Inside Jackson's chest, a musket ball is lodged just inches from his heart, a painful reminder of a duel seven years ago. His opponent shot first and scored a direct hit. Yet despite the hole in his chest and the blood pouring from his wound that would soon fill both his boots, Jackson managed to take a steady aim, then shot and killed his opponent. Doctors say that Jackson himself will die if the bullet is ever removed. Thus, it remains.*

With every step along the sidewalk, General Jackson and Colonel Coffee draw closer to Talbert's Tavern. Jackson knows there is a barroom on the ground floor, with a side hallway and a door leading to a back porch. A plan takes shape in his mind.

The two men stop directly in front of the hotel. Jackson quickly pivots to face Thomas Hart Benton.

"Now, you damned rascal, I am going to punish you," snarls Jackson, shifting the whip to his left fist.

Benton reaches for his pistol. At one time the young man idolized Jackson, whose successful career in the House of Representatives and Senate provided a road map to the sort of life Benton hopes to enjoy. Benton's own father died when he was just eight years old, and at first Jackson seemed to fill that void. In time, however, Benton longed to be more powerful, more famous, and even more beloved than the man nicknamed "Old Hickory." His respect turned into jealousy as Benton realized that his only chance of surpassing Jackson was to kill him.

But Thomas Hart Benton is nervous as he reaches for his gun. He has never drawn a weapon before. Benton fumbles to pull his eight-inch-long flintlock "pocket" pistol from his coat.

Andrew Jackson has no such problem.

The general smoothly draws his gun and presses the barrel against Benton's heart. Jackson pushes him backward into the tavern, toward

---

* Andrew Jackson fought that duel with his personal rival, Charles Dickinson, on May 30, 1806. Dickinson accused Jackson of reneging on a horse-racing bet and of being a coward, as well as slandered Jackson's wife with a charge of bigamy. (Rachel Jackson was previously married. Her divorce was not final at the time she wed Andrew Jackson.) The two men fought at Harrison's Mill in Logan, Kentucky. Dickinson was the better marksman and shot first, striking Jackson near the heart. Pressing his left hand over the wound to stop the blood flow, Jackson pulled the trigger of his own weapon, but the pistol misfired. Taking careful aim again, Jackson fired a second shot, which killed Dickinson.

the back door. Tennessee is still a lawless frontier state in many ways, but should Jackson opt to shoot the young plantation owner there can be no witnesses. Behind him, Colonel Coffee stands at the front door, blocking anyone from following Jackson out the back.

In all the commotion, Jesse Benton has been forgotten. Now, he slips from the tavern into a back hallway, where he takes up position behind Andrew Jackson and his older brother. Jesse fires his pistol. The first shot hits Jackson in his left arm, lodging in the humerus bone. The second shatters the general's shoulder blade. A third shot goes wild, stuck in the hotel wall.

Andrew Jackson pitches forward, firing as he falls. The powder burns Thomas Benton's coat. Though not hit, Benton tumbles backward down a flight of stairs. Colonel Coffee rushes to General Jackson's rescue and finds him facedown in a pool of blood. Bystanders follow Coffee, wrestling Jesse Benton to the ground and threatening to kill him. An irate John Coffee turns away from the prone Andrew Jackson and steps forward to pummel the younger Benton, but the crowd separates them. Thomas Hart Benton remains unhurt on the floor in the basement.

Now all eyes focus on Jackson. Colonel Coffee instructs the group of bystanders to help him carry Jackson back to his room across the square at the Nashville Inn. The general is losing so much blood that he soaks through a thin cotton mattress. When that cushioning becomes too saturated, it is replaced by another. Jackson's blood does not stop pouring from his wounds, and soon the second mattress is also a dark red.

Clearly, Andrew Jackson is dying.

The best doctors in Nashville arrive, called to care for the general. His left arm must be amputated; that much is clear. They hover over him, preparing the saw needed to cut away the shattered limb.

Suddenly, Jackson barks from the bed: "I'll keep my arm."

The doctors would ignore any other patient, but this is the great Andrew Jackson. It is determined that the ball lodged against the bone in his arm cannot be removed, meaning that the general now has two pieces of lead taking up permanent residence inside his body. A poultice made of slippery elm is applied to the wounds in Jackson's arm and chest, followed by a splint. There is nothing more to be done but let him rest.

Thus, Andrew Jackson remains bedridden for eight days, fading in and out of consciousness. His face turns a yellow gray. The Benton brothers have publicly denounced Jackson as a failed assassin, yet there is no way he can fight back. Jackson grows weaker with every passing day.

Then on Sunday, September 12, almost two weeks after setting out from southern Alabama, nineteen-year-old Samuel Edmondson gallops into Nashville with news about the massacre at Fort Mims. He bears a letter demanding that no less than General Andrew Jackson come to the immediate rescue of the beleaguered American settlers and fight the Creek Indians.

Jackson is strong enough to read the missive. It is an outrageous request, appealing to a lone man from Tennessee rather than the U.S. government to somehow bring the full force of military might to bear on the Creek aggressors.

Yet the general does not find it audacious. Rather, the letter is a tonic to his wounds. The general rises in bed and dictates a response. The call to battle appears in the September 14 edition of the *Nashville Whig*. In a letter addressed to "Fellow Soldiers," Jackson makes a call for the men of Tennessee to volunteer and follow him into battle.*

Enoch Parsons, a member of the Tennessee senate, proposes a bill authorizing the state to fund a war with the Creeks. He visits Jackson as a courtesy, informing the general that the bill will soon become law.

"I mentioned," Parsons would later write, "that I regretted very much that the general entitled to command, and who all would desire should command the forces of the state, was not in a condition to take the field."

"The devil in hell he is not," Jackson replies through gritted teeth.

The Benton brothers are forgotten for now. Andrew Jackson will deal with them later.

---

* More than three thousand men answer Jackson's call to battle. So many, in fact, that Tennessee earned the nickname "The Volunteer State," a title it holds to this day.

A second letter from Jackson is published on September 24. As panic about another Creek uprising spreads through the south, Andrew Jackson makes it clear that he is ready for war. "The health of your general is restored," he informs the people of Nashville, speaking in the third person. "He will command in person."

But Jackson is still frail. He returns to the Hermitage, his plantation ten miles outside Nashville, where he remains bedridden until the first week of October. The general wills himself to heal. The pain in his left shoulder is so great that he cannot wear his full military uniform, the weight of his epaulets causing extreme pain. His arm is still in a sling, making it impossible to mount a horse without help. Yet by the first week of October, just three weeks after being shot, Jackson is riding south to meet up with his new army. Colonel John Coffee has already led the force to the town of Fayetteville, Alabama, to await further orders.

"He was still suffering pain and was looking pale and emaciated from the wound received in the famous duel with Benton," one young lieutenant from Florida will later write of Jackson's appearance. "He was mounted on Duke, the brave old war horse that afterwards bore his gallant master so proudly on many glorious battlefields. His graceful, manly form, usually erect, was now bent with pain."

"His pallid cheek gave evidence of his suffering. Yet there was something in the lineaments of his face, a slumbering fire in his pale blue eye," twenty-one-year-old Richard K. Call will add, "that made me and everyone, recognize the presence of a great man."

Despite his misery, Jackson rides into Fayetteville on horseback. His army awaits. No longer an invalid, the wounded warrior is determined to once again lead men onto the field of battle.

But as he dismounts to greet his troops, even Andrew Jackson has no idea just how bloody that field will be.

Chapter Two

General Andrew Jackson prepares to "exterminate the hostiles." After spending five months conducting raids against the Creek Indians in central Alabama, Jackson is glad spring has arrived. He stands atop a small rise on this chilly Sunday morning, peering out at the enemy encampment through his collapsible brass spyglass. Finally, after a winter of war with the United States, the Creek nation appears to be trapped. As the sun rises, Jackson discerns smoke from cooking fires in the makeshift village. Houses large enough for twenty to thirty Indians back up to a line of trees. It is hard to count the number of Creek warriors milling about, but it looks to be close to one thousand. Jackson can also see hundreds of women and young children on the premises.

The one individual Jackson cannot see is William Weatherford. Since Fort Mims, the Creek leader has become notorious among Americans as the most feared and elusive chief in the South. Capturing or killing Red Eagle, as Weatherford is called by his warriors, would be devastating to the Indian cause. But this will not be easy. Just a few months ago, when U.S. forces thought they had Weatherford trapped, he boldly escaped by jumping his gray stallion off a tall cliff, falling into the Alabama River below.

Andrew Jackson is determined there will be no such flight today. William Weatherford must be captured.

The general wears full uniform, complete with epaulets and knee-high black riding boots. His jacket is slightly oversize, per Jackson's preference. His left arm still throbs painfully, but despite the musket ball lodged near his shoulder, the danger of amputation has passed.

All around him on this small hillside, Jackson's army stands at the ready, two regiments of Tennessee volunteers and another of U.S. Army regulars. Combined with the mounted cavalry led by John Coffee, now a general, and the renegade Cherokee warriors who have chosen to help Jackson annihilate the Creek nation, the general commands almost four thousand men—heavily outnumbering the Creeks.

But the Indians have chosen their defensive position wisely, opting to make their stand on a peninsula with a horseshoe shape. Their village is nestled within, bordered on three sides by the Tallapoosa River, a raging torrent whose ice-cold waters run to twenty feet deep.

Yet the river is not the most formidable obstacle protecting the Creek.

Rather than stealth and concealment, the Indians have chosen to wage war like the white man. In an act of ingenious military engineering, they have constructed perhaps the greatest fortress Jackson or his men have ever seen. As the general now observes, a thick and powerful wall reaches from one side of the peninsula to the other, directly across the open mouth of the horseshoe. This is not a feeble and hastily constructed barricade, like the doomed white settlers built at Fort Mims. A zigzag row of thick, rough-hewn pine logs stacked eight feet high stretches 350 yards across the valley, from the Tallapoosa River on the west side to the Tallapoosa on the east. Mud has been packed into the spaces between each log to hold them fast. Wooden firing platforms allow the Creek to take steady aim, then drop below the wall to reload, while narrow portholes allow the defenders to fire without putting themselves in danger.

The land in front of the wall has been denuded, offering no place for an attacking force to hide. Nothing but pine stumps and open ground lies between Jackson's army and the fortress. In the event

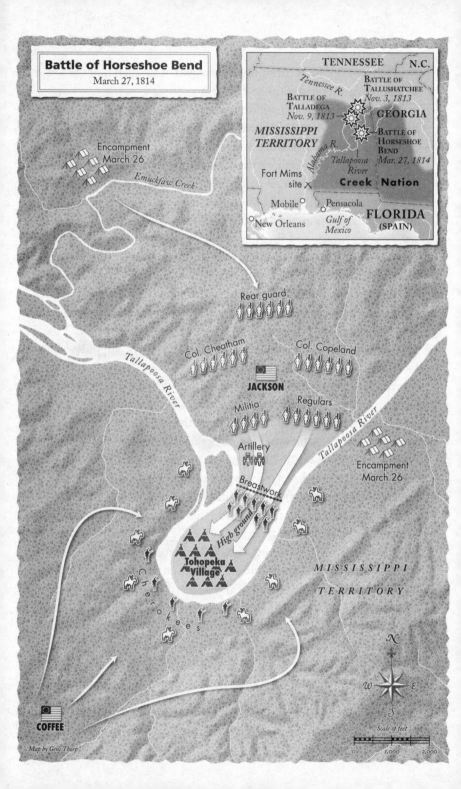

Battle of Horseshoe Bend
March 27, 1814

TENNESSEE   N.C.

Tennessee R.

BATTLE OF
TALLUSHATCHEE
Nov. 3, 1813

BATTLE OF
TALLADEGA
Nov. 9, 1813

GEORGIA

MISSISSIPPI
TERRITORY

BATTLE OF
HORSESHOE
BEND
Mar. 27, 1814

Alabama R.

Tallapoosa
River

Fort Mims
site

Creek Nation

Mobile   Pensacola
New Orleans   Gulf of
Mexico

FLORIDA
(SPAIN)

Encampment
March 26

Emuckfaw Creek

Tallapoosa River

Rear guard

Col. Cheatham

Col. Copeland

JACKSON

Militia

Regulars

Artillery

Tallapoosa River

Encampment
March 26

Breastwork

High ground

Tohopeka
Village

Cherokees

MISSISSIPPI

TERRITORY

COFFEE

N
W   E
S

Scale of feet

0   1,000   2,000

Map by Gene Thorp

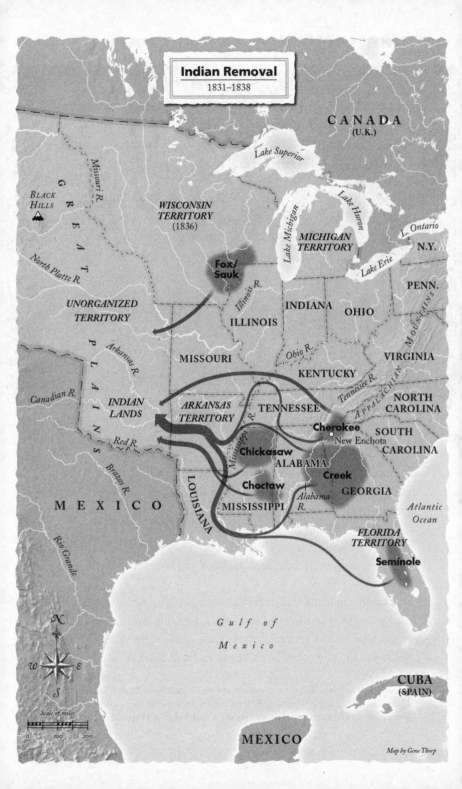

A Creek village

that Jackson's army makes it across this perfect killing zone, sharpened branches jut outward from the wall to impale those who would attempt to climb over.

Andrew Jackson is deeply impressed.

"It is difficult to conceive a situation more eligible for defense than the one they had chosen," Jackson will later write of the Creek fortress.

Making matters worse for Jackson is his army's morale. There is deep division within the fighting force: the men from Tennessee are loyal to the general, but they are undisciplined and prone to rebellion.* On the other hand, the men from the U.S. Thirty-Ninth

---

* Among the original Tennessee volunteers was a garrulous frontiersman named Davy Crockett. He enlisted shortly after the Fort Mims massacre and served until December 1813. He was not present for the Creek battle at Horseshoe Bend.

Infantry Regiment despise Jackson because he is not one of them. Aware of this, the general places the Thirty-Ninth at the center of his column, to spearhead the first wave of assault on the wall. These regulars are the general's best soldiers, and, as Jackson well knows, they just as surely will be the first to die.[*]

With the Creek finally trapped right before his eyes, the general must find a way to win. He believes the answer lies in his artillery. Jackson has two cannon at his disposal, a six-pounder and a three-pounder. They are aimed at the right side of the Creek barricade and will open fire from a distance of just eighty yards. This is point-blank range for cannon. Surely these artillery pieces can blast a hole in the stout Creek fortress.

The Tennessean uses the butt of his left hand to collapse his looking glass. There is nothing more to see. The artillery will not open fire for four more hours.

General Andrew Jackson's ingenious battle plan, however, is already in motion. The shape of the peninsula on which the Creek now make their stand resembles more than just a horseshoe. As shown on Jackson's maps, it also looks very much like a noose.

General Andrew Jackson is about to pull the knot.

꙰

Per Jackson's orders, General John Coffee is two miles away, moving his mounted cavalry into position. They are on the south shore of the Tallapoosa, strung out in a long line that will soon encircle Horseshoe Bend. When General Jackson orders his frontal assault on the Creek wall, the only avenue for the Creek to escape will be the river. But as they turn to flee, they will be met by the full force of the U.S. Cavalry.

Since answering the summons to war almost half a year ago, Coffee and Jackson have developed a very simple strategy for destroying

---

[*] Shortly after the Thirty-Ninth were ordered to join Jackson's command in January 1814, the general sought to quell the unruly behavior of his Tennessee volunteers by executing a soldier for misbehavior. Jackson ordered an eighteen-year-old private from the Tennessee militia shot by a firing squad. The charges against Private John Woods were false, but Jackson refused to rescind the order.

the Creek: surround a village with cavalry, then send infantry forward to kill as many Indians as possible. There is little imagination to this sort of envelopment. The Tennesseans have succeeded through sheer ruthlessness.

On November 3, 1813, Jackson ordered Coffee, newly promoted to brigadier general, to lead a group of nine hundred Tennessee mounted volunteers. This was the first act of vengeance for the massacre at Fort Mims. The engagement took place in central Alabama, in the heavily forested region between the Coosa River and the Georgia border. Coffee's mounted force marched through the night in complete silence, prepared to launch a dawn attack against a Creek settlement known to contain a few hundred warriors and their families.

"The surprise was complete," First Lieutenant Richard K. Call will write in his journal. As personal aide to General Jackson, Call was not actually present at the fight, basing his version of events on the recollections of his fellow soldiers. "The town was entirely surrounded early in the morning. So soon as our men were seen on one flank, the Indian drum sounded the alarm, which was answered by the wild war whoop of 180 warriors, who sprang to their arms."

The Indian counterattack was quickly suppressed. In what would become known as the Battle of Tallushatchee, Coffee's dragoons then surrounded the warriors and their families in their homes, killing 186 Creeks.*

"Shot them like dogs," is how Tennessee militia volunteer Davy Crockett will describe the battle.

When bullets were not enough, the houses were set ablaze. In one instance during the fighting, forty-six Red Sticks became trapped inside a house. Each was burned alive.

"The battle had ended in the village, the warriors fighting in their

---

* The advantages of a mounted fighting force were made clear early in U.S. history, with the successes of Francis "Swamp Fox" Marion and Henry "Light-Horse Harry" Lee in the Revolutionary War. However, it was not until March 1833 that President Andrew Jackson finally authorized the formation of a U.S. Army contingent of soldiers on horseback. They were officially known as dragoons, taking the name from similar French troops who rode into battle carrying a pistol bearing an imprint of a dragon.

board houses, which gave little protection against the rifle bullets or musket ball," First Lieutenant Call will write of the battle's final outcome. Call traveled through the night to enter the village the following morning so that he might report back to Jackson.*

"They fought in the midst of their wives and children, who frequently shared their bloody fate. They fought bravely to the last, none asking or receiving quarter, nor did resistance cease until the last warrior had fallen. Humanity might well have wept over the gory scene before us. We found as many as eight or ten dead bodies in a single cabin, sometimes the dead mother clasped the dead child to her breast, and to add another appalling horror to the bloody catalogue—some of the cabins had taken fire, and half consumed human bodies were seen amidst the smoking ruins. In other instances dogs had torn and feasted on the mangled bodies of their masters," Call will report.

That same morning, as Coffee's men loot the village in search of food, they discover a potato cellar. "We were all as hungry as wolves," Davy Crockett will write to his wife. "We found a fine chance of potatoes in it, and hunger compelled us to eat them, though I had a little rather not, for the oil of the Indians we had burned up on the day before had run down on them, and they looked like they had been stewed with fat meat."

Women had fought alongside their husbands, many times inflicting death with a bow and arrow. Inevitably, many were killed. One such woman lay dead, clutching her two-year-old son in her arms.

The boy, however, has survived the slaughter. Along with the small group of prisoners captured at Tallushatchee, he was brought before Andrew Jackson at his headquarters along the Coosa. Impulsively, Jackson decides to adopt the child, named Lyncoya, as his own. "I send on a little Indian boy," Jackson writes to his wife, Rachel, at home in Nashville. "All his family is destroyed."

Andrew and the former Rachel Jackson Robards have no children

---

* Call went on to serve as a nonvoting delegate in the U.S. House of Representatives representing the Florida Territory, which would not become a state until 1845. In 1836, he would be appointed territorial governor of Florida, courtesy of Call's friend and former superior officer, Andrew Jackson.

of their own. Theirs is a complex but deeply committed relationship. Rachel began publicly referring to herself as "Mrs. Jackson" long before their first wedding, in 1791. She did this while married to the violent and jealous Captain Richard Robards. Even after taking their vows, Andrew and Rachel were accused of bigamy because Rachel had failed to finalize her divorce from Robards. The two were legally married a second time in 1794. However, the charges of bigamy would be used to slander Andrew and Rachel Jackson for decades—with the ironic result of strengthening their bond. Upon Rachel's death from heart failure in 1828, at age fifty-one, Jackson will write to John Coffee: "My mind is so disturbed . . . my heart is nearly broke."

Between 1794 and 1809, as the Jacksons entered their forties without offspring, they made the choice to pursue adopting a family. The first of three boys who would take on the Jackson name entered their lives in 1809. Andrew Jackson Jr. was a twin, and the son of Rachel's brother, whom they adopted as a child. The reasons for splitting him from his twin are still uncertain, but it is believed that their mother was mentally ill. The young Creek child named Lyncoya will be the second son adopted by the Jacksons.*

This is a seemingly odd turn of events, for the general is currently in the midst of destroying every last vestige of the Creek nation. The bulk of his fortune and property holdings have come through successful land grabs from the Cherokee and Chickasaw tribes in North Carolina and Tennessee. Jackson considers Indians inferior and easily exploited, similar to the one hundred Negro slaves who work his plantation home outside Nashville. And just as Jackson zealously offers rewards for runaway slaves and uses the lash to inflict punishment, he also sees nothing wrong with his men trapping Creek warriors inside their homes and slaughtering every last one. The massacre at Fort Mims made it quite clear that men like Andrew

---

* Though he was educated in white schools and Andrew Jackson attempted to arrange an appointment to the U.S. Military Academy, Lyncoya was considered a "curiosity" and a "pet," in the words of Richard K. Call. He died of tuberculosis at the age of seventeen. The Jacksons had adopted a third son by then. Andrew Jackson Hutchings (1812–1841) was the grandson of Rachel's sister who was orphaned at the age of five, whereupon Andrew and Rachel Jackson adopted him. He ultimately married the daughter of Jackson's best friend, General John Coffee.

Rachel Jackson, wife of Andrew Jackson, in a painting
by Louisa Catherine Stroebel

Jackson are honor bound to protect the American way of life and the nation's westward expansion from tribes like the Creek.

However, in one very specific way, Andrew Jackson is just like the adopted boy named Lyncoya. The general's father died in a logging accident three weeks before his son's birth in 1767, his brother Robert died of smallpox, then his mother died of cholera while nursing American soldiers being held on board British prison ships during the Revolutionary War. Andrew Jackson was left orphaned and alone in the world at the age of fourteen. Thus, this hardscrabble frontiersman famous for his ruthlessness in business and war, fondness for settling disputes with fists and duels, and unrelenting determination to triumph in any situation, at all costs, has a singular sentimental weakness: family.

"He may have been given to me for some valuable purpose," Jackson will write to Rachel about adopting Lyncoya. "In fact, when I reflect that he as to his relations is so much like myself I feel an unusual sympathy for him."

In memory of his beloved mother, Elizabeth, who successfully pleaded for her son's release from a British prison during the Revolutionary War, then nursed the boy back to health after his near-death experience with smallpox, Andrew Jackson has a firm policy that his forces not "wage war on females."

Jackson, however, often makes this rule hard to follow.

✳

After his victory at Tallushatchee, the general's forces proceeded to the town of Talladega, Alabama. On November 9, 1813, Jackson ordered his troops to surround a Creek Indian settlement and slaughter its inhabitants. Two hundred and ninety-nine Creek Indians were killed, including women and children. Jackson lost fifteen American soldiers killed and eighty wounded.

Since that time, the Creeks have been fighting back ferociously. The enlistments of many volunteers have come to an end. Jackson has spent much of the winter waiting for reinforcements and supplies. There have been skirmishes with the Creek, with both sides extracting casualties, but no major battles.

Throughout these months, the name William Weatherford remained a cause of fear. The Creek chief appears to be everywhere and nowhere, launching attacks and disappearing just as mysteriously.

By January 22, 1814, desertions and mutinies had whittled Jackson's force to just two hundred men. In a remote and beautiful pine forest near Emuckfaw Creek, the general's army came under attack just before dawn. The men had risen at 4:00 a.m. and were enjoying a breakfast of coffee, bread, and cold meat when the Creek force surprised them, screaming in high-pitched war whoops.

"The enemy, yelling like demons, rushed on with great impetuity," Lieutenant Richard Call wrote of that attack. "They came within range of the [fire]light, and some of them so near that when they fell under the steady aim of our cool brave men, they fell in our fires."

The Creek warriors were repulsed and fled. General John Coffee and his mounted cavalry quickly gave pursuit. Lieutenant Call borrowed a horse and joins them.

"Approaching near their position, we halted," Call wrote. "Our spies, being experienced woodsmen, advanced to take a recognizance [*sic*] of their camp. We had examined our flints and priming so that by daylight we were ready for a fight . . . when they returned it was to report that the enemy was fortified by a high log wall extending from one side of the Tallapoosa to the other.

"Our men were anxious to make an attack," the lieutenant added. "Coffee—cool, deliberate, and resolute—determined not to do so. He ordered myself . . . to return and report to General Jackson that he thought the fortification might be taken only with the united section of the whole army."

It would be two more months until that attack would take place. But as General John Coffee accurately predicted, both sides are in for a fight.

✳

The Battle of Horseshoe Bend begins the morning of March 27, 1814. For the most part, the Creeks and Americans are equally armed, with both sides possessing accurate muskets and ammunition. But the Indians lack the advanced firepower of cannon, and as the bombardment begins, the general's contingent from the U.S. Thirty-Ninth Regimental Infantry stands ready to begin their dangerous run across open ground to the fortress. This attack will not commence until Jackson's three-pounder and six-pounder blast a hole in the wall.

But the cannon are ineffective. Instead of destroying the log walls, the balls are either going straight through the soft wood or becoming embedded. And even as Jackson's gun crews reload and take aim, the Creek are focusing their musket fire on the cannoneers. An hour passes. Then another. Women and children scream in terror as cannonballs miss the wall altogether and land in the camp.

Still, the fortress is unscathed. In addition to their musket fire, the Creek yell to their enemy above the sounds of battle, taunting their impotence.*

Cannon fire can be heard clearly by General John Coffee and his mounted men, poised along the banks of the Tallapoosa River with their Cherokee allies. They become eager as the time passes, determined to take part in the battle. The Cherokee finally snap into action. Spying Creek canoes concealed in bushes on the opposite shore, a small group attempts to cross the river. Despite the cold water and the powerful current, three Cherokee undertake the one-hundred-yard swim. Creek warriors on the bluff above open fire. One of the Cherokee, a man named Whale for his large size, is shot in the shoulder. But all three make it across, steal canoes, and paddle back to the other side. A system of ferrying men across the Tallapoosa now begins. Soon, more than one hundred of Andrew Jackson's Indian allies are waging war against the Creek village.

With American cannon firing from one side, and the Cherokee advancing on their village from the other, the Creek panic. Believing the wall to be impregnable, they turn their main force on the Cherokee.

At 12:30 p.m., Andrew Jackson orders a drumroll. Ironically, just as at Fort Mims, this is the signal to attack. In the center of the column, men of the Thirty-Ninth form into straight lines. They wear dark-blue jackets, white shirts, gray pants, and black boots. Each man holds a musket, to which a sharp foot-long bayonet is attached. At the front of each line are their officers, distinguishable by the scarlet sash across their chests and gold epaulets on their shoulders. Instead of a musket, these men carry a sword.

"I never had such emotions as when the long roll was beating," writes soldier John Reid in a letter to his wife. "It was not fear, it was not anxiety nor concern of the fate of those who were so soon to fall but it was a kind of enthusiasm that thrilled through every nerve and animated me with the belief that the day was ours."

---

* The Creek Nation was at a disadvantage because they had few horses. In fact, only their leaders usually rode. The southeastern part of the United States did not have large herds of wild horses available, so the Creek warriors were basically infantry.

The Battle of Horseshoe Bend, also known as Tohopeka,
Cholocco Litabixbee or the Horseshoe

The frontal attack begins with a sprint. Running toward the wall, Jackson's reinforced army of two thousand Americans race past the pine stumps. Many fall, killed instantly by Creek musket shots. But the rest push on, fearlessly, avoiding the sharpened branches projecting from the wall as they begin to scale up and over.

Major Lemuel Montgomery of the Thirty-Ninth is the first man to climb the barricade. He is immediately shot in the head.

Eventually, the regulars pour over the top, followed on the flanks by the Tennessee militia. In the hand-to-hand combat that ensues on the parapets, bayonets and rifle butts are swung by the Americans while the Creek wield tomahawks and their infamous war clubs. Hopelessly outnumbered, the Creek begin to fall back, sprinting for the perceived safety of their village, even though it is under intense attack from the other side by the Cherokee.

Soon the Creek are overwhelmed.

The massacre now begins.

The Creek are completely trapped within their own fortress. With the river behind them secured by General Coffee's cavalry and Jackson's men blocking their way forward at the wall, the Indians are penned in for the slaughter. The killing goes on for hours.

"The carnage was dreadful," General Jackson will write to his wife, Rachel. "It was dark before we finished killing them."

Hundreds of women and children are taken prisoner.

More than 850 Creek warriors lie dead as the battle comes to an end. The nose of each dead Indian is sliced from his head as a method of counting the fatalities. Some are scalped by the Cherokee to commemorate the victory. Gruesome as that might be, the volunteers from Tennessee are equally savage. Starting at the base of the heel, they use their knives to peel long strips of skin from the dead Creek to braid into bridle reins.

As the dead are counted, Jackson is satisfied with his triumph. American casualties at the Battle of Horseshoe Bend number 47 killed and 159 wounded. Another 23 Native Americans fighting on the side of the U.S. Army are also killed. The Creek Indians suffer an astonishing 857 dead and 206 wounded.

But General Jackson is all too aware that one man is missing.

There is no sign whatsoever of the infamous Chief William Weatherford.

Until Red Eagle is captured, the Creek resistance lives on.

※

For the next three weeks, General Andrew Jackson rides through the South, searching for William Weatherford. Jackson institutes a new policy, demanding that the Creek nation hand over Weatherford for hanging if they want peace. No Weatherford, no relief.

On April 18, 1814, a tall, bare-chested man wearing buckskin breeches rides through the Alabama countryside on a gray stallion. He spots a deer, shoots and guts the animal, then drapes it across his horse's neck to carry with him. Food is hard to come by now that the U.S. Army has made the forests their own. A plump deer will make for many good meals.

Reloading his musket, the warrior continues on his way, eventually riding into General Andrew Jackson's encampment at a place called Fort Toulouse. He asks directions to Jackson's personal tent. A soldier refuses to tell him, insulting the warrior in the process. An older gentleman standing nearby points the way.

The man on horseback is stately and serene. Soldiers and Indians walking through the camp stop and stare. Andrew Jackson himself steps from his tent.

"I'm Bill Weatherford," the man on the stallion says calmly.

"How dare you, sir, ride up to my tent," barks Jackson, "after having murdered the women and children at Fort Mims?"

"I do not fear you, General Jackson. I have nothing to ask for myself. I come to ask peace for my people. I am in your power. Do to me as you please. I am a soldier, I have done the white people all the harm I could. I have fought them and fought them bravely. If I had an army I would fight you but my people are all gone. I can do no more than to weep over the misfortunes of my nation. Once I could animate my warriors to battle but I cannot animate the dead. My warriors can no longer hear my voice. Their bones are at Talladega, Emuckfaw, and Tohopeka. On the miseries and misfortunes brought upon my country I look back with deepest sorrow and wish to avert still greater Calamities. You are a brave man and I rely on your generosity. I ask for peace for my people, not for Weatherford."*

Andrew Jackson is so stunned by Red Eagle's courage that he has no reply.

A crowd gathers around. Chants of "Kill him, kill him, kill him" fill the area surrounding Jackson's tent.

With a single sharp look from the general, the crowd goes silent.

"Any man who would kill a man as brave as that," says Jackson, "would rob the dead."

Andrew Jackson invites William Weatherford to join him inside for a brandy. Stepping from his horse, Red Eagle throws his freshly killed deer over his shoulder and accepts the invitation. He presents the animal to Jackson as a peace offering.

While inside, the two men talk peace between the Americans and the Indians.

It is a peace that will be extremely short-lived.†

---

* There are numerous versions of Weatherford's surrender story and his ensuing speech. All are based on hearsay, so it is impossible to know which is most accurate. The salient points—that Weatherford rode into Jackson's camp, surrendered with a great act of oratory, and was pardoned by Jackson—are all consistent. General Jackson will justify his actions to his good friend General Thomas Woodward, saying that Weatherford was "as high-toned and fearless as any man he had met with—one whose very nature scorned a mean action."

† Initially, the Creek were allowed to remain in the Southeast, but in 1836, President Andrew Jackson ordered them relocated to Indian Territory.

Chapter Three

A sitting president of the United States is about to doom the American Indian.

James Monroe's Seventh Annual Message to Congress is ready for delivery. Finally. The precise wording of the document has consumed America's fifth leader for months. Outside Monroe's second-story office window here in the White House, workmen and slaves are preparing to erect a new addition to the building known as the South Portico. This will change the physical shape of the mansion in the same manner that Monroe is altering the physical landmass of the United States with the document he now holds in his hands.

The weather outside is brutally cold. The sixty-five-year-old president is glad he doesn't have to make the two-mile journey to the Capitol to deliver the annual message in person. Monroe is a polished man, standing six feet tall, slender in girth. He has a full head of wavy brown hair, now turning gray. The president is deeply idiosyncratic in his dress, still wearing the ruffled shirts and buckled shoes that fell out of fashion after the Revolutionary War. Monroe's whole life has been devoted to public service, where he gained a foothold after serving in General George Washington's revolutionary army at Trenton. In that battle, Monroe bravely returned

James Monroe, 1817

to action after a musket shot severed an artery. Monroe continued showing his courage to Washington throughout the war, enduring a harsh winter at Valley Forge and making friends with the Marquis de Lafayette, the wealthy young Frenchman who so famously fought alongside the Americans. Just a year from now, early in 1825, Monroe will welcome Lafayette back to America to celebrate a half century of United States independence.

James Monroe is wed to a flamboyant woman named Elizabeth,

who actually smokes a pipe. They have two married daughters. A third child, James Spence Monroe, died of unknown causes when he was just sixteen months old.

Much like his mentor Thomas Jefferson, Monroe is a reserved man. He was raised in Virginia in affluence. Monroe knows he should deliver his annual address in person, but he resists doing that because, like Jefferson, he doesn't much enjoy public speaking.

The U.S. Constitution explicitly states that each president must periodically present a State of the Union address to Congress. George Washington, as America's first chief executive, met this requirement by delivering a formal speech to a joint session of the Senate and House of Representatives. Washington titled it his "Annual Message to Congress." John Adams, the nation's second chief executive, did the same. But upon succeeding Adams, Thomas Jefferson balked. The idealistic Virginian was shy and a poor public speaker. Using the excuse that a presidential speech was too much like the British monarchy's annual address to Parliament—and thus had no place in a democracy—Jefferson instead wrote his message by hand, then had the contents delivered to Congress to be read aloud.*

Twenty-two years and two presidents later, that tradition continues. The Eighteenth Congress met for the first time just yesterday. Now the president will have his say.

Monroe well understands that his message will be controversial all around the world. His vision favors what will become known as a "sea to shining sea" policy. That is, America will control all the lands between the Atlantic and Pacific Oceans, and no foreign power will intrude on U.S. policy governing that territory.

However, the North American continent is still sparsely populated west of the Mississippi River, and European powers are setting their sights on colonizing some of this land.

---

* This practice persisted until 1913 and the presidency of Woodrow Wilson. A speech has been standard practice since that time. Until 1934, the State of the Union address was delivered in December instead of January. It was called the "Annual Message" rather than State of the Union up until 1933. Calvin Coolidge delivered the first State of the Union address by radio in 1923, Harry Truman delivered the first by television in 1947, and Bill Clinton's 1997 State of the Union was the first ever sent over the Internet.

Monroe aims to stop that.

Left unsaid is that much of that western territory does not belong to the United States. It is home to hundreds of Indian tribes who have inhabited the land for countless generations. Monroe does not address Native Americans in his remarks, but it is clear that by demanding European powers cease the colonization of the West, he is stating that *only* the United States will dictate how the land is used.

President Monroe has a history of marginalizing Native Americans. Five years ago, he ordered General Andrew Jackson to quash Seminole Indian uprisings in Georgia and Florida. Jackson himself has become fantastically rich through speculative real estate deals, selling land gained from conquered Indian tribes. It is clear that James Monroe will continue these policies, and Andrew Jackson will play a major role.

Throughout America, Jackson has risen to the status of a hero. In 1815, he defeated the British Army at the Battle of New Orleans, thus putting an emphatic end to the War of 1812. Jackson's fame has become so great that some fear he will become an American Napoleon, a military leader so charismatic and invincible that he could possibly take over the entire country.

But this does not concern James Monroe at all. Andrew Jackson is useful to him, and he keeps the general away from Washington by continually sending him off to fight. When Monroe ordered Jackson to Florida to administrate the land for Washington, it still belonged to Spain. The Madrid government was outraged but could do little about it. In the Adams-Onis Treaty of 1819, Spain ceded Florida to the United States outright because it could no longer defend the territory from American intrusion.

As badly as the Spanish fared after Jackson's incursion, the Seminoles' defeat was even worse. Jackson's army ended the uprising by using overwhelming force, causing the Seminoles to completely give up all claims to land in Florida. Under the terms of the Treaty of Moultrie Creek, signed just three months ago in September 1823, the Indians are to be pushed out of their ancestral Florida homes to relocate to an area specified by the U.S. government. This turns out to be a small sliver of land in the center of Florida's peninsula.

Eventually, James Monroe and Andrew Jackson will forge a U.S. government philosophy dictating that the Seminoles, Creeks, and every single other Native American tribe are not sovereign nations and thus are not entitled to own land within the borders of the United States. It makes no difference that the Indians disagree.

This policy of "Indian Removal" formally begins in 1825, when James Monroe bows to demands from the state of Georgia that Cherokee Indians be banished. The president requests a "well-digested plan" to remove certain Indian tribes from all tribes to a location west of the Mississippi River. After that, the dominoes begin to fall.

❋

On this blustery December day, President Monroe's brutal vision of imposing the sea-to-shining-sea policy clashes with his high-minded rhetoric. A young courier borrows a horse from the White House executive stables and rides alone through Washington to hand-deliver the thick packet of paper to the clerk of the House of Representatives, Matthew St. Clair Clarke, who will read it aloud to the House. The same duty will fall to New Hampshire's Charles Cutts in the Senate.

President Monroe is rightfully considered one of America's few living Founding Fathers. As those who read his Seventh Annual Message will soon learn, the promise of this great nation is as vibrant to him now as it was five decades ago. It is also clear from his message that the expansion will come at the expense of the Indian tribes.

President James Monroe will leave office in 1825. He will be virtually penniless after a lifetime of public service and forced to live with his daughter until his death in 1831. Monroe's presidency will be overshadowed by those of the four great men before him—Washington, Adams, Jefferson, and James Madison—and the two ideological warriors immediately afterward: John Quincy Adams and Andrew Jackson.

Monroe's message, dated December 2, 1823, will be scarcely noted by Europe's great powers, and in time it will almost be forgotten.

But out of that address will come the "Monroe Doctrine," as it will be labeled in 1850. That doctrine will shape America for centuries to come.

The sea-to-shining-sea vision is easily described on paper. But to make that policy a reality will not be easy. For the next sixty years, torrents of blood will be shed. And America's legacy will endure controversy forever.

Chapter Four

Abraham Lincoln waits for destiny.

Twenty-three and unemployed, the lanky former store clerk and flatboat operator stands next to his rival. Both Lincoln and wealthy sawmill owner William Kirkpatrick have answered the call to war. Sauk Indians under the command of a chief named Blackhawk are said to be on the rampage. Forced by the U.S. government to relocate from their homeland in central Illinois, Blackhawk and his eight hundred warriors have now returned to claim their land.

The Sauk were once a prosperous tribe, farming the fertile Illinois soil in the summer and traveling south to hunt in the winter. The Indians mined the ground for lead, which they smelted and sold to traders for a profit. But as settlers like Abraham Lincoln moved into the lands the Sauk have occupied for centuries, conflict began.

Illinois governor John Reynolds is calling for the state's volunteer militia to take up arms against the Indians. The tall, self-important career politician who prefers the nickname "Old Ranger," earned as a private during the War of 1812, knows that few issues will galvanize his electorate more than taking a strong stand against the Indian population. In addition to the Sauk, other tribes such as the Fox,

Winnebago, and Potawatomi call Illinois home. Like most white residents, Governor Reynolds wants *all* Indians banished from the state forever.

Yet the militia is the reason conflict exists in the first place. One year ago, Blackhawk and his warriors made a similar warlike move. Public fears of an uprising were rampant. The U.S. Army scrambled six infantry companies up the Mississippi River from St. Louis to quell the unrest.* In reality, Blackhawk had no intention of waging war. He wants to make peace with the soldiers. However, the presence of the unruly militia among the more disciplined regulars unsettled the Indians. Blackhawk feared his entire tribe would be massacred once the U.S. Army returned to St. Louis. Rather than surrender, the Sauk temporarily fled to safety west of the Mississippi.

Now Blackhawk and his men have returned. No violence has yet occurred, but Governor Reynolds has once again put out the call for men to fight the Indians. Abe Lincoln and sixty-seven other local volunteers immediately signed up and have just been sworn in as soldiers. In all, twenty-one hundred men throughout the state will volunteer for a thirty-day enlistment. These amateurs will be placed under the command of the U.S. Army.

However, at the insistence of the vainglorious Governor Reynolds, two volunteer battalions will remain under his command.

This will become a disaster.

Most men standing on the village green here in Richland are filthy and unshaven, preferring dark calico garments that hide their grimy appearances. They see themselves as frontiersmen, comfortable with the hardships of wilderness living. These are exactly the sorts of violent men Blackhawk fears. The new volunteers are hard individuals; many drink heavily and are illiterate. They are not the sort to take orders from anyone. Yet militia policy stipulates that these men must elect officers who will lead them.

---

* Congress is so suspicious of America maintaining a standing army that it has mandated the nation's fighting force be reduced to a legal limit of exactly 6,183 officers and troops. The nation's military academy at West Point continues to graduate would-be officers, but few actually receive a commission. Thus, when trouble arises, a volunteer militia is the fastest way of raising a fighting force.

There are two candidates to lead: lumber magnate William Kirkpatrick and the inexperienced Abe Lincoln, who was thrust into the election because a number of the militiamen remember the epic wrestling match six months ago between Lincoln and a hulking giant named Jack Armstrong. The bout was a draw, but the thin and deceptively strong Lincoln fought with such determination that he earned their lasting admiration. So rather than let Kirkpatrick run unopposed, "Honest Abe" Lincoln is nominated.*

The voting process is simple: Kirkpatrick and Lincoln stand alone on the village green. Each volunteer lines up behind the candidate of their choice. The man with the longest line will become captain.

Lincoln was at first reluctant to run. His temperament is not at all like most of the other volunteers', and it is unclear if he is cut out to be a leader. In 1831, shortly after moving to New Salem from Indiana, Lincoln morosely described himself as a "friendless, penniless, uneducated boy, working on a flatboat for ten dollars a month."

All that has changed. Though prone to bouts of dark depression, Honest Abe is also warmhearted, makes friends easily, and is known for his sharp intellect. While he is enthralled by the idea of holding elected public office, his first foray into politics did not go well. Just last month, in March 1832, Lincoln ran for the Illinois state legislature. His candidacy was derailed by his awkward public speaking style and the fact that his employer's business had just gone bust. Making matters worse, Denton Offutt's store was more than just a source of employment to Abe Lincoln; it was his home. He and fellow employee William C. Greene, who also volunteered to join the militia, slept on a single cot in the store. Abraham Lincoln isn't volunteering to fight Indians out of a sense of public duty but because he needs money and a roof over his head.

He won't get much. For his six-month enlistment, Abraham Lincoln will be given forty acres of land.

As Lincoln stands on the common next to William Kirkpatrick, he is amazed to see man after man lining up behind him. Even

---

* Lincoln earned this nickname while working as a store clerk in New Salem. After mistakenly overcharging a customer, he traveled several miles to refund the money.

those who originally supported the sawmill owner are changing their minds and stepping over to Lincoln's line.

Almost thirty years from now, Abraham Lincoln will look back on this moment and recall it as "a success which gave me more pleasure than I have had since."

Right now, however, Abraham Lincoln's emotions are not so easily contained.

"I'll be damned, Bill," Lincoln exclaims to William C. Greene as it becomes clear he has won his first election. "I've beat him."

✷

Chief Blackhawk is not so easily defeated. It is the afternoon of May 14, 1832—three weeks after Abraham Lincoln enlisted in the militia. The sixty-five-year-old Blackhawk and his tribe of one thousand men, women, and children are camped on the banks of a place called Sycamore Creek. The land is flat, dotted by creeks and thick forests. The youngest Sauk warriors are currently miles away, hunting for game. Blackhawk himself is eating a meal of dog when one of his advance scouts gallops into camp to report that a group of white men on horseback are approaching.

"I immediately started young men with a white flag to meet them, and conduct them to our camp that we hold council with them," Blackhawk will later remember. He has just forty warriors in camp at the moment and is in no position to fight an enemy force.*

Despite white fears, Blackhawk did not return to Illinois to wage war. Instead, the Sauk believe they might once again find a place to call home. The population of white settlers has increased from 40,000 in 1818, when Illinois became the twenty-first state, to more than 250,000 today. A land so vast and wild surely has enough room for Indians and settlers alike. However, Blackhawk has been unable to find food or refuge for his people, who are now starving. Even as

---

* In perhaps the first example of a Native American voice being published for a white audience, Blackhawk's version of events appears in an 1833 autobiography: *Life of Ma-Ka-Tai-Me-She-Kia-Kiak or Black Hawk*, published in Cincinnati and edited by John B. Patterson.

the scout returns with news of an approaching militia, Blackhawk has already made the sad choice to leave Illinois. The chief is determined to once again cross back over the Mississippi—this time for good. The Sauks have committed no hostile acts during their foray, and the abundance of dependents in camp makes it clear this is not a war party.

After sending off the three warriors bearing a flag of truce, Blackhawk orders five others to trail behind and observe the proceedings from a distance.

Meanwhile, the two rogue battalions of Illinois militia that remain under the command of Governor John Reynolds are making camp in a swampy wooded valley known as Old Man's Creek. Though the governor is not currently traveling with his army, these 275 men are under orders to kill on sight as many hostile Indians as they can.

The earth is muddy from the previous day's rains. The volunteers long ago filled their canteens with whiskey. Unruly and undisciplined, prone to firing their rifles for fun during moments of drunkenness, they immediately start shooting at the sight of the approaching Indians, taking prisoner all three warriors bearing the white flag.

Twenty more mounted militia attempt to capture the five observers. Gunshots are exchanged. Subsequent depictions of the fighting offer differing views. But there is no denying that one, if not two, Indians drop from their horses, dead. The others turn quickly and ride hard for Sycamore Creek, covering the seven miles at a full gallop with the militia right behind.

The Sauk warriors arrive, bringing news of their dead. Dusk is falling.

Chief Blackhawk has had enough. It is a basic tenet of Sauk custom to seek clan revenge on anyone who harms his people. This belief, along with years of degradation, lies, and theft of tribal land by white settlers, has led to this point of no return.

"Some of our people have been killed," the chief cries out. "We must revenge their death."

The few Sauk warriors remaining in camp mount their horses.

A plaster model of Abraham Lincoln
by sculptor Charles Keck. The photograph was given to
Frederick Hill Meserve in 1951.

Knowing it is a suicide charge, they ride straight into the oncoming militia. To their great surprise, the white men turn and flee in terror. "The enemy retreated," Blackhawk will long remember, "in the utmost confusion and consternation before my little but brave band of warriors."

As night falls, the Sauk press their advantage. With their women and children at great risk from a militia reprisal, they launch a preemptive attack on the encampment at Old Man's Creek. Greatly outnumbered, fighting in pitch-dark conditions, the stealthy Indians quickly spread terror. For although the white volunteers consider themselves superior outdoorsmen, their skills hardly compare with those of Blackhawk's warriors.

"As if by magic, each tree and stump appeared to send forth a band of savages," Illinois volunteer James Stephenson will later recount. "The swampy ground, the surprise, the retreat of the whites, threw everything into confusion."

Twelve militia soldiers are immediately killed. The rest run for their lives. The volunteers desert the battlefield so fast that the fight will come to be known as "Stillman's Run," in a humiliating depiction of militia commander Major Isaiah Stillman's personal flight.

The corpses of the dead militia bear the brunt of the humiliating rout. Heads are cut off. Tongues are sliced away. Legs, arms, and even hearts are chopped from bodies. The entire camp is looted.

Abraham Lincoln is among the soldiers who will arrive within days to bury the dead. Surveying the scene, he will later write of what he saw: "The red light of the morning sun was streaming upon them as they lay head towards us on the ground. And every man had a round red spot on top of his head, about as big as a dollar where the redskins had taken his scalp. It was frightful, but it was grotesque, and the red sunlight seemed to paint everything all over."

※

Vengeance can be a two-way street, and now it is Blackhawk's turn to run. He guides his band northeast, away from Illinois. He leaves panic and confusion in his wake, for the militia have lost their will to fight and are deserting en masse. Indian tribes throughout the region are deeply inspired by Blackhawk's victory, leading to gruesome uprisings. Settlers and militia alike are murdered, their bodies mutilated beyond identification. On May 19, militia volunteer William Durley is shot from his horse. The bullet enters his groin, slicing open his femoral artery and killing him before he hits the ground. His corpse is later discovered with his nose cut off and head nearly sliced from his body.

A group of travelers bury Durley's body in a shallow grave, only to find themselves surrounded by thirty Indians. Just three settlers manage to escape. The others are killed, later discovered in a field of tall grass with their hands and feet cut off.

At a place called Big Indian Creek, the home of settler William Davis is surrounded by seventy Indians. The house is filled with friends and neighbors who have come to the Davis residence seeking protection, hoping their large numbers will protect them from attack.

They are wrong.

A guest named William Pettigrew sees the approaching Indians through an open window and protectively lifts his infant daughter into his arms. He is instantly shot dead.

Two teenage girls, Rachel and Sylvia Hall, try to run. The advancing warriors capture them and carry them back to the house, where the settlers are being slaughtered like cattle.

Fifteen men, women, and children are butchered. Their screams for mercy are ignored. Blood spatters the walls and puddles on the wooden floor of the Davis home. Everyone, even William Pettigrew's infant child, is scalped. The women are hung upside down by their feet and sexually assaulted before their limbs, breasts, and heads are hacked from their bodies. No corpse, man or woman, is left intact.

Only Rachel and Sylvia will live to tell the story. After witnessing the horror, they are kidnapped and taken back to Blackhawk's camp.

However, the massacre is not Blackhawk's doing, and he orders both young women released. In reality, it is the Potawatomi tribe who carry out the brutal attack on the Davis household to permanently settle a long-lasting dispute. But Blackhawk is assumed to be

Blackhawk's War skirmish marker on the Black Hawk Trail to Bad Axe, Wisconsin

responsible. The collective Native American fury in the face of an advancing America is embodied in the viciousness of their attacks. It is now Blackhawk who becomes the public face of that horror.

Thus the name: "Blackhawk's War."

By June, that title becomes a self-fulfilling prophecy. Blackhawk stops running. He now chooses to fight, sending his warriors on raids that result in the massacre and scalping of settlers and soldiers. Whites flee the frontier in terror, overwhelming the city of Chicago in their search for safe refuge. Governor Reynolds's militia hunts in vain for the elusive chief, but Blackhawk's ability to attack makes a fool of the self-important politician.

In Washington, President Andrew Jackson has had enough. He authorizes a new armed force under War of 1812 hero General Winfield Scott to crush the Indians.

When it comes to Indians, Old Hickory is once again determined to have the final say.

※

Soon it is over.

The U.S. military arrives in Illinois with cannon, a weapon the Indians cannot defend against. Blackhawk's tribe begins to die at an alarming rate. In just two days of fighting in early August at the Battle of Bad Axe, an estimated five hundred Sauk men, women, and children are slaughtered—many after trying to surrender. Making matters worse, the Dakota Sioux have crossed the Mississippi to join the fight against Blackhawk, taking sixty-eight scalps from the fleeing Sauk. Blackhawk himself narrowly escapes death by retreating alone from the battlefield in disgrace, even as the fighting continues.*

Just five U.S. soldiers are killed in that same engagement.

On August 27, 1832, the chief surrenders and is taken into American custody. His head is clean-shaven, save for a single lock of graying hair, as he is placed in chains. The remaining members of his tribe are allowed to cross the Mississippi to find a new home.†

※

To impress upon the five foot five Sauk chief that rebellion against the United States is futile, authorities take Blackhawk to the great cities of Baltimore, Philadelphia, and New York City, in order that he might see for himself the enormity of America's power.

To his great surprise, Blackhawk is greeted by large crowds wherever he goes, eager to witness the defeated chief in person. Yet it is not because Blackhawk fought for his people, but because he exemplifies what academics and intellectual society are now calling

---

* This band of Sioux were mercenaries working on behalf of the U.S. government to defeat Blackhawk.

† U.S. military officers Zachary Taylor and Jefferson Davis are the men who take charge of Blackhawk after he surrenders. Taylor will go on to become president of the United States, while Davis will become president of the Confederate States during the Civil War.

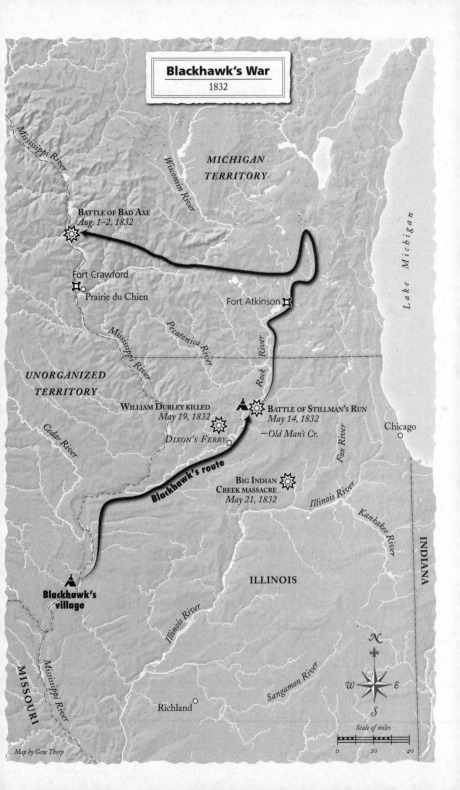

Blackhawk's War
1832

Mississippi River

Wisconsin River

MICHIGAN TERRITORY

BATTLE OF BAD AXE
Aug. 1–2, 1832

Fort Crawford

Prairie du Chien

Lake Michigan

Fort Atkinson

Pecatonica River

Mississippi River

Rock River

UNORGANIZED TERRITORY

WILLIAM DURLEY killed
May 19, 1832

BATTLE OF STILLMAN'S RUN
May 14, 1832
—*Old Man's Cr.*

Cedar River

DIXON'S FERRY

Chicago

BIG INDIAN CREEK massacre
May 21, 1832

Fox River

Illinois River

Kankakee River

Blackhawk's route

Blackhawk's village

ILLINOIS

INDIANA

Illinois River

MISSOURI

Mississippi River

Richland

Sangamon River

N
W E
S

Scale of miles

0   20   40

Map by Gene Thorp

"the noble savage." This, of course, insults the proud warrior. And just as that moniker trivializes his very existence and the reasons he sought a homeland for his people, the ease with which the U.S. government put an end to his dream shows that resistance to an expanding America is futile.

Blackhawk's most important stop is Washington, D.C. There he meets face-to-face with President Andrew Jackson, the man who signed the Indian Removal Act of 1830. This law allowed the forceful relocation of tribes to lands west of the Mississippi. Both men are the same age—sixty-five—but Old Hickory towers over the diminutive chief. When Blackhawk attempts to explain why he went to war, Jackson shows little interest. He merely wanted to see the infamous Chief Blackhawk in person. Jackson is certain the little man is no threat to America.

The meeting is over within minutes.

✳

The United States was so certain of victory over Blackhawk that men like Abraham Lincoln were actually mustered out of military service a full month before the war ended. Lincoln never fought in battle nor fired a single round at the enemy, but Blackhawk's War is the making of him. The friends, connections, and even leadership skills gained during his short time as a soldier will propel him to public office and, eventually, the presidency.

In time, Abraham Lincoln will stand before Congress and reflect upon Blackhawk's War as nothing more than a minor skirmish.

"I had a good many bloody struggles with the mosquitoes," Lincoln states, trivializing Blackhawk's acts of defiance. "And although I never fainted from the loss of blood, I can truly say I was often very hungry."

Chief Blackhawk is imprisoned briefly in Virginia, where he languishes for one month. Upon his release, he is stripped of all authority among the Sauk and allowed to return to his tribe, who are now living on the banks of the Iowa River. Blackhawk dies in 1838, a broken man.

He will not be the last.

Chapter Five

The truce is over.

The morning desert air is bone cold. Chokonen warriors completely surround a small Mexican military presidio. The Indians have been here before, sometimes taking hostages, other times stealing cattle. Today they have come for the horses. There are at least fifty in small corrals. The plan is to steal as many as possible, then drive them north, into the Chiricahua Mountains, where the tribe makes its home.

The leaders this morning are Pisago and Relles, two of the group's most audacious fighters. Among the younger Indians is Cheis—"Oak"—a warrior in his late twenties with a perfect Roman nose. His ears are pierced with steel hoop earrings in the belief that he will hear better. Long black hair, which he grooms fastidiously, falls to his shoulders. The son of a tribal leader, Cheis has been targeted for power and trained in the art of war since the age of seven.

The Chokonen have not yet encountered white American settlers. That conflict is still twenty years away. It is the Spanish and then the Mexicans who have intruded upon the tribe's lands for almost three centuries, building their forts and Catholic churches wherever they settle. The two have waged war for just as long. It is

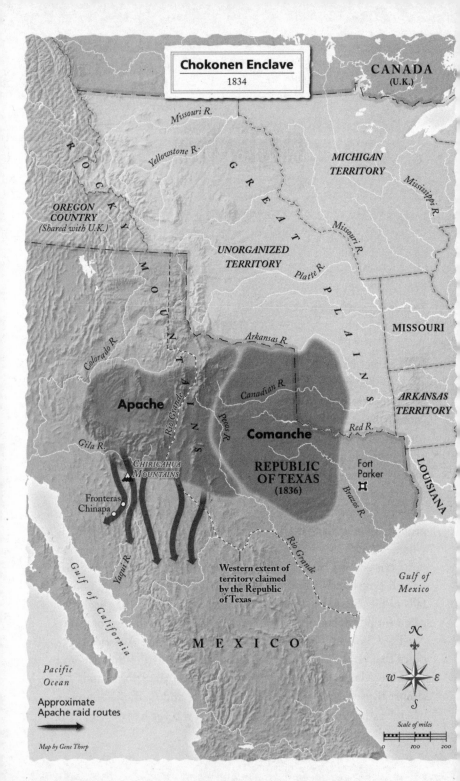

Chokonen Enclave
1834

CANADA
(U.K.)

Missouri R.

Yellowstone R.

R
O
C
K
Y

MICHIGAN
TERRITORY

Mississippi R.

OREGON
COUNTRY
(Shared with U.K.)

UNORGANIZED
TERRITORY

G
R
E
A
T

M
O
U
N
T
A
I
N
S

Missouri R.

Platte R.

MISSOURI

Colorado R.

Arkansas R.

P
L
A
I
N
S

Apache

Canadian R.

ARKANSAS
TERRITORY

Gila R.

Rio Grande

Pecos R.

Comanche

Red R.

CHIRICAHUA
MOUNTAINS

REPUBLIC
OF TEXAS
(1836)

Fort
Parker

LOUISIANA

Fronteras
Chinapa

Braxos R.

Yaqui R.

Western extent of
territory claimed
by the Republic
of Texas

Rio Grande

Gulf of
Mexico

M E X I C O

Gulf of California

Pacific
Ocean

𝒩

𝒲   𝓔

𝒮

Scale of miles

**Approximate
Apache raid routes**

0   100   200

Map by Gene Thorp

from these enemies that the Chokonen tribe has learned the art of torturing captives in a most horrific fashion. Cheis is a kind man, but as a warrior he is a student of this new knowledge and capable of inflicting pain and mutilation when needed.

For the last fifty years, the Chokonen and Spanish peoples have been at peace. But relations have been strained since Mexico gained its independence over a decade ago. Tired of new treaties that limit their freedom of movement, starve their people, and seek to make them dependent on Mexican alcohol, Indian tribes throughout this desert region are in revolt. The uprisings take the form of raiding parties. Theft among tribe members is forbidden, but stealing from an enemy is a traditional part of the Chokonen lifestyle. It is a rite of passage for a young man to take part in raids. Indeed, until a boy has shown courage in four such excursions, he cannot call himself a warrior.

Moving quickly and stealthily on horseback, the Chokonen approach the Presidio of Santa Rosa de Corodéguachi, as the adobe fort is formally known. Each Indian is armed with a hunting knife and rifle. Some also carry a bow and arrow.

The presidio is built into the base of a hill, facing outward at the desert. Roughly fifty Mexican soldiers live in the barracks. These Caballería de las Fronteras—"cavalry of the frontier"—give the presidio its more commonly used name.

The warrior Cheis, standing almost six feet tall and weighing a lean 175 pounds, is keen to distinguish himself this morning. He must be aggressive and appear fearless, willing to kill the enemy and take a scalp if that is required to complete the mission. Cheis has honed himself for battle through long-distance running, wrestling, riding, and becoming an expert marksman. As a young man, one test of his mettle was to run many miles with a mouthful of water—but not swallow a drop. He abstained from sexual relations until the tribe declared him a warrior and still practices a strict regimen of self-control that forbids gluttony, drunkenness, and dishonesty.

Cheis is not alone. His tribe's warriors all adhere to this code. For that reason, and for their utter ruthlessness in war, they are widely renowned and just as widely feared. The Zuni tribe calls Cheis's people "enemy." Their word for that term is "Apachu."

The Yuman tribe refers to them as "e-patch," or "man."

The Mexicans blend both terms together, giving the tribe of Cheis the name that will become infamous: "Apache."*

❖

The surprise is complete. Even as Mexican soldiers pour out of their barracks, half-dressed, fifty prime horses are being galloped away from Fronteras.

But not every horse has been stolen. Mexican captain Bernardo Martinez rallies a small group of his men to follow the Apache band east, where they have completely disappeared into a notch in the mountains.

The pursuit is a grave mistake. Anticipating they will be followed, the Apache have halted their flight to hide in the pink soil and low shrubs just a half mile from the presidio. Captain Martinez gallops into this trap, only to be shot dead. Three other Mexican soldiers are also killed and scalped before the others are driven off.

It is not the goal of the Apache to take land or forts from their enemy. But through terror and intimidation they hope to encourage the Mexicans to abandon any claims to lands that have long belonged to the Apache tribes. In this way, they are like Blackhawk and his Sauk Indians. But the Apache band, also known as the Chiricahuas, will not bend so easily to the white man.

So now, rather than merely herding their spoils north to their homeland, young Cheis and his band maraud through northwest Mexico. The ranch of a man named Narivo Montoya is plundered of food and livestock until there is nothing left to steal. Eight Mexican settlers unlucky enough to be traveling down the same road as the

---

* The Apache are descended from Athabascan tribes originating in Canada and Alaska. Their migration southward likely took place before the year 1100. They do not function as a single tribe but as many autonomous bands defined by region. The Eastern Apache number the Jicarilla, Chiricahua, Mescalero, Kiowa, and Lipin bands. The Western Apache are comprised of the Cinecue, Mimbreno, Coyotero, and Mogollon Apache. In times of war, it is common for several bands to be under the leadership of a single chief.

Six tribal leaders on horseback in ceremonial attire (l to r):
Little Plume (Piegan), Buckskin Charley (Ute), Geronimo (Chiricahua Apache),
Quanah Parker (Comanche), Hollow Horn Bear (Brulé Sioux), and
American Horse (Oglala Sioux). Photograph by Edward S. Curtis, circa 1900.

Apache are shot and scalped, their bodies left to bloat in the desert sun. The town of Chinopa is destroyed. Knowing that stealing the local cattle will slow them down, the Indians simply butcher those they wish to eat, then set the others loose into the wilderness.

The Apaches eventually return home to the Chiricahua Mountains, located in present-day Arizona. Their families await them on the small ranches where the Indians can raise their livestock, grow mescal, and feed their horses. There will be no more raiding until the

Cochise's Head, a rock formation in Arizona named after
the chief of the Chiricahua Apache, circa 1950

need for more provisions becomes apparent. Or, should the Mexican Army find them, the Apache will once again take up arms to fight for their land.

This deadly back-and-forth will continue for decades, defining daily life for Cheis and the members of his tribe. In time, Mexicans will no longer be the enemy, replaced instead by Americans continuing their western settlement. By all accounts, Cheis is a happy man during peacetime, raising his sons and taking just one wife, believing all the while that it is possible to avoid warfare. Ultimately, he makes peace with the Mexicans, and later with the new wave of settlers. For a time he even sets aside his warrior training and makes a living providing firewood to a local American stagecoach company.

But war is inevitable. By then, Cheis will be the leader of his tribe. He will also be known by another name: Cochise.

And until the day he dies, Cochise will never suffer defeat in battle.

Chapter Six

Seventy-eight-year-old John Parker knows he may soon be facing death. On this warm spring morning, a band of Native Americans numbering in the hundreds gallops toward his family's fortress. Even their women are on horseback. Parker was warned that this moment was coming. Yet he is a prideful man and ignored those messages. Now Parker, and perhaps his entire family, are just moments away from paying for his foolishness.

It was two years ago when Congress passed a law making it illegal for white men to settle west of the Mississippi River. If necessary, the U.S. Army is authorized to arrest anyone found in violation of the 1834 Act to Regulate Trade and Intercourse with the Indian Tribes, and to Preserve Peace on the Frontiers. Passed into law two decades after the massacre at Fort Mims, this legislation fulfilled Andrew Jackson's long-held ambition to permanently separate Indians and whites by creating a Native American sanctuary west of the Mississippi.

But settlers like Parker, who treat the Indians with contempt and believe the land is theirs as a gift from God, do not respect the U.S. government or any laws that may inhibit their ambitions. So while John Parker's fort and eighteen-thousand-acre farm is more

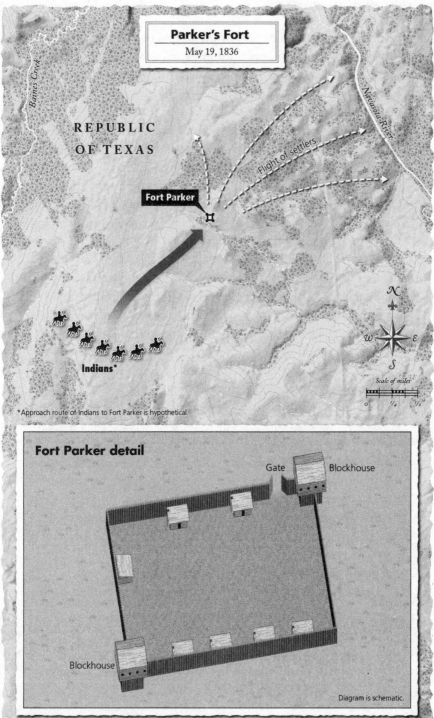

Parker's Fort
May 19, 1836

Baines Creek

REPUBLIC
OF TEXAS

Navasota River

Fort Parker

Flight of settlers

Indians*

N
W E
S

Scale of miles
0   ¼   ½

*Approach route of Indians to Fort Parker is hypothetical.

Fort Parker detail

Gate   Blockhouse

Blockhouse

Diagram is schematic.

Map by Gene Thorp. Diagram by Gene Thorp and Kate Thorp

than four hundred miles west of the Mississippi, he has made sure this new law does not apply to him. For Parker no longer resides in the United States of America but in the Republic of Texas, a sovereign nation that declared its independence from Mexico just two months ago.*

John Parker was born in Maryland and grew up in Virginia. In his youth, he fought in the Revolutionary War, battling Native American tribes loyal to the British alongside Daniel Boone. The legendary frontiersman made such an impression on Parker that upon marrying Sarah "Sallie" White in 1779, he named his first son Daniel. John and Sallie Parker moved to Georgia in 1785, seeking to escape the Indian attacks that bedeviled Virginia and its governor, Patrick Henry. Parker made a name for himself for his bravery fighting Indians but longed to flee the hostilities. From Georgia the family traveled to Tennessee, then on to Illinois. John became a widower in 1825, but remarried soon after to a woman whose name is also Sallie, though she is known most frequently as Granny.

The relocation to Texas came three years ago. Enticed by the prospect of free land, John Parker migrated south with a caravan of thirty oxcarts, bringing his grown children, their spouses, and his grandchildren to this vast land of rolling hills and thick oak forests. Parker's homestead is not just any western settlement but absolutely the westernmost location of any fort in the Republic of Texas. The closest white settlement is sixty miles east. And because Parker no longer resides in the USA, he does not enjoy the protection of the U.S. Army. In the event of an Indian attack, the refuge they have built is their only hope to stay alive. The one-acre stockade is designed to repel any assault. Blockhouses, an ample number of gun ports, and walls fifteen feet high make this a true fortress. The front gate has been extensively reinforced so that it is bulletproof.

In all, six families made the journey to Texas with John Parker.

---

* The law's full name is "An Act to Regulate Trade and Intercourse with the Indian Tribes, and to Preserve Peace on the Frontiers." Congress passed it on June 30, 1834, declaring that no whites were allowed to settle on Indian land or trade with the Indians. The mandate was so ineffective that a second law establishing "A Permanent Indian Frontier" was passed in 1840. This law, too, was ignored.

A portrait of Penateka Comanche chief Milky Way, also known as Asa Havi or Bird Chief, holding a bow, 1872

More than half are women and children. Fifty-seven-year-old Daniel Parker is not among the Parker clan, having parted ways with his father in a schism over their religious fundamentalism years before.

It is a separation that will save Daniel Parker's life.

For in the aging John Parker's thirst to possess this small kingdom on the Texas frontier, he is taking an enormous risk. Texas is a land of tornadoes, thunderstorms, searing heat, poisonous snakes, bloodsucking insects, and snapping turtles. There is an abundance of warlike Indian tribes as well, among them the Cherokee, Tawakoni, Kichai, and Caddo. It is the Caddo who have named this vast land "Taysha," which the Spanish spell as Tejas.

To the Caddo, "Taysha" means a friend or an ally. But of all the tribes in Texas, one band stands alone as no one's amigo. These Indians call themselves Numinu ("People") and are so warlike that the Ute tribe has christened them Komantcia, which translates to "anyone who wants to fight me all the time." Whenever sign language is utilized to communicate between tribes that do not speak the same tongue, the speaker places his forearm flat in front of him and wriggles it back and forth to describe the Komantcia. This is also the sign word for snakes.

Once again, the Spanish changed Komantcia to a word they could understand better. Thus, this tribe, so legendary for the atrocities they inflict upon their victims, is fearfully known as the Comanche.

For months, the Comanche have been terrorizing ranches and settlements in eastern Texas. There have even been two separate reports from friendly Indians that Fort Parker will be attacked, one of them stating the morning of May 19 as the time it will occur. Because of this, Texas governor Sam Houston has ordered Parker to evacuate his property—a demand the settler ignores.

Now, the Comanche are two hundred yards outside Fort Parker.

And, as at Fort Mims, someone has carelessly left that bullet-proof front gate wide open.

Eleven of the fort's male inhabitants are far out in the fields, leaving just six men inside to defend the eight women and nine young children—all of whom are now in a panic. Mothers grab their children by the hands, rushing toward the low doorway of the back gate, hoping to escape into the nearby woods. Recognizing that he has been a fool, old John Parker grabs Granny's hand and races after them.

Some will make it.

Most will not.

And some will suffer horrendously.

※

The Comanche sit patiently atop their mounts. The morning air is eerily silent. Conversations are muted, and their well-trained horses remain still. In addition to rifles, knives, and a battle-ax tipped with a two-pound flint stone, each man is armed with a sharpened steel-tipped lance seven feet long, in the manner of a European knight. This is a weapon best suited for combat on horseback, and the Comanche are trained to impale even the smallest of prey at a full gallop.

A white flag of truce is held high for the inhabitants of Fort Parker to see. An attack right now would easily overwhelm the whites, and the open gate would certainly make this raid easier than most. But despite their reputation, these Comanche warriors want nothing more than a cow to slaughter and directions to a well where they might water their horses.

This is not their first visit to Parker's fort, although it is the first time the settlers have seen them. These Comanche have long hunted and raided in eastern Texas and watched from afar as John Parker built his fortress in the midst of a prime hunting ground. The Comanche people once resided in the Snake River region of the Rocky Mountains and were part of the Shoshone tribe. But the two bands split centuries ago, for reasons that remain unclear. The Shoshone drifted farther north, into what is now Idaho, living a subsistence lifestyle. The Comanche traveled south, to lands controlled by the Spanish and the Apache, a direction that would change their fate dramatically.

Once a band of nomads who traveled on foot in search of food, the Comanche soon learned to ride the horses the Spaniards first introduced to North America in the late 1600s. It is impossible to overestimate the profound change these animals made to the Comanche and to every other tribe west of the Mississippi. The horse gave them mobility, allowing them to hunt and raid wherever they pleased. Escaping from enemies became much easier. No longer confined to the mountains, the Comanche made a life for themselves on the broad expanse of the plains, once too vast for them to cross easily. Horsehair could be woven into ropes and bridles. Prior to the horse, dogs were used to transport personal belongings on special harnesses known as travois. But dogs lack the power of a horse and cannot feed on the grass and bark found in abundance on the plains. In the rare event of starvation, a horse could be slaughtered and eaten. Not so a dog, against the eating of which the tribe had a religious superstition.

The Comanche are now among the very best horsemen in the world, trained to ride from a young age. At a full gallop, a Comanche warrior is capable of leaning all the way down to the ground, grabbing a human being, and pulling the person back up onto horseback.

Because of the horse, and then the rifle, there is nothing that now stops the Comanche from reigning over the entire southwestern plains. They live in tepees made of buffalo hide, supported by as many as eighteen poles, that can be taken down and reassembled quickly. The Comanche will forage for nuts and berries if necessary, but their primary source of food is buffalo, for which they roam hundreds of miles to hunt.

The Comancheria, as the land of the Comanches is known, extends thousands of square miles from Texas all the way to Santa Fe, New Mexico, and into the nation of Mexico. This territory was not granted to them outright but acquired through a century of war that established Comanche dominance. First the Utes, then the Kiowa, Osage, Arapaho, Tawakoni, Wichita, Waco, and Kichaies were either conquered or settled for a peace that allowed the Comanche to live and hunt wherever they pleased.

France had designs on pushing west of the Mississippi from its stronghold in Louisiana. So, too, the Spanish, with their hope of connecting territorial claims in the Pacific Northwest with their large holdings in Mexico. Despite a century of attempts to pacify, evangelize, or crush the Comanche outright, both nations failed to expand their empires. Regular Comanche raids on European settlements throughout the eighteenth and early nineteenth centuries soon forced most to be abandoned. Spanish horses were the coveted plunder of these surprise attacks, enriching the Comanche through trade with other tribes too timid to attempt such larceny.

It is the Apache, however, whom the Comanche have devastated the most. There was a time when the Apache lived in New Mexico and Texas, but the Comanche migration put that to an end. While the Comanche roam the prairie unafraid, the Apache were forced to retreat to desert mountains far to the south. This is the only terrain where they hold superiority over the Comanche, and yet the warring attacks continue. Regular Comanche raids against the Apache net slaves, horses, and mules, all of which are used for barter—most frequently for bullets and rifles. In addition to trade with tribes north of the Comancheria, these weapons were also acquired from the French and Spanish, despite the hostilities between them and the Comanche. After the Louisiana Purchase of 1803 by the United States, followed by Mexican independence in 1821, Spain and France abandoned any claim to the Southern Plains.

In their place came the Americans.

At first the Comanche were eager to trade with the new white settlers. In 1825, an American trade expedition met peacefully along the banks of the Brazos River with a Comanche delegation. Prior to Texas becoming an independent republic, a delegate from the United States named Sam Houston met with the Comanche to discuss a peace treaty. It was Houston who went over the wall against the Creek Indians at the 1814 Battle of Horseshoe Bend and was shot in the leg as a result. The war hero's negotiations with the Comanche did not initially result in success. But on August 24, 1835, an agreement was reached between the Comanche and the United States of America allowing tribes relocated from land east of the Mississippi to hunt in peace on Comanche lands in Texas. The Choctaw, Chickasaw, and Creek tribes are already being relocated. Without this permission from the Comanche, Andrew Jackson's landmark

Act to Preserve Peace on the Frontiers, forever dividing America into Indian and white, would be impossible.

But Texan independence rendered the 1835 agreement useless. And as more settlers moved into the new republic, building their homes near clear water—a rarity in Texas, where sediment clouds most rivers and lakes—and on the pastures best suited for feeding Comanche horses, the tribe chafed at the presence of the newcomers. Rather than be at peace with the whites, the Comanche began raiding their settlements just as they once terrorized the Spanish and French.

So it is that the settlers of Texas live in fear.

Most of these guerrilla actions take place during daylight, but during the blinding full moon of October, when the night sky is bright, Indian raids take on a brand-new form of terror. This "Comanche Moon" period means attacks can come at any time.

Wherever the Comanche raid, whether by night or day, a trail of violence follows. Vengeance-seeking warriors mutilate and murder most of the men, gang-rape the women, and slaughter the infants, if only because babies are difficult to carry while making a quick escape on horseback.

But for young boys and girls captured during these raids, there is a different fate: kidnapping. The Comanche's wandering ways and long days on horseback make it difficult for their women to carry babies to term. Snatching young girls and boys from other tribes, then raising them as Comanche, keeps the tribal population high.

Now, well aware that women and young children reside within Fort Parker, the Comanche watch as a middle-aged man steps alone from the split-cedar walls of Fort Parker and begins walking through the tall grass to speak with them.

❋

As cocksure as his father, forty-eight-year-old Benjamin Parker boldly ventures forth to negotiate. His younger brother Silas remains behind with his teenaged sister Rachel Parker Plummer, a married eighteen-year-old with bright-red hair who has chosen not to flee the fort with her baby.

Benjamin Parker's decision to approach the Comanche is arrogant on the surface, for the Indians clearly have the upper hand. But this selfless maneuver is also incredibly brave: the longer Benjamin can stall, the more time the women and children will have to flee and hide should the white flag be a hoax.

The Comanche remain on their horses as Benjamin walks forward. Looking down at the white settler, they tell him their demands for a cow and directions to water.

Benjamin negotiates in the Comanche language. In his mind, he has no doubt the Indians know their way to the local creek, and giving them a cow is out of the question. If he did that, the Comanche would demand all the cows. Instead, Benjamin offers to provide them with flour and salt. Despite being surrounded by men on horseback, all of whom are armed, Benjamin Parker boldly turns his back on them and walks to the fort, promising to return with these staples.

Fort Parker is now all but deserted. Whether out of foolishness, arrogance, or loyalty, only Benjamin Parker, his sister Rachel, the father-and-son pair of Samuel and Robert Frost, and thirty-two-year-old Silas Parker remain to protect the fortress. Silas Parker's wife, Lucy, has already fled toward the cornfields with their four children, among them a ten-year-old, blue-eyed daughter named Cynthia Ann.

Benjamin Parker's arms are full of foodstuffs as he returns to parlay once more. Silas watches from the relative safety of the fort, Rachel at his side.

"I know they will kill him," whispers Silas to his sister.

He is correct.

※

The Comanche are insulted.

They know where to find grapes, walnuts, pecans, and persimmons. In the absence of buffalo, the tribe can easily shoot deer or antelope. What they want is red meat, not the sundries this settler carries in his arms.

Yet the Comanche remain patient, allowing Benjamin Parker to make that two-hundred-yard walk from the fort. Only then do they surround him, their horses almost touching the defenseless settler.

There is no hand signal, no nod of the head. In the Comanche world, the lance is a symbol of leadership. So it is that the warrior in charge of this small band—for the Comanche do not travel as a single tribe but as compact fighting units—suddenly thrusts his lance clean through Benjamin Parker. In an instant, every man surrounding Parker does the same.

Yet Benjamin Parker is still alive as blows from the Comanche battle-axes then rain down on his head and arrows are shot into his torso from just three feet away. Finally, Parker is scalped.

Giving great war cries, the Comanche then gallop into the fort to kill its remaining inhabitants. Others Indians gallop around the back to stop anyone from escaping. Rachel Parker Plummer has belatedly rushed out the back of the fort, just an instant before her brother Silas is murdered and scalped. She carries her infant son, James, in her arms. But her escape is short-lived. The Comanche knock her to the ground, steal the child, and drag her by the hair back into the fort.

Three-quarters of a mile from the fortress, the Comanche catch up to John and Granny Parker, along with Granny's widowed daughter. All three are stripped of their clothing. John Parker is beaten with tomahawks. Granny is forced to watch as her husband's genitals are cut off and he is scalped. The two women are then raped by several men. Daughter Elizabeth Kellogg is deemed young enough to kidnap and is thrown onto the back of a horse. Granny, however, is left to die on the Texas prairie, a Comanche knife thrust deep into her breast.

In the nearby cornfields, the four children of Silas Parker huddle quietly with their mother, Lucy. Their father is being scalped at this very moment, though they cannot possibly know he is suffering this fate.

Thundering hooves mark the arrival of the Comanche, who plunge headlong into the cornfield, knowing they have nothing to fear. The panic and terror build for Lucy Parker and her children. Captivity is imminent as the horses thrash through the tall green stalks, cutting off all avenue of escape. Down in a nearby riverbed, a group of women and children, along with the men who spent the

Waneda Parker, the daughter of Quanah Parker,
the chief of the Comanche Indians

day working in the fields, remain hidden from the Comanche, never to be discovered.

The same is not true for Lucy Parker and her children.

Soon enough, the Comanche have them. Being taken captive by the Comanche is harrowing. It begins with beatings to intimidate the victim, followed by whippings, and often the removal of clothing to make the prisoner feel vulnerable.

Back inside the fort, the Comanche are shooting cattle, scavenging for plunder in the small cabins where the Parker families once lived, and then setting fire to the buildings. It is here that Lucy Parker and her four children are taken. She is wounded and left to die. Amazingly, in the chaos, two of her children manage to escape once again and flee safely to the riverbed.

Their siblings will not be as lucky. The Comanche take five prisoners today. Rachel Parker Plummer is outside the fort as Lucy Parker and her children are brought back, being stripped and whipped by Indian women. Rachel will be placed naked upon a horse, her wrists tied in front of her, ankles bound beneath the animal's belly, and forced to ride hours in the hot Texas sun, before spending a night of depravity so vile she will never speak of it again. This abuse will continue well into her captivity. "My own soul becomes sick at the dreadful thought," Rachel will later write, adding that "anyone who said that a good woman died before being violated had not been forced to run naked tied by a rope to a horse for a day or two in the sun."

As Rachel Parker Plummer is defiled, again and again through the long night as warriors dance around a campfire, her agony will be made worse by the terrified sobbing of her young son, James. "I could hear his cries," she will also write, "but could offer him no relief."

The final two prisoners will become legends: ten-year-old Cynthia Ann Parker and her two-year-old brother, John. Their wrists and ankles are bound by their kidnappers as they begin a new phase of life.

It is May 19, 1836. Cynthia Ann and baby John Parker, once the children of white settlers, are being sized up for adoption into the Comanche tribe. Within days they will be hundreds of miles from Fort Parker and all vestiges of white society. The search for the young children, however, will never end.

And one day, Cynthia Ann and John Parker will finally be found.

Chapter Seven

Ralph Waldo Emerson is angry.

Two thousand miles from the Texas prairie, the lanky thirty-four-year-old philosopher sits alone in his first-floor study, penning a letter to President Martin Van Buren. Emerson firmly believes in the power of the individual to determine his own fate, and that all men are created equal. But even as he writes, the U.S. Army is marching to Georgia to strip the Cherokee nation of lands they have inhabited for centuries. Emerson finds these policies immoral. The tribe will be placed under arrest en masse and imprisoned in internment camps. Then, under armed guard, the Indians will be force-marched a thousand miles west to forge a new life in lands north of Texas.

Taking pains to hide his disgust, an irate Emerson tells President Van Buren why this is wrong.

"The newspapers now inform us that, in December, 1835, a treaty contracting for the exchange of all the Cherokee territory was pretended to be made by an agent on the part of the United States with some persons appearing on the part of the Cherokees; that the fact afterwards transpired that these deputies did by no means represent the will of the nation; and that, out of 18,000 souls composing the [Cherokee] nation, 15,668 have protested against the so-called treaty. It now appears that the government of the United States chooses to hold the Cherokees to this sham treaty, and are proceeding to execute the same. Almost the entire Cherokee Nation stand up and say, 'This is not our act. Behold us. Here are we. Do not mistake that handful of deserters for us;' and the American President and the Cabinet, the Senate and the House of Representatives, neither hear these men nor see them, and are contracting to put this active nation into carts and boats, and to drag them over mountains and rivers to a wilderness at a vast distance beyond the Mississippi."

Ralph Waldo Emerson makes his living writing about social justice. He will become a mentor to Henry David Thoreau and other New England philosophers. But Emerson knows he is fighting a losing battle with the federal government. The 1829 discovery of gold in Georgia sent thousands of speculators flooding into that state, trespassing on Cherokee lands. As the white population swelled, the newcomers pressured the state legislature to remove the Cherokee. Georgia responded by passing laws stripping the tribe of their farms, then held lotteries granting those properties to the new white arrivals. When a delegation of Cherokee tribal leadership traveled to Washington to protest, U.S. officials took advantage of their absence to convince a handful of tribal dissidents to sign a new treaty exchanging all their land in the east for land west of the Mississippi. This Treaty of New Echota, named after the Cherokee nation's capital in Georgia, was overwhelmingly opposed by the rest of the tribe. Yet the U.S. Senate ratified the accord in May 1836, setting in motion the removal of every single Cherokee living in Georgia, Texas, Tennessee, Alabama, and North Carolina.*

Ralph Waldo Emerson knows the depth of the Indian Removal corruption and desperately seeks to make Martin Van Buren sympathetic to the Cherokee. He writes of "a general expression of despon-

---

* A census of the Cherokee nation conducted by the U.S. War Department in 1835 counted the total tribal population as 16,542 full-blooded Cherokee, 201 intermarried whites, and 1,592 African American slaves. Though the tribe was never allowed to vote on the Treaty of New Echota, more than 13,000 signed a petition against the accord in February 1836.

Ralph Waldo Emerson, photographed in London, 1873

dency, of disbelief" among America's citizens about this "barbarous" policy.

Led by the powerful voice of former president John Quincy Adams, many residents in the Northeast are coming down hard against Cherokee removal. Southern states, meanwhile, insist the policy is necessary. The result is a growing divide between north and south.

Emerson's full letter is six pages long. At a time in history when the nation is at a crossroads about treatment of all Native Americans, Emerson makes a plea that the president do the right thing, setting a precedent for generations to come.

"I write thus, sir," Emerson concludes, "to pray with one voice more that you, whose hands are strong with the delegated power of fifteen millions of men, will avert with that might the terrific injury which threatens the Cherokee tribe.

"With great respect, sir, I am your fellow citizen."

✳

It is unclear whether Martin Van Buren ever read Ralph Waldo Emerson's letter. But in truth it was a waste of good ink and paper, for Van Buren is wholeheartedly behind the Indian removal. The fifty-four-year-old New Yorker will serve just one term in office. The time from 1837 to 1841 is a period when America is mired in a great economic depression. Van Buren refuses to utilize federal intervention to stop this financial crisis, ensuring that it will continue for five more years, spike unemployment rates to 25 percent, and doom his presidency.

Yet Van Buren has no such qualms about utilizing the power of the U.S. government to enforce Andrew Jackson's Indian Removal policy. Old Hickory was an inspiration to the portly Van Buren, whose bald forehead is framed by thick tufts of white hair. During Jackson's time in office, Van Buren served first as secretary of state and then vice president. His admiration for Old Hickory transcends mere loyalty, venturing into the realm of worship.

"No man ever entered upon the execution of an official duty with purer motives, firmer purpose or better qualifications for its performance," Van Buren once wrote glowingly of Jackson. The new president is aware that there is popular opposition to the Cherokee plight, but he considers Indian Removal "the settled policy of the country" and ignores any suggestion that it be discontinued.

Or, as Martin Van Buren makes clear in his annual Message to Congress: "A mixed occupancy of the same territory by the white and red man is incompatible with the safety or happiness of either."

So it is that on May 26, 1838, under the supervision of U.S.

Army general Winfield Scott, four thousand members of the Georgia State Militia descend upon New Echota to arrest any and all members of the Cherokee nation.

The "Trail of Tears" has begun—and in a most violent fashion.

✷

General Winfield Scott tells himself he is just obeying orders. Though personally not in favor of the Indian Removal policy, Scott allows members of the militia under his command to evict entire Cherokee families from their homes. The fifty-one-year-old Scott's order that the militia treat the Cherokee with "every possible kindness" goes unheeded. Children scream as they are torn from their mothers' arms, the soldiers bawl commands at gunpoint, and innocent Cherokee families are prodded toward internment centers at the tip of a bayonet. Those who defy the military order are beaten with fists and rifle butts, as the soldiers ignore their commander's order.

The date is May 28, 1838. This moment has been coming for three years, ever since the ratification of the Treaty of New Echota. So it is fitting that this surprise morning raid marking the beginning of military intervention takes place in the town of the same name.

General Scott has taken great pains to assure the Cherokee leadership that the men under his command will be gentle. "If, in the ranks, a despicable individual should be found capable of inflicting wanton injury or insult on any Cherokee man, woman or child, it is hereby made the special duty of the nearest good officer or man . . . to seize or consign the guilty wretch to the severest penalty of the laws," Scott previously promised the Cherokee leaders.

But the Georgia militia are rabble. Scott is powerless to stop the mostly illiterate soldiers from abusing the Cherokee nation. These men have long despised the Cherokee culture and coveted their vast acres of prime farmland. Even now, as they root out the tribe from their homes, the militia steal Indian cattle and loot before setting their houses ablaze.

"The work of capture commenced," the *New-Yorker* (a short-lived predecessor to the *New-York Tribune*) will report. "And continued with unfeeling rigor, until the entire rightful and legitimate of the country were divested of house and home, and reduced to a state of abject poverty. In most cases, the humane injunctions of the commanding general were disregarded.

"The captors sometimes drove the people with whooping and hallowing, like cattle, through a river, allowing them no time even to take off their shoes and stockings. Many, when arrested, were not so much as permitted to gather up their clothes . . . the horses brought by some of them were demanded by the Commissioner of Indian property, to be given up for the purpose of being sold. The owners refusing to give them up—men, women, children, and horses were driven promiscuously into one large pen, and the horses taken out by force, and cried to the highest bidder."

The Cherokee masses arrive at a hastily erected stockade with the few worldly possessions they have been able to carry and just the clothes on their backs. There they will remain throughout the long summer. More than 350 will die from dysentery and cholera before the long march west begins on a cold, drizzling October morning. The Cherokee will travel on foot and in wagon trains, "loaded like cattle or sheep," in the words of Private John G. Burnett of the U.S. Army. They will soon endure one of the coldest winters in memory, a season so frigid that streams will freeze over with six inches of ice.

"On the morning of November 17th," writes Burnett, who traveled alongside the Cherokee to enforce their removal, "we encountered a terrific sleet and snow storm with freezing temperatures. And from that day until we reached the end of the fateful journey on March 26, 1839, the sufferings of the Cherokee were awful. The trail of exiles was a trail of death. They had to sleep in the wagons and on the ground without fire."

Private Burnett adds: "The long painful journey to the west ended . . . with 4,000 silent graves reaching from the foothills of the Smoky Mountains to what is known as Indian Territory in the west."

Among the dead are the parents of Samuel Cloud, a nine-year-old Cherokee. He will never forget this journey, passing his emotions down from generation to generation, until his great-great-grandson will finally put the words onto the page.

Cherokee Indians are forced from their homelands during the 1830s

"I know what it is to hate," Cloud states. "I hate those white soldiers who took us from our home. I hate the soldiers who made us keep walking through the snow and ice toward this new home that none of us ever wanted. I hate the people who killed my mother and father. I hate the white people who lined the roads in their woolen clothes that kept them warm, watching us pass. None of these white people are here to say they are sorry that I am alone. None of them care about me or my people. All they ever saw was the color of our skin.

"All I see is the color of theirs.

"And I hate them."

Chapter Eight

Lieutenant Hiram Ulysses "Sam" Grant is homesick.

A soft morning breeze wafts in from the Gulf of Mexico as the five hundred men of the U.S. Fourth Infantry assemble. The future president is twenty-three, a five-foot-eight, clean-shaven graduate of the U.S. Military Academy, Class of 1843. Surrounded by swarms of black flies, the enlisted men and officers divide into lines by company. The Mexican border is just 130 miles south. After seven horrendous months on these Texas sands, buffeted by a winter of torrential rains, this fighting force is just days away from becoming the first army in U.S. history to invade another nation.

Silently, Sam Grant wishes the Fourth Infantry was marching in the other direction. He is lonely and afraid. Last year, just before shipping out from the Jefferson Barracks in St. Louis, Grant swam his horse "Fashion" through a river at flood stage to say farewell to Julia Boggs Dent, the nineteen-year-old daughter of a Missouri plantation owner. The young officer soon proposed marriage, offering his West Point ring as a symbol of love. The brown-eyed Julia is pretty—though one of her eyes does not align with the other, a condition known as "walleye." She has plenty of suitors and has

*General Ulysses S. Grant at his Cold Harbor, Virginia, headquarters, June, 1864.
Photograph by Egbert Guy Fowx.*

already refused to marry Grant once. But this time her answer was yes. As a reminder that she would wait for him, Julia gave Sam Grant a lock of her hair.

The young Ohioan carries it with him now. Grant pines to be at Julia's side and writes love letter after love letter. He is so desperate to be with his fiancée that Grant has seriously contemplated resigning his commission. But that would be an act of cowardice, a shame he would carry the rest of his life. So U. S. Grant soldiers on.

One year ago, Texas ceased being a sovereign nation and became America's twenty-eighth state. The border between Texas and Mexico is still in dispute, so the Fourth Infantry has occupied Corpus Christi to keep the peace. But an enraged Mexican government has sent troops into these borderlands, providing an excuse for President James K. Polk to order the army south under the command of General Zachary Taylor.

Victory is hardly assured. The decade since the U.S. Army battled Blackhawk and his Sauk Indians has been mostly a time of peace. There is grave concern within the ranks that the Americans are not as battle ready as the Mexican forces. But in truth, Mexico's army has been equally absent from combat. The Comanche and Apache tribes have become increasingly bold in their raids on Mexican settlements, stealing thousands of cattle and murdering and kidnapping hundreds of homesteaders. But the Indians have become so fierce in this region that Mexico's federal government does not want to fight them. Citizens have been urged not to set foot outside their settlements unless accompanied by at least thirty armed men. The Comanche's dominance of Texas and northern Mexico is so profound that between July 1845 and June 1846—the same period of time in which American and Mexican troops are saber rattling along the Rio Grande border—Comanche raids into Mexico will account for more than 650 deaths. Farther to the west, Apache tribes steal and murder with the same impunity.

And no one can stop them.

Though Lieutenant Sam Grant and his fellow soldiers don't know it, protecting the border will not be enough to satisfy President James K. Polk. He quietly covets not just Texas but also the territo-

Oregon Trail reenactment

ries of New Mexico and California to the west. For the former Tennessee governor and protégé of Andrew Jackson fervently believes in an expansionist vision known as "Manifest Destiny."*

This philosophy, dreamed up far from the dusty plains of Texas in the cozy confines of a Washington salon, by a young idealist born into privilege and deeply smitten with the philosophies of Andrew Jackson, will soon lead to fifty years of war and death.

In an 1839 article for the *United States Magazine and Democratic*

---

* In a nod to his close relationship with Andrew Jackson, Polk's nickname was "Young Hickory." He was a gifted orator whose life was marred by a childhood surgical procedure to prevent urinary stones. A hole was drilled in his prostate gland without the use of anesthetic, leaving him permanently impotent.

Review, political writer John L. Sullivan first argues that America is "the great nation of futurity." Expanding upon the theme in an 1845 essay entitled "Annexation," Sullivan writes that it is "our manifest destiny to overspread the continent allotted by Providence for the free development of our yearly multiplying millions."

President Polk is on board with that. The United States is already taking advantage of a new route west known as the "Oregon Trail": settlers on horseback and in covered wagons are traveling to establish farms and towns in territory on the Pacific Coast jointly occupied by the United States and Great Britain.

There is no concept of intruding on Indian land because, according to the U.S. Supreme Court, Native American tribes are not sovereign nations, therefore not entitled to any protections at all.

So even though the Comanche and Apache have total control of the Mexican-American border and much of the land in Texas, New Mexico, and California, no consideration is given to negotiating with either tribe.

Lieutenant Sam Grant does not give the Comanche a second thought. Not once does he mention the Indians in his many letters home. Grant's only worry is the Mexican Army—and making it home safely to Julia. "Fight or no fight," he writes her, "everyone rejoices in leaving Corpus Christi."

But Sam Grant will not have the luxury of ignoring Native Americans and the lands they own much longer. For the Mexican-American War and the concept of Manifest Destiny will set into motion a horrible chain of events. During Grant's lifetime, the simmering conflict between whites and the many Indian nations across the American West will erupt into a powerful confrontation. Among those who will perish is a fellow native of Ohio, a man who presently is just a seven-year-old boy. It will be left to the future president Grant to break the news to the country about this man's massacre at a place called Little Bighorn.

But that is thirty years into the future.

After the gold rush.

Chapter Nine

President Polk is satisfied.

He makes that clear in his Annual Message to Congress, in which he presents his view: "Peace, plenty, and contentment reign throughout our borders, and our beloved country presents a sublime moral spectacle to the world."

After a two-year fight, James K. Polk forced the Mexican government to sign a peace treaty ten months ago, on February 2. U.S. forces under the command of General Zachary Taylor and then General Winfield Scott routed the enemy, eventually occupying the capital of Mexico City. Sam Grant started the war as a quartermaster, responsible for the logistics of feeding and supplying the army. But then he became a hero at the Battle of Monterey when he rode his horse through sniper-filled streets to deliver an urgent message. He did not sit upright in the saddle but "adjusted [him]self on the side of the horse furthest from the enemy, and with only one foot holding to the cantle of the saddle, and an arm over the neck of the horse exposed," he galloped through the city.

"It was only at street crossings that my horse was under fire, but these I crossed at such a flying rate that generally I was past and under cover of the next block of houses before the enemy fired."

Grant's heroics, however, were in vain. The advance position he had been sent to warn was overrun.

On August 18, 1847, the Mexican War offered Sam Grant yet another encounter. He had just returned to General Scott's headquarters after a day of foraging for food to feed the troops. His uniform was unbuttoned, and his face was covered in dust and grime. A colonel approached, his uniform spotless, and he sharply scolded Grant for his slovenly appearance. The man spoke with a Virginia drawl and insulted Grant so completely that the memory would never fade.

In this way, Ulysses S. Grant and Robert E. Lee met for the first time. They will not speak again until 1865, at a remote farmhouse in the Virginia village of Appomattox Court House, where Grant will accept the surrender of Lee's Confederate troops, bringing the American Civil War to an end.*

President Polk was the direct beneficiary of the American army's effectiveness—and he knew it: "Within less than four years, the annexation of Texas to the Union has been consummated; all conflicting title to the Oregon Territory south of the forty-ninth degree of north latitude, being all that was insisted on by any of my predecessors, has been adjusted, and New Mexico and Upper California have been acquired by treaty."

Polk then adds: "The Mississippi, so lately the frontier of our country, is now only its center. With the addition of the late acquisitions, the United States is now estimated to be nearly as large as the whole of Europe."

※

For the Apache and Comanche tribes, the Mexican War allows them an unchallenged opportunity to raid, steal, and kill. The Indians took advantage of white men fighting each other to grow even stronger. In fact, one provision of the war-ending Treaty of Guadalupe Hidalgo is that the United States will be responsible for policing the border, protecting the country of Mexico from future Indian incursions.

---

* A total of 1,733 Americans were killed in the war with Mexico. More than 4,000 were wounded. The Mexican Army suffered more than 10,000 dead.

Obviously, Mexico City wants no part of the Comanche and Apache.

＊

President Polk's Manifest Destiny policy quickly pays off in another area. Shortly after the Mexicans capitulate to the United States, gold is discovered in Northern California. Had Mexico still controlled that area, the giant strike would have been theirs.

Polk quickly encourages Americans to head west to seek their fortune. Within months, thousands of young men answer his call. They travel overland by horse or even sail around South America in tall ships. Men flood into Northern California through a small fishing village known as San Francisco. They then proceed to the Sierra Nevada, which is home to a variety of Indian tribes. But President Polk does not care about the Native Americans. And the millions in gold soon extracted by the so-called 49ers does not benefit the tribes at all. In fact, the opposite is true. Indian land is being destroyed. More than twelve billion tons of earth will be moved in the gold exploration—reducing the depth of San Francisco Bay by three feet after rivers wash silt into that body of water.*

But as with the Georgia gold rush of 1829, the influx of white speculators will soon lead to tragedy. Fearful of Indian attacks while searching for gold, the prospectors take brutal measures to completely rid California of Native Americans.

Prior to Polk's announcement, more than 150,000 Indians are estimated to live in California. These are not warring nomads like the Comanche; they are fishermen and hunters who maintain a peaceful existence along the ocean and in the mountains. But rather than move these tribes to reservations, or negotiate a treaty that might benefit the Indians, the gold miners simply attack.

A shocking policy of extermination, land theft, and enslavement soon decimates the Native American population in California. Local

---

* Mercury was commonly used by miners to separate gold embedded in rock. The mercury was then washed downstream into San Francisco Bay. California gold miners used so much of this toxic metal that more than 150 years later, many restaurants in San Francisco still refuse to serve fish caught in the bay due to high mercury levels.

militias are paid a cash bounty for murdering and scalping Native Americans.

On May 15, 1850, at a place north of San Francisco known as Clear Lake, the federal government under the new president Zachary Taylor unofficially sanctions genocide. More than two hundred old men, women, and children of the Pomo tribe are surrounded and massacred by a regiment of federal troops called dragoons. In all, an estimated one hundred thousand Indians will die in the first two years of the California Gold Rush.*

"A war of extermination will continue to be waged between the two races until the Indian race becomes extinct," California governor Peter Hardeman Burnett tells the legislature in 1851, soon after the region is granted statehood. The newest addition to the Union has been admitted as a "free" state, but this protection does not extend to Native Americans. Thus, Indian children are commonly sold into slavery, forced to work on California farms and in the mines.

"While we cannot anticipate this result but with painful regret," Governor Hardeman concludes, "the inevitable destiny of the race is beyond the power or wisdom of man to avert."

But while the Indians of California are easily defeated, that will not be the case for other Native American tribes.

Especially the seething warriors of Cochise.

---

* The Pomo were massacred after taking revenge on white settlers who had raped their daughters and attempted to enslave the adults.

Chapter Ten

The most feared man in Mexico is home.

Cochise, the Chiricahua Apache chief, stoops low to exit the doorway of the small domed structure where he and his principal wife, Dos-teh-seh, have shared the night. The morning air is cool, and Cochise wears a cotton shirt with long pants. As the day becomes warmer, the chief will strip down to a simple loincloth. Sitting near the breakfast fire, he pulls on buckskin moccasins that come up to his knees to protect his legs from thorns and snakebite. A thick, durable sole curled up at the toe makes it easier to walk over rocky terrain.

Now in his forties, the strikingly handsome Cochise has spent the winter raiding for cattle and horses deep into Mexico. He has presided over months of plunder and murder, with few eyewitnesses left behind. Almost everyone in Mexico who encounters Cochise dies. The Apache speaks little Spanish but well understands the screams of his victims until the moment they are murdered.

This mountain stronghold is an oasis from all that, its lush meadows and oak forests a stark contrast to the barren mesquite and grasses of the surrounding desert. While the Apache are often spoken of as synonymous with desert living, they are in truth mountain

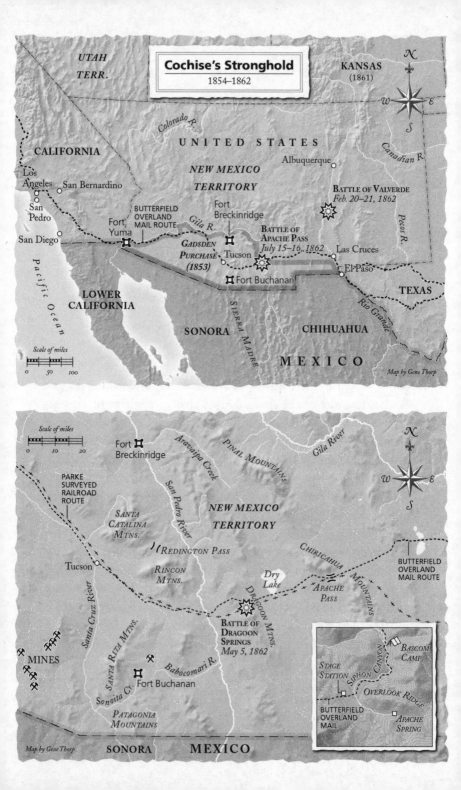

Cochise's Stronghold
1854–1862

UTAH TERR.

KANSAS (1861)

CALIFORNIA

Colorado R.

UNITED STATES

NEW MEXICO TERRITORY

Albuquerque

Los Angeles

San Bernardino

BUTTERFIELD OVERLAND MAIL ROUTE

Fort Breckinridge

BATTLE OF VALVERDE
Feb. 20–21, 1862

Canadian R.

San Pedro

Fort Yuma

Gila R.

Pecos R.

San Diego

GADSDEN PURCHASE (1853)

Tucson

BATTLE OF APACHE PASS
July 15–16, 1862

Las Cruces

El Paso

Pacific Ocean

LOWER CALIFORNIA

Fort Buchanan

TEXAS

SONORA

SIERRA MADRE

CHIHUAHUA

Rio Grande

MEXICO

Scale of miles
0   50   100

Map by Gene Thorp

Scale of miles
0   10   20

Fort Breckinridge

Aravaipa Creek

PINAL MOUNTAINS

Gila River

PARKE SURVEYED RAILROAD ROUTE

SANTA CATALINA MTNS.

San Pedro River

NEW MEXICO TERRITORY

CHIRICAHUA MOUNTAINS

BUTTERFIELD OVERLAND MAIL ROUTE

Tucson

REDINGTON PASS

RINCON MTNS.

Dry Lake

APACHE PASS

DRAGOON MTNS.

BATTLE OF DRAGOON SPRINGS
May 5, 1862

Santa Cruz River

SANTA RITA MTNS.

MINES

Fort Buchanan

Babocomari R.

Sonoita Cr.

PATAGONIA MOUNTAINS

Map by Gene Thorp

SONORA   MEXICO

Inset:

STAGE STATION

SIPHON CANYON

BASCOM CAMP

OVERLOOK RIDGE

BUTTERFIELD OVERLAND MAIL

APACHE SPRING

dwellers. The "lost" mountains of this region, so called by American surveyor William H. Emory because they rise dramatically from the desert floor and seem to have no apparent connection to one another, not only allow a wide vista for Apache sentinels to see the dust of approaching enemies but also feature clear skies, fresh air, and plenty of timber for firewood.

Apache Pass is also a place for family. Cochise and Dos-teh-seh, like most Apache, make camp and share food with several generations of their clan—perhaps up to forty people. But Cochise's time here will be short, for he and a band of two hundred warriors are riding south again in one week. Cochise is a product of the harsh desert environment in which he was raised, possessing cruelty in abundance and pity not at all. Such harsh behavior is considered virtuous among the Apache. But here at the pass, where no outsiders are present, the chief is a different man. Cochise has a keen sense of humor, enjoys laughter, and is known for being cheerful. He can relax because he knows most Mexicans are terrified of entering Apache Pass, calling it *el Puerto del Dado*—"the Pass of Fate"—as entering will almost surely result in death. Thus, safe in this Chiricahua stronghold, Cochise can spend the next few days at leisure.

The Chiricahua have been coming to Apache Pass for centuries. A map of the region shows that this land belongs to Mexico, but in truth the Apache are in complete control. They are a tribe in name only, preferring to live and travel in bands composed of several family groups, which come together with other clans to raid and fight. The Chiricahua Apache domain extends well north into New Mexico and hundreds of miles south to the Sierra Madre range in the Mexican state of Sonora. Using a strategy of surprise attacks and unrelenting cruelty toward enemies, the Chiricahua have established themselves as the most feared of all Indian bands in this region. Their reign of terror is so absolute that no new American or Mexican settlements are established within Apache lands. The growing cities of Tucson, Albuquerque, and El Paso are purposely located on the outermost fringes of Apache territory, to avoid citizens having cattle stolen, homes burned, and their very lives snuffed without warning.

＊

While Cochise has been away these past months, Dos-teh-seh has raised their teenage son, Taza. In time, Dos-teh-seh will give birth to a second boy, both of whom will be raised to succeed their father as a chief. Cochise also has a second wife, whose name has been lost to history, who will bear him two daughters.

The man is the head of every Apache household, but in truth the women make most decisions. Like Cochise, Dos-teh-seh wears knee-high buckskin moccasins as she prepares the morning meal, very often an acorn stew. She is clad in a skirt and cotton shirt but, like other Apache women, prefers to wear no top at all when the day gets warm.

It is Dos-teh-seh who builds the traditional wickiup shelter from tree branches and grass. It is a task she undertakes every time the family moves, and the process can be accomplished in less than two hours. The ceiling is always low, and there is no furniture because objects are a hindrance when it comes time to move. In the winter, animal hides are placed atop the small roof structure to keep out the snow, wind, and rain that so often buffet Apache Pass and other mountainous camping areas within the Chiricahua domain. The floors of the shelter are covered with animal-hide blankets, but the space is so cramped that there is just room enough for Cochise, his wife, and his son.

When it comes time to move the family campsite, it will most likely be Dos-teh-seh who makes the decision, whether to avoid danger or because she simply wants to visit relatives. The ability to find food is of utmost concern. Dos-teh-seh is always on the hunt for agave, which is the staff of life to the Apache. The versatile plant can be eaten, made into rope, or pounded into a pulp to produce soap. She also collects wild berries, mesquite beans, walnuts, and cactus that can be eaten raw or fermented to make drinks. These are placed in baskets woven from cottonwood twigs which have been lined with pitch to make them waterproof. And whether gathering firewood or searching for acorns, Dos-teh-seh never travels alone. Wild animals, the rare enemy, and the threat of injury by falling in this harsh terrain are hard facts of Apache life. Male or female, no one goes far without company.

Case in point: if an Apache woman is captured alive, the Mexican government will pay a bounty of 150 pesos. This "Fifth Law" went into effect on May 25, 1849. The price for a male Apache scalp is 200 pesos. The price for a captured male warrior is 250 pesos. It is a maxim of Apache life that the world is their enemy, and only other Apache can be trusted.

For this reason, during this short interlude at home, Cochise teaches Taza not just how to behave but also the location of the best trails, sources of water, and even places to hide. He shows his son how to craft his lance from the straight stalk of the spiny evergreen sotol plant and how to make a hunting bow from a mulberry tree branch, using the sinew of a deer's leg to fashion the drawstring. They also hunt together. Deer, pronghorn antelope, rabbit, and even mountain lion are primary sources of food, but rats and squirrels will suffice when other game is scarce.

Taza is growing to his father's height of five foot eleven, but he carries an extra twenty-five pounds of muscle like his grandfather, the giant chief Mangas Coloradas, who stands six foot six. Despite his bloodline, there is no certainty Taza will become a chief. The Apache have more than one chief at any given time, and they are ruthless in their democracy, promoting a man if he is a true leader but also ignoring him and robbing him of authority if he fails in battle.

So though he is devoted and loving while at home, Cochise is cruel when raiding. It is not enough to steal cattle and burn homes—or even murder. Sometimes, as when revenge is taken against a Mexican who has shot an Apache, or when interrogation is necessary to extract vital information, Cochise makes a point of asserting authority by killing his enemies slowly. Some are placed atop an anthill, where their bodies are then smothered in honey. Others are tied upside down to a tree branch until their head is just two feet off the ground. Cochise is fond of building a very small fire under these prisoners, just enough to slowly burn their scalp and fry their brains. Sometimes, if Apache women are present, Cochise allows them to skin the victim alive. This is the fate of many a Mexican who has blundered into Apache Pass.

Another favorite method of torture is more insidious: A one-inch incision is made at the base of the prisoner's leg. The first layer of skin is then peeled away, all the way up the legs and back to the top of the head. Most men scream during this ordeal, which makes Cochise despise them. The Apache are trained to suffer in silence and expect the same from their prisoners. Screaming and begging are signs of weakness.

So it is that there are two sides of Cochise. And while the sanctuary here at Apache Pass allows him the luxury of relaxation, he cannot be soft when it is time to plunder. The slightest slip or strategic blunder will lead to his demotion from the position of tribal chief. He must use all of his authority to protect himself and his band.

Because if he falls into Mexican hands, he will surely be killed.

Cochise will not allow that to happen.

✳

Of all the reasons Cochise enjoys life here at Apache Pass, the most sublime is a cool freshwater spring gushing forth from a shaded rock. The flow pours forth in a torrent, producing the stream that waters the valley below, keeping it green all year round. The Mexicans like to describe the Apache as a dirty people, but that is because they only encounter the Chiricahua after they have ridden hundreds of miles on horseback. But here, where water is plentiful, Cochise and the other Chiricahua can scrub away the trail dust. The powerful apache chief is known for his scrupulous personal appearance, unlike many Indians and whites at the time.

Inevitably, in a place as dry as the desert, where a traveler can go weeks without finding a drop of water, the Apache Spring, as it is known, is not a secret. But that knowledge was limited to just Mexicans and Indians until 1849, when a pair of guides suggested that a party of white settlers bound for the California gold fields lead their wagon train through Apache Pass. "The road was tolerable good,

Apache Pass, spring 2019

until we reached the pass, which was indeed a romantic one," wrote settler Robert Eccleston, part of a group from New York who passed through on October 24, 1849. Like most whites traveling from the East Coast, Eccleston prefers to call himself an "emigrant" rather than a settler, as if he is leaving one country and entering another. "The road was overshadowed by handsome trees, among which I noticed the pecan, the ash, oak, and willow."

Eccleston published his diary shortly after his arrival on the West

Coast. *Overland to California on the Southwestern Trail* revealed the secret of Apache Pass and its clear running waters. Soon the route became the preferred southern passage for white travelers. Unlike his treatment of Mexican trespassers, Cochise is bemused by the white man and allows the infrequent wagon trains to pass through his territory.

But less than five years after Robert Eccleston exposed the oasis at Apache Pass, there is talk of a southern transcontinental railroad that would travel directly through this Apache sanctuary. Despite the fact that this land is owned by Mexico and controlled by the Chiricahuas, the U.S. Army Corps of Engineers has sent a survey team to explore this possibility. Led by Second Lieutenant John G. Parke, they camp in Apache Pass early in March 1854, shortly before Cochise returns home from his winter raids. Parke chooses a camp-site on a small rise at the very center of the valley, allowing him and his team a complete view of the circle of peaks ringing the pass. Having no idea that Parke is grading the land in order to run a railroad through the center of their most prized hideaway, the Apache basically leave Parke and his men alone, even selling them mules.

※

As Cochise and Dos-teh-seh enjoy life together before he once again rides south into Sonora, troubling events are taking place thousands of miles away in Washington. A treaty is being voted on in the U.S. Senate. The pact is between Mexico and the United States. The "Gadsden Purchase," as it is known, will secure Apache Pass and the lands a hundred miles to the south and west from Mexico for $10 million. Secretary of War Jefferson Davis is one of the leading proponents, hoping that a new rail line to California will ensure the expansion of slavery into the western territories of the southern United States.

Cochise will never meet Jefferson Davis. And the Chiricahua chief knows nothing about the politics of slavery now roiling the United States of America. But when the Gadsden Purchase takes effect on June 8, 1854, the lives of Cochise and the Apache people will be forever changed.

Apache Pass is now part of the United States of America. It is only a matter of time before American soldiers are sent to police these lands and, in the process, confront Cochise and the Chiricahua.

When that day comes, the U.S. Army will meet an enemy unlike any other in American history. For Cochise will never surrender and never be defeated.

Ever.

Chapter Eleven

Texas Ranger Sullivan Ross is terrified.

Yesterday at sunset, the twenty-two-year-old captain received word that the Comanche band he has been hunting is located on the north Texas plains, at the confluence of the Pease River and a tributary called Mule Creek. Rather than wait until morning to begin his march, Ross has pushed his contingent of twenty Rangers along with a squad of twenty-one U.S. Army dragoons through the night, hoping to launch an ambush at first light. Captain Ross is well aware that his young age has some believing he is incapable of halting the Comanche rampage. In moments, Ross's mettle will be tested, for his goal is nothing less than a complete annihilation of this rogue band.

Captain Ross and his combined force have been tasked with tracking down a notorious Comanche chief named Peta Nocona, who is thought to be responsible for several recent raids on white towns, as well as the slaying and scalping of a pregnant woman. Nocona is thought to have five hundred warriors, and the band has sparked terror throughout north Texas. Hundreds of white settlers have been murdered or kidnapped by the Comanche, whose methods of torture are as brutal as anything ever seen on the North American continent. If Peta Nocona is cornered, no mercy will be shown.

Positioning his men atop a ridgeline looking down on the Comanche, the captain cannot help but recall his last encounter with the Indians. Two years ago, at a battle called Wichita Village, in the midst of an epic five-hour fight, Ross and three of his Texas Rangers were surrounded by more than two dozen warriors. The captain was shot through the shoulder with an arrow, then took a rifle bullet to his chest from close range. As a Comanche warrior stepped forward to take his scalp, suddenly U.S. soldiers appeared and shot the Indian dead, saving Ross's life.

But his trauma was not over. For five days, the then twenty-year-old Ross lay in the shade of a small tree, too wracked with pain to be moved. His wounds became infected, and he cried out for his men to shoot him. Finally, Ross was deemed strong enough to be placed in a litter and carried to safety. News of the captain's exploits made the newspapers in the new settlement at Dallas, and he was hailed as a hero. But rather than remain in Texas to bask in celebrity, the traumatized Ross wanted nothing more to do with fighting Comanche. He fled east to the safety of Alabama to attend college.

Born in Iowa but raised in Texas, Sullivan Ross eventually changed his mind and returned to settle his score with the Comanche. Three months ago, Governor Sam Houston commanded the young Ranger captain to assemble a team of mounted volunteers to protect white settlers and to destroy the Comanche population. "You are strictly ordered to regard all Indians this side of the Red River as open enemies of Texas," reads Houston's written order. That effectively authorizes Ross to slaughter any Native American captured between Louisiana and the Pacific Ocean.

Sullivan Ross has faith in his Texas Rangers, knowing that these men are expert horsemen and brave under fire. They travel light, long-barreled Colt .45-caliber "Peacemaker" pistols tucked snug in their holsters. Rifles lie across the pommels of their saddles, with some men preferring the breech-loading Sharps, while others carry the brand-new lever-action Henry rifle, capable of firing sixteen rounds without reloading. The Rangers wear no uniforms but all seem to dress alike, protecting their heads from the burning sun with large-brimmed felt hats and wearing thick pants and boots as a buffer against rocks and thorns. Almost to a man, a chaw of tobacco is tucked between cheek and gum.*

But the small Ranger band is no match for the Comanche. So help has been requested from the U.S. Army at nearby Camp Cooper. The twenty-one troopers on horseback will not even the odds, but their presence is most welcome.

The mounted soldiers represent a new breed of Indian-fighter known as "cavalry." Ross takes comfort in knowing these men are second only to the Texas Rangers as a fighting force. This was not always so. Until five years ago, the U.S. Army's horseback forces were known as dragoons. Using tactics borrowed from similar European units, they rode into battle but dismounted and fought on foot like the infantry—a style of combat well-suited to the smaller battlefields of Europe but foolish on the wide-open plains of Texas, where mobility is often the key to victory.

Comically, the dragoons wore a uniform based on a design favored by French soldiers: orange caps, blue and orange jackets, and white pantaloons. As one Texas Ranger dryly noted, the only danger a dragoon presented to a Comanche was if the funny uniforms and abominable horsemanship caused the Indian to laugh himself to death.

In 1855, Secretary of War Jefferson Davis created a new type of horse soldier. The West Point graduate and commander of troops in the Mexican War was convinced that America's westward expansion depended upon military mobility—and that meant the horse. Davis authorized the creation of an elite fighting force that would soon

---

* The Texas Rangers were formed by Stephen F. Austin in 1823 to protect white settlers from Indian attack. This occurred during a time when Texas was still part of Mexico, giving the Rangers no legal authority. However, upon the creation of the Texas Republic in 1836, President Mirabeau Lamar formalized their role as protectors of the frontier. The Rangers were disbanded after Texas became a state, but concerns about the U.S. Army's inability to protect settlers from Indian attack led to their reinstatement in 1857. The Rangers still exist today as a law enforcement agency focused on investigating crime and protecting the governor of Texas.

U.S. Cavalryman shooting Apache sheepherders in a canyon

roam the prairies of the American West as skillfully as any Indian tribe, riding into battle and remaining in the saddle to fight.

Thus was born the American cavalry. The term "dragoon" is still used interchangeably to describe mounted soldiers, but the cavalry is an entirely different force. Officers and enlisted men are handpicked for their courage, leadership, and skill on horseback, and their primary role is the protection of American settlers. Many were born and raised in southern states and in the European nations of Ireland and Germany. Cavalry units live in solitary forts out on the plains, far from creature comforts, coming to know the landscape just as completely as the Comanche and Texas Rangers. Their horses are colored according to company: browns, grays, bays—for easy distinction in battle. Officers even wear an ostrich feather in their caps to denote their status. As Jefferson Davis is fond of noting, a cavalry unit costs three times as much to maintain as infantry but is ten times more effective.*

So it is that even though Sullivan Ross's Texas Rangers and the men of Second Cavalry will be outnumbered more than ten to one as they attack the Comanche settlement here at Pease River, there is every hope that surprise and professionalism can win the day.

Yet as Ross studies the Comanche encampment, he is surprised. The captain sees tepees being dismantled, and horses laden with buffalo meat and hides, as if the Comanche are in the process of relocating. If that is the case, Ross's inclinations were correct, and he was smart to ride through the night. But the captain notices no warriors, only women, children, and old men wearing buffalo robes to stave off the cold. And rather than five hundred warriors, he counts just fifteen in the camp.

Nevertheless, Captain Ross has come to kill. His final orders make his intentions quite clear.

---

* The average infantry regiment costs $500,000 a year to maintain. The feed and care of horses added $1 million each year to that cost. It should be noted that America's first true cavalry regiment was named the Second Cavalry, for reasons known only to bureaucracy. Their first commander was Lieutenant Colonel Robert E. Lee, famous for his later role as a general in the Civil War, who kept a rattlesnake for a pet in his Texas headquarters.

"I promise a pistol and a holster to the first man to bring back a Comanche scalp."

✴

First Sergeant John Spangler guides the Second Cavalry into position to block any Comanche escape, as Captain Ross and his men charge into the camp. The Comanche women, as adept on horseback as their men, immediately mount the only available horses and gallop across Mule Creek. But their mounts are too heavy from their cargos of meat and hides, and the soldiers catch them quickly. Each woman is shot dead. "Killed every one of them, almost in a pile," Texas Ranger Charles Goodnight will later write in his official report.

An older Comanche man throws a young girl onto the back of a horse and attempts to flee, but Ross shoots the girl dead. As she falls off the horse, the old man topples to the ground with her. Captain Ross fires again, hitting the older Indian in the arm but not killing him. Dismounting, Ross fires two more times, and still the old Comanche will not die. Instead, the aging warrior clings to a mesquite bush and chants his death song. Rather than fire again, Ross allows his Mexican servant to shoot the Indian in the head, whereupon two Rangers take the man's scalp and cut it in two, so that each might have half.

As the ambush comes to a quick ending, the Rangers and cavalry walk through the camp, scalping all the dead. Two troopers keep a tight hold on a Comanche woman clutching a young daughter who has been spared. She is filthy, her hair matted and sun-bronzed skin covered in dirt. The woman's hands are greasy from stripping meat from buffalo hides. At the sight of the Comanche dead she begins moaning and wailing in grief. As the Rangers set the tepees ablaze, their horses literally trotting over the corpses sprawled awkwardly on the ground, her face becomes a mask of pain.

For Captain Sullivan Ross, this ambush has been a frustrating failure. Clearly, Peta Nocona and his warriors are off hunting and raiding. His men have slaughtered women doing manual labor and preparing for the hard winter ahead, tasks the Comanche fighters consider beneath the dignity of a man.

Even as the Rangers and cavalry loot the encampment, taking any souvenirs and foodstuffs they can find, it is clear that this wailing woman and her daughter are the only Indian survivors. The fact that they have spared the woman is something of a mystery, for all the other squaws were killed without a chance to surrender. She will be interrogated about the whereabouts of Peta Nocona, but beyond that, her fate is uncertain. The same is true for the Indian child. There is a good chance that mother and daughter will be separated.

In time, Sergeant Spangler notices something unique about the woman: she has blue eyes. A closer look at her face shows freckles, and that the parts of her body not exposed to the sun are pale white.

The squaw is questioned about her ethnicity. She speaks only Comanche and broken Spanish, so Captain Ross's Mexican servant does much of the interrogating. Two shocking facts soon come to light.

This woman is the wife of the feared Peta Nocona and mother of his children. She is known among the Comanche as Naduah—"Someone Found"—and her eighteen-month-old daughter is Topsannah, meaning "Prairie Flower."

But upon further questioning, the woman's true identity is revealed.

Shockingly, she is Cynthia Ann Parker, who was kidnapped twenty-four years ago in the notorious attack on Fort Parker. She was just a child when a Comanche band decimated the family stockade, killing and dismembering her grandfather, murdering her father, and kidnapping four other relatives. Ironically, among the warriors committing this slaughter was a tall, muscular sixteen-year-old whose Indian name means "Lone Wanderer:" Peta Nocona.

James Parker, an uncle who survived the massacre in 1836, devoted several years to searching for Cynthia Ann and his other missing relatives. In time, he would become legendary as "the man who searched for the Parker captives." He successfully found and purchased the freedom of his sister-in-law, Elizabeth Kellogg, for $150 from a band of Delaware Indians three months after the massacre.

It took another year, but James Parker was also successful in ran-

Cynthia Ann Parker, also known as Naduah

soming his daughter. By then, Rachel Parker Plummer had endured more than a year in Comanche captivity as a slave before being accepted as a full-fledged member of the tribe. Her son, James Pratt, was taken from her on the night of her kidnapping and she never saw him again. Rachel had a second child during her time in captivity, a boy of Comanche blood. But when it became clear that she doted too much on the infant, the newborn was tied to a rope and dragged through cactus until dead.*

On June 19, 1837, Rachel was sold to traders acting on behalf of her father and was reunited with her family in February 1838.

Cynthia's brother John, who was two at the time of the attack on Fort Parker, was ransomed back to white society after six years with the tribe. His return went against his will, and he tried on several occasions to rejoin the Comanche.†

Eventually, James Parker discontinued the search for Cynthia after more than a decade of hunting and nine courageous forays into the Comancheria. But rumors that she lived in captivity continued. There were several sightings of a blue-eyed woman now living as a full member of the Comanche tribe.

After one such sighting, Captain Randolph B. Marcy of the U.S. Army, who had come to map Texas and find more optimal routes for westward settlement, confirmed that Cynthia Ann Parker was alive. Yet he made no attempt to bring her back to the white world. "This woman has adopted all the habits and peculiarities of the Comanches; has an Indian husband and children, and cannot be persuaded to leave them," reported Marcy.

It was none other than Cynthia's brother John who relayed this sighting to Captain Marcy. At his mother's behest, the young man bravely traveled back into Comanche territory looking for his sister. John Parker stated that he spoke with Cynthia Ann, and that she was very happy in her new life. "There she should remain," Parker told U.S. authorities.

And it was true. In the more than two decades since her kidnapping, Cynthia Ann Parker has totally assumed the ways of the Comanche. She and Peta Nocona have three children, among them

---

* Rachel was soon reunited with her husband. She published a book about her captivity shortly after her release from the Comanche. *Narrative of Twenty-one Months Servitude as a Prisoner Among the Comanche Indians* is considered one of the most accurate portrayals of daily life on the prairie with an Indian tribe. Rachel Parker Plummer died from childbirth complications on March 19, 1839.

† John Parker eventually fought for the Confederacy in the Civil War. After that, he moved to Mexico, where he lived until his death in 1915.

a boy named Kwihnai—"Eagle"—who is destined to succeed his father as a great chief. Cynthia keeps the family lodge clean and organized, butchers buffalo and tans hides to make robes, and packs the horses when it comes time to move camp. Her love for Peta Nocona is real, and he reciprocates by not taking a second wife. And on the day that Texas Rangers ride through the Comanche camp at Mule Creek, Cynthia wails for the slain members of her tribe. As the soldiers and Texas Rangers scalp the dead before stuffing saddlebags with dried buffalo meat and stealing the robes she has spent hours scraping and tanning, Cynthia Ann Parker takes a small degree of comfort in knowing that she and her young daughter, Prairie Flower, have been spared from death.

But now, against Cynthia's will, both she and her daughter are being returned "home" to white society.

However, that will not end her story.

Chapter Twelve

February 4, 1861
Apache Pass, New Mexico Territory
5:00 P.M.

Betrayal is coming.

Lieutenant George N. Bascom of the U.S. Army waits impatiently for the arrival of Cochise. The twenty-three-year-old officer from Kentucky has summoned the vaunted Apache chief to his campsite to explain the kidnapping of a white child from a nearby settlement. It has been more than a day since Bascom demanded that Cochise come to meet him. As the sun begins to set, the lieutenant grows angrier by the minute. He has marched a column of fifty-eight soldiers from Company C, U.S. Seventh Infantry, forty miles east from the outpost at Fort Buchanan to confront the Apache. His orders are to find twelve-year-old Felix Telles and twenty head of cattle stolen by Indians. Bascom and his men arrived in Apache Pass yesterday, a Sunday. They made camp at Siphon Springs, just a mile from the heart of the pass. After arranging their tents in precise rows, Bascom sent a messenger informing the nearby Apache that he wished to speak with Cochise.

George Bascom is an imperious man who finished second-to-last in his class at West Point. He has no experience in negotiating with Indians but shares the belief of many whites that the Apache are an inferior people, prone to lying and theft. Based on hoofprints found along the Babocomari River, Bascom is convinced he has successfully tracked the culprits in the kidnapping back to Apache Pass. There is no doubt in Bascom's mind that Cochise and the Chiricahua band now hold young Felix.

Suddenly, as Lieutenant Bascom's soldiers sit down for their evening meal, Cochise walks into the American camp. He brings with him a small group of Apache warriors, his wife Dos-te-seh, his young daughter Dash-den-zhoos, and his four-year-old son Naiche to signal his intent that the meeting be peaceful.

"How, how," Cochise says, using the traditional greeting.

"How, how," Bascom replies.

Lieutenant Bascom offers Cochise a cup of coffee and suggests they go inside his tent to talk. Cochise's brother, Coyuntura, is also invited. John Ward, the Irish-born stepfather of the missing boy, will act as interpreter. Dos-teh-seh, the children, and two other warriors are taken to the mess tent to eat.

Lieutenant Bascom closes the flap to begin their meeting. Armed soldiers with bayonets affixed to their rifles form a ring around the shelter.

The great Cochise is now trapped.

⁂

What will go down in history as the "Bascom affair" begins one week before the meeting between Cochise and the lieutenant. On January 27, eleven miles south of Fort Buchanan, two bands of Apache successfully raid the Ward ranch. Felix Telles is three hundred yards from the house when he is grabbed and taken, never to be returned. Ironically, this horrific incident will be the making of him. In time, the boy will be raised as a warrior in the Apache way. He will take on the nickname Mickey Free, reenter white society, and earn notoriety as a scout, interpreter, and bounty hunter. But on this day he is just a terrified twelve-year-old whose kidnapping will soon ignite all-out war between the United States of America and the Chiricahua Apache nation.

John Ward, the Irishman who married a Mexican woman named Jesusa Martinez and raises her children as his own, is away

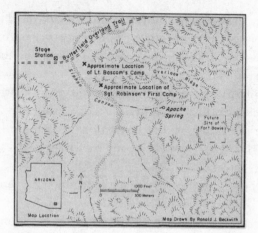

Map of Apache Pass

on business when the raid occurs. But upon his return the following day, he immediately sets out for Fort Buchanan to report the attack. Even without the Apache raids, tension is high in this Arizona region of the New Mexico Territory. Just a few months ago, in April 1860, delegates to a convention in the city of Tucson voted in favor of creating a Territory of Arizona, separate and independent from the New Mexico Territory. Miners have flooded into the region following the discovery of gold and silver, creating tension with the Apache bands that have long made this land their home.

More ominously, the United States is close to civil war. Southern states in favor of continuing the practice of slavery are on the verge of seceding from the Union. The Americans living in the New Mexico Territory have already chosen to side with the south, and there is talk of renaming the region "Confederate Arizona." There is uncertainty about what would happen to the U.S. Army soldiers stationed at Fort Buchanan and the newly built Fort Breckinridge, ninety miles north. But one thing is certain: troopers who have sworn their loyalty to Abraham Lincoln, the Illinois lawyer and former soldier in Blackhawk's War who has just been elected America's new president, will no longer be welcome in Arizona.

As in other regions of the west, the U.S. military presence serves mainly to protect settlers from Indian attacks. But the lands of Southern Arizona appear to be peaceful. Cochise is recognized as the preeminent Apache chief, and since his first encounters with white Americans in the fall of 1858, he has shown every intent of forging friendly relations. The Apache have largely confined their raiding to Mexico, and miners in the Santa Rita and Patagonia Mountains go about their business without fear of attack.

Perhaps the greatest evidence of Cochise's desire to keep the peace is the presence of a regular stagecoach route through the heart of the Apache homeland.

The Butterfield Overland Mail coach departing from San Francisco for Tipton, Missouri. Published in Harper's Weekly, *December 11, 1858.*

The Butterfield Overland Mail Route stretches twenty-eight hundred miles from St. Louis to San Francisco, delivering the U.S. mail and ferrying passengers across the continent. More than two hundred way stations have been established along the route, averaging roughly twenty miles apart. Amazingly, Cochise has allowed a Butterfield stop to be built in Apache Pass and routinely provides the whites with firewood, as well as grass for their horses.

The stone and adobe station rests in the center of the valley, just a half mile from Apache Springs. It is manned by three Butterfield employees and fortified with Sharps rifles and ammunition in case of trouble.

But until January 27, 1861, there was no trouble at all. Cochise has made it plain that his warriors "would not molest the whites" provided the settlers "not interfere with Apache incursions into Sonora."

The kidnapping of Felix Telles changes all that.

One day after the abduction, Lieutenant George Bascom and Lieutenant Richard Long are dispatched to find the perpetrators. Within hours, they locate the trail used by the Apache as an escape route. It heads east, into Apache Pass. This confirms to both lieutenants that Cochise and his men are the culprits. The Chiricahua are the only band known to use this route.

Unbeknownst to either officer, the construction of Fort Breckinridge to the north has caused other tribes to alter their traditional paths when returning from raids in Mexico. To avoid U.S. Army patrols, Coyotero, Pinal, and Western Apache no longer travel via Sonoita Creek and Redington Pass. Instead, they now follow the same route as the Chiricahua along the Babocomari River.

Had Lieutenant Bascom known of these changes, he might not have been so certain Cochise is guilty. But as he lures the chief into his tent on February 4, just before sundown, Bascom's plan is simple: keep Cochise hostage until Felix is returned. The lieutenant is sure Cochise's band is holding the boy. A simple prisoner swap will put the matter to a successful end.

But Cochise vows he is innocent. Through translator John Ward, he swears that neither the boy nor the twenty stolen head of cattle are in his possession. Cochise suspects that a band of Western Apache has done the kidnapping. He asks for ten days to find the kidnappers and bring the boy home safely.

The lieutenant is equally convinced Cochise is lying. Bascom informs the chief that he is now a prisoner of the U.S. Army, not to be freed until the Chiricahua return Felix Telles to his parents. Coyuntura will be sent to find the boy and bring him back. Cochise's wife and children will remain in custody with him.

The confinement should have produced fear in Cochise. The tent is heavily guarded. The chief appears to be unarmed, holding a coffee cup in his left hand. Lieutenant Bascom stands with his back to the tent flap, blocking any path to escape. Most men would have conceded defeat there and then.

Cochise is not most men.

☀

The code of the Apache is stealth and self-preservation. Producing a heretofore unseen knife, Cochise quickly slices open the tent wall and runs for his life. Coyuntura, who also holds a hidden knife, slits open another tent wall and sprints after him.

"Shoot them down!" cries Bascom. John Ward is the first to open fire, but soon all the sentries are shooting. Cochise has been told that the rifles are not loaded, but that is obviously not the case.

In haste, Coyuntura trips on a tent rope and is soon set upon by soldiers.

Cochise escapes. Gunshots ring out as the chief sprints across the meadow and up a hill. He has been trained since a very young man to quickly bound up these rocky hillsides and run long distances for hours on end. So even as his lungs burn with effort and his legs grow heavy from the steep incline, Cochise is unstoppable. Only when he crests the summit and knows for certain that he has escaped does the chief realize he still clutches a coffee mug in his fist.

☀

One hour later, Cochise appears atop a different hill and looks down upon the American camp. He loudly calls out, demanding that

Coyuntura and his family be released. Cochise's demand is met with a volley from Lieutenant Bascom's soldiers.

The chief raises his hand and cries out in his native tongue: "I will have my revenge."

✵

Fearing his campsite is not well fortified, Lieutenant Bascom moves his detachment into the Butterfield stage station. The thick rock walls will endure bullets and prevent a frontal assault. Bascom adds to the fortifications by dragging supply wagons around the perimeter, then tilting them on their side to form a barricade. The men then dig trenches behind the wagons as fighting holes. Strategically placed bags of flour and grain form an additional shield. The Americans have enough rations for twenty days, but the nearest water is up the valley at Apache Springs.

Cochise is also hard at work, attempting to kidnap three Butterfield employees to hold hostage. One escapes, and one is mistakenly shot by American soldiers while running to the safety of the station, but the third man, stage driver James Wallace, is captured by the Indians. The Massachusetts native is thirty-three and newly married. His bride remains behind at their home in Tucson. She will never see him again.

Just after noon on February 5, less than one day after the incident that would go down in Apache history as "cut the tent," Cochise stands atop a summit known as Overlook Ridge next to James Wallace. The stage driver has a noose around his neck and his hands are bound behind his back. Cochise offers to exchange Wallace and sixteen mules he has recently stolen from the army in return for his family and friends.

Lieutenant Bascom refuses. There will be no negotiation. Either Cochise delivers the boy or there is no deal.

Cochise is growing more frustrated with each passing hour.

On the morning of February 6, the chief orders his warriors to attack a wagon train en route to Las Cruces, New Mexico, loaded with flour. After surrounding the wagons, Cochise's men take three Americans and nine Mexicans prisoner. Cochise has a lifelong disdain for Mexicans and chooses to kill them all. First, they are tied to wagon wheels and tortured. Then the wagon wheels are set afire, burning the men to death.

The Americans, however, are useful leverage for Cochise. Sam Whitfield, William Sanders, and Frank Brunner are brought back to the Apache camp, where they join Wallace under guard. But as the days pass and it becomes clear the Americans have no intention of bargaining, the hostages lose their value. Cochise and his band make plans to leave Apache Pass. The four prisoners, however, will not be joining them.

The methods of torture used upon Wallace, Whitfield, Sanders, and Brunner are undocumented, though there is some evidence that Apache women were allowed to work on the men with knives—a hellish fate reserved for only the most hated enemy.

In any event, the four men all die a brutal death and are not found until long after the Chiricahua move on from Apache Pass.

* * *

It is February 18, 1861—almost two weeks after they are killed—when the four Americans are discovered dead. Lieutenant Bascom's infantry troops have been extensively reinforced, but the additional men are unnecessary. Not for the first time, Cochise and his Apache band have slipped away, preferring to wait and fight another day. Corpses of the hostages are buried beneath a large oak tree near the western edge of Apache Pass.

Left unsaid is that Cochise has abandoned his family and close friends.

It is decided by the American officers that Cochise's wife and children will be set free. But not the warriors—they are to be hanged.

The Indians ask for whiskey before they are dispatched.

This is denied.

They ask to be shot instead of hanged.

Again, denied.

So it is that a small squad of U.S. Cavalry throws their lariats up and over the high branches of the same four oak trees under which the American prisoners were recently buried. "The Indians . . . were hoisted so high by the infantry that not even the wolves would touch them," notes one eyewitness.

The Americans return to their forts, thinking the incident is over, not realizing that this confrontation will soon lead to all-out war.

"Tread on a worm and it will turn," writes one soldier who was in Apache Pass as witness to the conflict. "Disturb a hornet's nest and they will sting you. So with savage Indians: misuse them and you make revengeful foes."*

---

* To this day, it is not known exactly why the U.S. contingent allowed Cochise's wife and children to live. After their release, they returned to Apache territory, eventually finding Cochise high in the mountains.

Chapter Thirteen

B revet General George Armstrong Custer is in a bad place.

It is day three of the battle that will go down in history as simply "Gettysburg."

The twenty-three-year-old Custer has spent the day in the saddle, leading Union cavalry into battle for the first time since his promotion just one week ago. Custer is not really a general but was given the temporary "brevet" title in recent Civil War battles.

Autie Custer, as he likes to be called, is an intense man who has had a colorful military career. He finished last in his class at West Point, causing the military academy much grief with his insubordination and mischief making. But now Custer is facing the challenge of his life.

Today's attacks and counterattacks against Confederate forces have been intense. Custer has already had one horse shot from under him. But the young general is invigorated by the fighting, even though he is exhausted, having slept little over the past week. Autie Custer wears a uniform of his own design, with tanned leather gloves and a red cravat around his neck. A thick blond mustache covers his upper lip, and his wide-brimmed hat is pressed down tightly over his shoulder-length locks.

General George Armstrong Custer, circa 1870

The men of Custer's Michigan Brigade have taken heavy losses in the last two hours. By day's end, more than 250 men and horses will perish, cut down by Confederate gunfire, artillery, or, in many cases, hand-to-hand fighting. But more death is near. Right now, on the opposite side of this property belonging to farmer John Rummel, Confederate cavalry under the command of General J. E. B. Stuart gather en masse, a mounted force of more than five thousand strong. Custer has just four hundred men. But his cavalry is all that stands between the Confederates and the rear of Union lines. The men of Michigan must not fail.

The cry of "Battalions, forward" peals forth from the Confederate lines—the signal for Stuart's cavalry to advance. They ride forth from the woods in tight columns, a spectacle of flashing sabers and polished carbines glistening in the afternoon sun. Up front ride the Second Carolina Cavalry, a unit bearing the motto "Honor and Immortality."

Union artillery opens fire, but the Confederate cavalry only increases its pace—first a walk, then a canter, and finally a full gallop. The rebels make no attempt to feint or whirl in their efforts to pierce the Union lines, riding straight at Custer and his men. Even as canister rounds and shells from the Union guns rain down in their midst, eviscerating rider and horse alike, the Confederate cavalry closes gaps to keep their ranks tight, charging closer and closer to the Michigan Brigade.

Custer can wait no longer. He draws his saber and throws his hat to the ground, revealing the long yellow hair that makes him so distinguishable on the battlefield.

"Come on, you wolverines," shouts the general, spurring his horse.

George Armstrong Custer leads the way as his men gallop across the open field, racing into the Confederate columns at full speed. On the rebel side, the Second Carolina does not flinch or scatter, instead spurring their animals to charge even faster. The "honor" of their regimental maxim is never in doubt. However, the "immortality" will be sorely tested.

Distance between the two cavalries narrows quickly. The horses gallop at the pace of a locomotive. What was once a mile becomes a half mile, then a quarter, then just one hundred yards. Pistols are unholstered. Rifles are drawn. The air is rent by the thunder of thousands of hooves.

Fifty yards. The horses lather, shoulders and necks covered in white sweat brought on by exertion and fear.

Twenty yards. Not a single man pulls back on the reins.

Five yards.

Saber raised, General George Armstrong Custer braces for impact.

✳

Two thousand miles away, in the land of Cochise, this strange war between the whites from the north and the whites from the south gives the Apache chief freedom to do whatever he pleases. For Cochise no longer has an enemy to fight. It is just eight years since the U.S. Army formed its first cavalry units with the intention of protecting white settlers from Indian attack. The American government has built forts throughout Texas, New Mexico, and Arizona and filled them with soldiers trained to be the equal in the saddle of any tribe.

But now those forts are empty. The vaunted cavalrymen have taken their horse skills east, where they use the tactics learned on the plains and deserts to fight the Civil War. Jefferson Davis, the former secretary of war whose vision foresaw the need for a mounted force to take control of the American West, is now president of the Confederate States, a secessionist faction of southern governments that have left the Union. Robert E. Lee, one of the U.S. Army's original cavalry commanders, is now leader of all Confederate troops. Lee's belief in the cavalry is total; he uses them as scouts to suss out the location of Union forces prior to battle, then uses their speed to penetrate enemy lines once shots are fired.

Up and down the prairie, as soldiers leave their frontier posts and march east, ranchers, miners, and farmers are forced to abandon their now unprotected land. Since the gold rush of 1849, white settlers have flooded across the prairie on their way west. Even after gold fever abated in California, new discoveries in Colorado and Montana lured prospectors. The land west of the Mississippi once considered "Indian Territory," an inviolable place where no whites were to be allowed, is completely disrespected by the new settlers. The Oregon and Santa Fe Trails extend from starting points in Missouri to the destinations from which they take their names. So many settlers make the journey by oxen-drawn covered wagons that it has become possible to voyage without map and compass—one has only to follow the wheel ruts heading west. However, the Civil War slows that migration significantly.

The war affects tribes all across America, though in vastly different ways. Tribes such as the Cherokee and Seminole in the southeast have owned black slaves for decades and align themselves with the Confederates. In 1861, the Creek nation, long ago relocated from Alabama and Mississippi to Arkansas, signs a peace treaty with the Confederacy meant to last "as long as grass shall grow and water run." Later that year, tribes loyal to the Union murder seven hundred Creek, forcing the tribe to relocate again, this time to Kansas.

On the Texas plains, the Confederacy is also eager to sign a treaty of peace with the Comanche. But though the Comanche eventually enter into a treaty with the south, they also form an alliance with the Union, in the hope of extracting gifts and food from both sides. It becomes common Comanche practice to raid Texas ranches of their livestock, then sell it to the U.S. Army. More than ten thousand head of cattle are stolen and sold in 1863 and 1864 alone.

The departing soldiers represent a chance for the Comanche to reclaim their way of life. Not only have the Union troops left, an additional sixty-two thousand able-bodied Texas males have also departed and are now fighting far from home for the Confederates. There are just twenty-seven thousand white men between sixteen and sixty remaining in the entire state—most too old or too young to fight, and hardly enough manpower to stop the Comanche from riding across the prairie uncontested, lords of all they survey. The Comanche way is anathema to whites, who cannot imagine living off the land and having no permanent place to call home. But there is beauty and even romance in this lifestyle, as evidenced by the plight of Cynthia Ann Parker. The kidnapping victim who spent twenty-four years among the Comanche before being forcibly returned to white society tries again and again to escape back to the tribe. Each time she fails.

Even more than the Comanche, the departure of U.S. soldiers emboldens Cochise and the Chiricahua Apache in Arizona. The tribe is no longer content to merely raid and plunder. Since the Bascom affair, Cochise has been at war with all whites. In one bold attack on a wagon train of settlers fleeing Arizona, Cochise steals more than thirteen hundred head of cattle. Prior to his feud with

Bascom, Cochise would never dare a frontal assault on a heavily fortified caravan.

Further emboldening Cochise is the closure of the Butterfield stagecoach station in Apache Pass. The move was actually not related to the Indians; Congress did not want the U.S. mail traveling through Confederate Texas and chose a new route farther north. But Cochise sees this as an Apache victory, a fact further reinforced by the departure of soldiers from Fort Buchanan and Fort Breckinridge. The army burned both forts so they wouldn't fall into Confederate hands, making their departure appear all the more final to the Apache.

Without the stage line and army, the citizens of Arizona have lost a significant source of income. Businesses that sell food and whiskey to the forts, as well as men who provide services as teamsters, blacksmiths, farriers, and even harness makers are no longer needed. The growing city of Tucson, now without a stage line, sees hotels and restaurants languish.

Most settlers leave Arizona, some traveling east to the Confederacy while others depart for the free state of California, now part of the Union. Some whites choose to remain, but doing so means turning their homes into fortresses. "Every farm and rancho is abandoned," writes one Arizona mine owner. "The loss of property is immense. I am holding my place at great expense. In fact, it is a garrison. . . . I am constantly prepared for a fight."

On February 14, 1862, the Confederate Congress in Richmond, Virginia, votes to make the Territory of Arizona part of the Confederacy. In theory, this land is now under the governance of Jefferson Davis. But as Cochise solidifies his control over the region through raids and attacks, there is no doubt who controls life in Arizona. This is made clear on May 5, 1862, when Cochise and his warriors defeat a Confederate force at the Battle of Dragoon Springs, killing four, stealing horses and livestock, and suffering no Apache dead.

On July 15, 1862, white soldiers once again march into Apache country, this time on behalf of the Union. In what will become known as the Battle of Apache Pass, the Chiricahua under Cochise's command launch a surprise attack against the column of Union infantry and cavalry who have traveled from California to drive Confederates out of Arizona. The use of artillery by U.S. forces ends the battle in a stalemate but deeply impresses Cochise's aging father-in-law. Several months later Mangas Coloradas approaches a U.S. fort in southwest New Mexico under a white flag of truce. The seventy-year-old leader seeks peace for his people, knowing the Americans have the firepower and numbers to exterminate the tribe completely if given enough time.

The chief immediately regrets this decision.

"He looked careworn and refused to talk, and evidently felt he had made a great mistake in trusting the paleface on this occasion," a local miner who was present on that day will remember.

Rather than broker a treaty, fort commander General Joseph R. West secretly orders the execution of Mangas Coloradas, telling guards he wants the Apache dead by morning. That night, as the aging chief lies down to sleep on the ground, his captors heat their bayonets in the campfire and prod him. When he rises up and curses the soldiers in Spanish, telling them he is not a child to be played with, the guards empty their guns into the chief—first with rifles, then pistols. He is then scalped and decapitated. His body is then thrown into a ditch.

The official U.S. Army report will state that Mangas Coloradas died while attempting to escape.

The Bascom affair at Apache Pass certainly started Cochise's war against the whites, but it is the death of Mangas Coloradas that will fill him with the rage to take intense revenge. Cochise will long grieve the death of his friend and fellow warrior, even as Mangas's demise gives him unmatched power in the Apache nation.

However, for all his power, Cochise will never have the one piece of personal retribution he truly desires. For on February 21, 1862, at the Battle of Valverde between Confederate and Union forces in New Mexico, his nemesis, Lieutenant George Bascom, is shot and killed. The Kentucky-born West Point graduate chose to honor his vow to preserve the Constitution of the United States rather than switch sides and fight for the Confederacy.

It is unclear if Cochise ever learns of Bascom's death. As whites leave Arizona for a less threatening place, Cochise and the Chiricahua Apache are at war in name only, their opponents busy fighting one another thousands of miles away.

But Cochise knows the white man will return.

And on that day, the chief will once again seek revenge.

❋

Far to the north of Cochise, a vicious war between the United States and a band known as the Sioux nation begins in August 1862. The Sioux reign over the northern prairie, from Minnesota all the way west to the newly discovered gold fields of Montana. Frustrated and starving because Washington has broken a treaty and reneged on a promise to provide them food, an eastern band known as the Santee Sioux leaves their reservation to attack federal storehouses. Within weeks, seven hundred more settlers are dead as the tribe rampages throughout Minnesota. White women are forced into mass rapes by Santee warriors before being mutilated and then murdered. Terrified they will be the next to die, more than forty thousand whites flee, turning local farm roads into an endless column of refugees.

In time, the war between the whites and the Sioux nation will escalate, making it necessary for the Union to actually use Confederate prisoners of war to man the local forts. But as the conflict with the Sioux begins, a local militia is formed to confront the violence. Four months later, these Minnesota volunteers successfully catch and publicly hang thirty-eight Sioux warriors on a snowy day after Christmas in Mankato. The number would have been greater had not President Abraham Lincoln personally pardoned more than three hundred other captured Sioux.[*]

The Indian rebellion finally comes to an end seven months after the hangings, when the leading Sioux instigator is shot dead by two white settlers. The body of fifty-three-year-old Little Crow, as he is known, is immediately scalped. Lighted firecrackers are placed in his ears and nostrils. The chief's remains are dragged through the streets of Hutchinson, Minnesota. Only then is the corpse discarded in a

---

[*] Lincoln's decision was based on the belief that all men must be granted equal fairness under the law, regardless of race. His pardons were granted to all those for whom guilt could not be confirmed. Regardless, it appears that those Sioux hanged were chosen at random.

On August 18, 1862, a group of about thirty-five missionaries, mission workers, and government employees fled from the Lower Sioux Agency.

slaughterhouse and the chief's head severed from the torso so that it might be placed on public display.*

The death of Little Crow comes on July 3, 1863—the same afternoon General George Custer leads his fateful cavalry charge against the Confederates at Gettysburg.

This is the first time the personal history of Custer is intertwined with that of the Sioux nation.

It will not be the last.

❈

---

* The Minnesota Historical Society acquired the scalp and skull of Little Crow. These remains were put on display at the Minnesota State Capitol building in 1879. They were viewed by the public until 1915, when they were removed from display at the request of Little Crow's descendants. It wasn't until 1971 that Little Crow's remains were returned to his family for burial at the First Presbyterian Church in Flandreau, South Dakota.

It is hell on earth at Gettysburg.

General George Custer threads his horse through a wall of Confederate cavalry, hacking downward with his saber at any man in his path. He is among the lucky, for he remains in the saddle as the fight begins. But the full speed, head-on collision of horses and men is not so

The final phase of the Battle of Gettysburg

kind to others. It is a sound like falling timber. "So sudden and violent was the collision that many of the horses were turned end over end, and crushed their riders beneath them," one Union officer will later write.

All around Custer, the air is thick with the screams of men and horses as the two great armies fight in the saddle and dodge bullets fired at point-blank range. There are demands for surrender and terrified cries for help from fallen men being trampled.

Quickly, the fighting becomes hand-to-hand. Men grab hold of one another for leverage, swinging their sabers down, slicing any piece of flesh they can find. After the battle, property owner John Rommel will come upon "two men . . . who fought on horseback with their sabers until they finally clinched and their horses ran from under them. Their head and shoulders were severely cut. And when found, their fingers, though stiff with death, were so firmly embedded in each other's flesh that they could not be removed without the aid of force."

In twenty minutes the battle is over. Union infantry, held in reserve, breaks from a tree line and attacks the Confederate cavalry. Even more Union soldiers pivot to attack the rear of the rebel lines. Nearly surrounded, their dead men and horses littering Rommel's farm, the rebels have no choice but to retreat.

George Custer and the Michigan Brigade have held the line.

"I challenge the annals of warfare to produce a more brilliant or successful charge of cavalry," General Custer will write in his report. He is prone to the dramatic and to self-aggrandizement, but in this instance the general is correct.

His victory assures the young officer that he is invincible. That assurance will eventually be challenged in a climactic way.

The Civil War will end in two years' time, as Confederate general Robert E. Lee rides to a small house in Appomattox Court House, Virginia. Union general Ulysses S. Grant, who spent the Mexican War as a homesick lieutenant, will dictate the terms of surrender. General George Custer will be among the Union army cavalry officers granted the privilege of being in the room to witness this historic event. In time, Custer will even come to own the very table upon which the surrender is signed.

For many, the end of the Civil War brings a close to their fighting days. Not so for George Custer. He is a soldier to the core, a man who needs a battlefield. So as the war concludes, and the American army once again turns its focus to protecting settlers from Indian attacks, Custer forever leaves the battlefields of the east for the wide-open plains of the west.

There, George Custer has a rendezvous with history.

There, the American Indian is waiting.

Chapter Fourteen

Crazy Horse is ready to fight.

It is the first day of winter. The sky is growing dark from an approaching blizzard. The twenty-five-year-old Sioux warrior sits astride a brown pony, armed with a simple steel hatchet, a thick red blanket draped over his shoulders. He is a man of medium height, with hair and skin so light there were once rumors that he had been kidnapped from white society as a child.

Spread out on the ridgeline to Crazy Horse's right and left are nine other warriors, specially chosen for their courage and the speed of their ponies. Like Crazy Horse, they remain out in the open, so unafraid of the American soldiers down below that they choose not to conceal their presence.

As Crazy Horse well knows, this impending attack has been months in the making. The U.S. government has built a brand-new fort on Indian land, greatly angering the Sioux nation. This corner of the Dakota Territory is prime hunting ground and considered sacred by the Sioux and other tribes.

Fort Phil Kearny is being constructed alongside a new settlers' route known as the Bozeman Trail, leading north to the Montana gold fields. This rectangle six hundred feet by eight hundred feet is

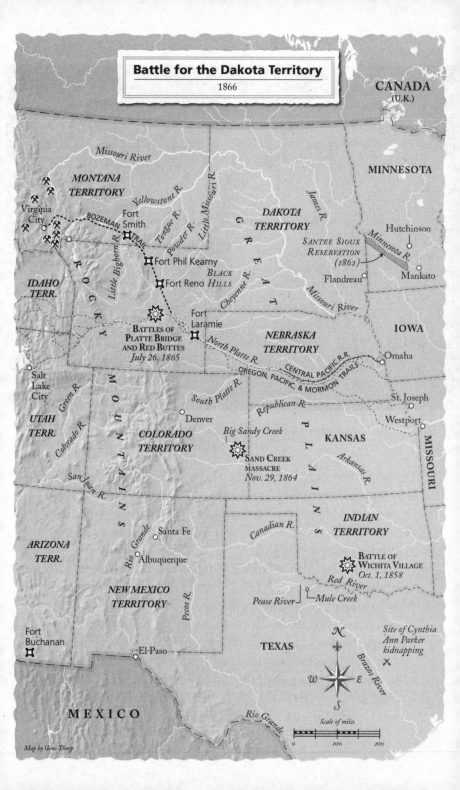

Battle for the Dakota Territory
1866

CANADA
(U.K.)

MINNESOTA

Missouri River

MONTANA
TERRITORY

Yellowstone R.

DAKOTA
TERRITORY

James R.

Virginia
City

Fort
Smith

BOZEMAN TRAIL

Tongue R.

Powder R.

Little Missouri R.

SANTEE SIOUX
RESERVATION
(1862)

Hutchinson

Minnesota R.

Fort Phil Kearny

Little Bighorn R.

Fort Reno

BLACK
HILLS

Flandreau

Mankato

IDAHO
TERR.

Cheyenne R.

BATTLES OF
PLATTE BRIDGE
AND RED BUTTES
July 26, 1865

Fort
Laramie

Missouri River

IOWA

NEBRASKA
TERRITORY

North Platte R.

Salt
Lake
City

Green R.

CENTRAL PACIFIC R.R.

OREGON, PACIFIC, & MORMON TRAILS

Omaha

UTAH
TERR.

Colorado R.

South Platte R.

Denver

Republican R.

St. Joseph

Westport

COLORADO
TERRITORY

Big Sandy Creek

KANSAS

Arkansas R.

MISSOURI

San Juan R.

SAND CREEK
MASSACRE
Nov. 29, 1864

ARIZONA
TERR.

INDIAN
TERRITORY

Santa Fe

Rio Grande

Canadian R.

Albuquerque

Pecos R.

NEW MEXICO
TERRITORY

BATTLE OF
WICHITA VILLAGE
Oct. 1, 1858

Red River

Pease River

Mule Creek

Fort
Buchanan

El-Paso

TEXAS

Site of Cynthia
Ann Parker
kidnapping

Brazos River

N

W   E

S

MEXICO

Rio Grande

Scale of miles

0   100   200

Map by Gene Thorp

*Low-angle view of the incomplete Crazy Horse Memorial
in Black Hills, South Dakota*

the largest stockaded fort on the frontier, ringed by eleven-foot-long logs sunk three feet into the ground. Each log is twelve inches in diameter. The tops are sharpened to a point for the purposes of defense and to prevent water from pooling atop the surface. A low platform runs along the inside of the walls for soldiers to stand upon when firing outward at advancing intruders. They will stand five feet apart should this happen. A firing notch carved into the top of every fifth log ensures this precise separation.

Each morning, soldiers leave the safety of the fort and ride by wagon to the closest forest to gather firewood and chop lumber. The distance can be as much as seven miles. However, it is a grave strategic mistake on the part of the army to build the fort so far from a source of timber. Each day soldiers expose themselves to possible attack. Crazy Horse and the combined force of the Sioux, Chey-

*The Indian battle and massacre near Fort Phil Kearny,
Dakota Territory, December 21, 1866*

enne, and Arapaho nations have a plan to exploit this weakness.
Only freshly cut "green" timber is used in the fort's construction,
thus ensuring the need to undertake this long and dangerous task
every working day. Currently, the army is hurrying to create winter
quarters for incoming troops and finishing the fort's new hospital
before heavy snowfall makes the timber detail impossible until the
spring thaw.*

The woodcutters and their armed escort left the fort an hour

---

* The location of Fort Phil Kearny is in modern-day Wyoming. The "Dakota Territory"
was a construct of the U.S. government, extending from what is now North and South
Dakota west through Montana and Wyoming. A separate and unique Wyoming Territory was not created until 1868. Of note: the name "Wyoming" was not the name
the Native Americans called the region. Instead, Congress named it for the Wyoming
Valley in Pennsylvania, site of a 1778 battle during the Revolutionary War.

ago. Crazy Horse can see the wagon train from his high vantage point atop Lodge Trail Ridge—a long line of interconnected hills offering an unobstructed view of Fort Phil Kearny and most of the valley below. The fort is to the south—his left. A wide frozen and cottonwood-lined creek known as Big Piney runs between the stockade and the base of Lodge Trail Ridge. As Crazy Horse knows from the prebattle planning sessions, the Indian assault on the woodcutters from his well-hidden fellow warriors will commence when the caravan is roughly three miles from the fort. Crazy Horse will not take part.

And so it begins. High-pitched war whoops and the irregular pop of gunfire shatter the morning silence. Crazy Horse is engaged by the battle, but only for a moment. Then he turns his gaze to focus his attention on Fort Phil Kearny.

Where there is no sign of activity.

So Crazy Horse waits.

A quick glance back at the battle shows the American wagons drawing into a tight defensive circle. Sioux warriors charge their mounts in close before launching their arrows. The sound of fighting captivates Crazy Horse—that endless commotion of gunfire and battle cries carrying miles on the wind and cold air. If he can hear the commotion high up on this ridge, then surely the soldiers inside Fort Phil Kearny can hear it as well. Will they respond by sending reinforcements, or will they let their brethren endure the attack alone?

The success of Crazy Horse's mission depends upon the American response.

Crazy Horse continues to wait. Five minutes pass. Then ten.

Finally, an answer: the stout wooden gates of Fort Phil Kearny open wide.

Fifty armed foot soldiers march out to rescue the woodcutters, accompanied by a single officer on horseback. The gates immediately close behind them. Shortly afterward, the gates are pushed open once again. This time, a large contingent of cavalry gallops from the fort, led by a young officer riding a white horse. Crazy Horse smiles—he saw the same brash soldier in combat two weeks ago. The man is impulsive under fire.

Crazy Horse makes a quick count: in all, eighty-one Americans now hasten to the woodcutters' defense. A regimental dog escapes from the fort at the last minute, eager to follow the American soldiers, wherever they might be going.

It seems the whites have taken the bait.

Even better, the soldiers do not hurry west, toward the battle. Instead, in an attempt to cut off an Indian retreat, the Americans travel northward.

Straight toward Crazy Horse and his nine brave companions.

Just as expected.

The white soldiers outnumber Crazy Horse and his small band by a margin of eight to one. The Americans carry better rifles, have slept the night in warm cabins rather than on frozen ground, and enjoy the full backing of the U.S. government as they sally forth with intent to kill.

Crazy Horse likes his odds.

＊

The distance from Fort Phil Kearny to Crazy Horse's position on top of the hill is a little more than two miles. At a quick march, it will take Captain William J. Fetterman and his men forty-five minutes. Historians will long debate whether or not Fetterman disobeyed orders by not traveling straight to the woodcutters' rescue. But what's done is done. Fetterman has now committed his troops to cutting off the Indian retreat rather than marching to the battlefield.

The thirty-three-year-old captain is mounted, keeping his horse to a slow walk as his infantry columns march northeast along Big Piney Creek. He shouts encouragement and orders, demanding his troops to march faster. The trail goes through the valley lined with cottonwoods. The captain has been described as a "fire-eater" and longs to extract a victory over the Indians. Captain Fetterman carries a six-shot revolver but prefers to ride with his M1860 light cavalry saber drawn.

The son of a West Point graduate, Fetterman's own application to the U.S. Military Academy was rejected for reasons unknown fifteen years ago. He worked as a banker before the Civil War finally allowed him to fight for his country. Captain Fetterman served four years with distinction as a Union officer and chose to remain in the army once the war ended. Aggressive and intense, with a long, curving mustache and receding hairline, Fetterman arrived at Fort Phil Kearny six weeks ago. Shortly after the first of the year he is due to take sole leadership of the fort. When that happens, he plans to change the passive leadership approach of the current commanding officer, Colonel Henry B. Carrington. The two men know each other well from their years together during the Civil War, but Fetterman prefers to take the fight to the Indians rather than let them dictate terms, as is so often the case at Fort Phil Kearny.

The captain leads his men through a grove of cottonwoods along the banks of Big Piney. The creek is a frozen sheet of ice with snow covering the surface. Lodge Trail Ridge rises steeply to its right. At the top, just out of rifle range, two Indians wrapped in red blankets watch Fetterman's advance. This is the third time in three weeks that the Eighteenth Infantry Regiment has left the safety of Fort Phil Kearny to relieve a besieged party of woodcutters. Two weeks ago, the captain took part in a bruising engagement between his soldiers and the Sioux, in which the Indians used decoy riders to lure the Americans into a trap. Two soldiers were killed. The corpse of one popular young cavalry officer, Lieutenant Horatio S. Bingham, was pierced by more than fifty arrows.

Afterward, Fetterman admitted that the Indians were better fighters than he once believed, saying, "This Indian war has become a hand-to-hand fight, requiring the utmost caution."

The Sioux, Arapaho, and Cheyenne tribes have been relentless in their raids on Fort Phil Kearny. In addition to attacking the woodcutters, more than fifty attacks against the fort have taken place in the last five months, with two dozen Americans killed. Almost as devastating has been the theft of oxen, cattle, mules, and especially horses. The fort is home to four hundred men but is down to just fifty serviceable mounts, thus the need to march.

It is just as well. The soldiers under Fetterman's command this morning are inexperienced and unruly. Each man wears a heavy greatcoat, dark-blue shirt, light-blue trousers, and ankle-high brogans

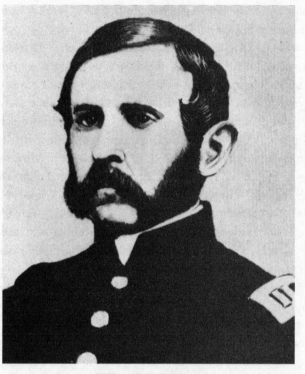

William Judd Fetterman

known as Jefferson boots. Most can barely march in formation, let alone ride a horse into combat.

Single, and with no heirs, Fetterman is perfectly suited for life on the frontier. The same cannot be said of his troopers. Since the demobilization of the U.S. Army after the Civil War, the sort of man who volunteers for duty in Indian Country is likely to be running from the law or new to America. Indeed, twenty of the men marching forth with Fetterman are Irish-born immigrants. Soldiers are forbidden from leaving the fort by themselves, or even in small groups, to explore the local hills in their free time. Swearing is absolutely prohibited, they are not allowed to walk on the grass of Fort Phil Kearny's parade ground, and every soldier is confined to their barracks at dusk. Life is lonely and harsh for these men, far from home, with no women or social life to distract them from the monotony and loneliness of a small military fort, within which they are essentially prisoners.

It was once thought that a posting to a frontier garrison would be romantic, and the army still encourages officers to bring their wives and children. But the truth is that the constant threat of sudden death from an Indian attack has brought discipline and morale at Fort Phil Kearny to an all-time low. It is common for each man to sleep in his clothes, lest a surprise raid come at night. The few remaining horses are saddled and ready to ride from dawn to dusk.

Lack of proper weaponry only adds to the disgruntlement. Rather than rifles that fire several rounds before the need to reload, as were common during the Civil War, the Dakota Territory soldiers are mostly armed with single-shot .58-caliber muzzle-loading rifles—a weapon that has changed little since George Washington waged war against the Indians of the East Coast.

Strangely, the only group within Fort Phil Kearny armed with the modern Spencer repeating rifle are members of the regimental band. History records no reason why that is the case.

Just before breaking through the ice to splash across Big Piney Creek, Fetterman is joined by twenty-seven members of the Second Cavalry under Lieutenant George W. Grummond.

At the end of the Civil War, Grummond chose not to return home to his wife and two children in Michigan, preferring to marry a young woman he met while serving in Tennessee. The two were already wed when a Detroit judge handed down a $2,000 judgment for neglect against Grummond. The lieutenant did not pay, instead accepting this posting at Fort Phil Kearny in an attempt to flee his past. Grummond has since shown a fondness for drunkenness and insubordination. He has even been court-martialed.

But a lack of young officers has forced fort commander Colonel Carrington to reluctantly allow the controversial Grummond not only to remain on duty but now to accompany Fetterman's infantry column. The young lieutenant rides a white horse so that his men might see him more easily during battle. Like Fetterman, he is armed with a saber and pistol.

Each cavalry trooper was issued twenty-eight rounds of ammunition. Fetterman had the forethought to liberate the Spencer seven-shot repeating rifles from the regimental band, then distribute them out to his troopers. The riders all carry a saber, as well.

Lieutenant Grummond has orders to place himself under Fetterman's command. But at the sight of the two Indians wrapped in red blankets atop the ridgeline, all thoughts of compliance disappear. Lieutenant Grummond orders his bugler to sound the charge. The cavalry begins climbing the steep hill to the summit.

Fetterman then orders his foot soldiers to march double time, realizing the need to remain as close as possible should the cavalry get in trouble. Rather than straight columns, the men spread out in skirmish formation, marching abreast in a ragged line. Each soldier is well aware that even when the Indians move into rifle range, they must be extremely deliberate when choosing to fire their weapons— ammunition supplies are so low that each foot soldier carries just forty bullets.

Captain Fetterman has gone on record as boasting that "with just eighty men" he can "ride through the Sioux nation."

Right now, Fetterman commands exactly eighty men.

※

At the sight of the U.S. Cavalry galloping across Big Piney Creek, then up the Lodge Trail Ridge, Crazy Horse orders all nine of his fellow warriors to move forward, so they might easily be seen among the rocks, dead grass, and scattered pine trees of the slope. They are all mounted and aggressively ride their ponies slowly downward toward the approaching American cavalry.

The U.S. Army likes to believe the Indians fight without strategy, relying on impulse and nerve to launch attacks in random fashion. But as Crazy Horse can attest, battles are planned well in advance. Discipline is paramount to success. Warriors who fail to execute their roles are subjected to a public tribal beating. For today's fight, the Sioux chiefs Red Cloud and High Backbone have orchestrated a meticulous scheme. The goal is to kill as many Americans as possible, then burn Fort Phil Kearny. But there can be no battle unless Crazy Horse and his nine companions convince the Americans that they are the main force, a small band of renegade warriors who will be easily defeated.

The soldiers open fire, shooting and riding at the same time as they charge up the steep hill toward Crazy Horse. Predictably, the bullets go high. The Indians fall back, taking care to remain just out of range.

Suddenly, the soldiers halt. Though Crazy Horse and his men remain in plain sight, the Americans appear to be having second thoughts. Crazy Horse can clearly see Captain Fetterman and the infantry continuing their march up to the summit of Lodge Trail Ridge, but the cavalry is no longer advancing. Lieutenant Grummond seems to have learned a hard lesson two weeks ago and refuses to ride any farther.

Crazy Horse must now seize the initiative.

Though still a young man, Crazy Horse has been killing opponents in combat for more than a decade. The warrior was given the name of Cha-Oh-Ha—"Among the Trees"—at birth, but his pale skin and locks led to the childhood nickname of Light Hair. Some even called him Curly. The name Crazy Horse was actually that of his father, a medicine man. But as the young warrior grew in stature, his father renamed himself Waglula—"Worm"—passing along his former title to his son as a display of honor. Though not a chief, Crazy Horse is a valued wartime commander. He is a complicated man, often aloof and quiet, while also deeply spiritual. Just yesterday, Crazy Horse was overcome with emotion when a shaman prophesied that today's battle would result in the murder of one hundred U.S. soldiers.

Crazy Horse longs for that to happen.

Signaling his nine other warriors, Crazy Horse directs them to act confused. One warrior dismounts and tends to his horse's forelock, as if the animal is lame. Another trudges up the hill dragging his mount by its buffalo-hide bridle, suggesting the horse is too exhausted to be ridden. Crazy Horse dismounts and scrapes snow and ice from his pony's hooves, taking his time even when the white men advance within rifle range. He even makes a small fire and warms himself.

The ruse works. The American advance resumes. Crazy Horse

takes care not to move too quickly, lest the whites once again sense a trap. Soon, he and his warriors reach the summit. They then turn and open fire, screaming taunts at the American soldiers.

Crazy Horse watches eighty-one blue-clad soldiers approach. The first part of the battle plan is coming together.

Just to be sure the Americans do not have second thoughts about advancing, Crazy Horse orders a warrior named Big Nose to commit an act of enormous bravery. Without hesitating, the young Cheyenne gallops his black pony directly at the Americans, braving withering gunfire. Incredibly, not a single round strikes Big Nose as he circles around the Americans and then races back up the ridge, where Crazy Horse awaits.

※

Captain Fetterman watches the lone Cheyenne warrior on the black warhorse gallop to catch up with his companions. He counts ten Indians in all, not more than three-quarters of a mile up on the ridge. There are no other warriors in sight, giving Fetterman a momentary sense of calm. If it *had* been a trap, he would have arrived to find many Indians waiting.

Fetterman's orders are not to descend the other slope of Lodge Trail Ridge as he gives pursuit. So far, he has followed those orders by remaining atop the summit. As long as he remains there, no harm, he believes, can come from chasing down ten Indians.

Finally, Captain Fetterman orders a charge. The cavalry gallops toward the small band. The infantry marches double time in the same direction. Many of the men grab onto the stirrup of a cavalry saddle and jog beside the horse and rider in the hopes of getting to the fight quicker. The trail descends the other side of the ridge, then flattens on a plateau near the forks of a stream known as Peno Creek, allowing cavalry and infantry to move with all haste toward their enemy. Technically, Fetterman is now disobeying orders, for he has descended the far side of the ridge. He continues to follow the ten Indians on horseback as their path takes them onto another narrow ridgeline, this one no more than fifty yards wide in some places, with steep slopes descending into a valley on both sides. This new path is actually a section of the Bozeman Trail. Wagon-track ruts form a winding dirt path atop its surface. Fetterman has a clear view of not just the finger of land in front of him but thirty miles more to the north. And other than the ten Indians on horseback, the captain sees not a single warrior.

Lodge Trail Ridge now rises behind Fetterman's command like a high wall, blocking any chance of rescue or escape to the rear. A hard wind reddens his cheeks, portending the coming storm. The sky blackens as the clouds move closer. No one at Fort Phil Kearny can see him—or save him. Fetterman orders his men to move forward.

Soon, Captain Fetterman and most of his foot soldiers are more than a half mile behind the galloping cavalry. The entire force of the U.S. Army patrol is isolated on this narrow stretch of the Bozeman Trail, which drops off steeply on both sides. In the distance, to his great disbelief, the ten Indians turn their horses and charge directly at the American mounted force.

※

Crazy Horse splits his band of warriors into two separate lines of five riders. Each man knows this part of the plan well, for it is a moment that will require extreme bravery. Even more than their ability to lure the Americans into a trap, this is why they were selected to serve as decoy riders. It is suicide to charge their horses straight at the American cavalry, but as each warrior quirts the flanks of his steed on Crazy Horse's command, there is no turning back.

"Hoka-he," cries Crazy Horse as they ride hard into the bitter cold wind. "Today is a good day to die."

The warriors charge toward the soldiers in two single file lines. On a predetermined signal, they turn their horses and weave among one another.

"Hoka-he!" yells Crazy Horse.

"Hoka-he!"

※

Cavalry commander Grummond gallops his white horse toward the two approaching lines of Indians. He hears the sound of "hoka-he," knowing the exhortation is a traditional Sioux rallying cry. There is a moment of confusion for Grummond, followed by great confidence that the approaching warriors' hubris will soon come to an end.

But as Grummond and his cavalry rush along the Bozeman Trail toward the small band of ten Indians, the lieutenant is stunned to see hidden Indians rising up from the slopes on both sides of the trail. Everywhere the lieutenant looks, there is danger. To his amazement, many warriors from a variety of tribes have hidden themselves in the rocks and small gullies. These Indians laid here on the cold hard ground for hours, many even pinching the nostrils of their ponies to ensure the horses did not whinny and give away the element of surprise.

The terrifying screech of battle cries echoes across the land as Indians pour forth, shooting their bows and arrows, instantly killing American soldiers and their horses. Some Indians have firearms they have stolen from the whites in previous battles. Many prefer to carry a nine-foot lance with an iron point, while others use a stone war club. Each warrior carries a steel-bladed knife, for when the time comes to take scalps. But the main weapon of these warriors is a four-foot-long bow that fires iron arrows more than two feet long. Amazingly, some forty thousand arrows will be launched before this surprise assault is done.

Many of the cavalry immediately see the attack for what it is. Surrounded on all sides, they quickly dismount and take cover behind their horses, using the Spencer repeating rifles to great effect. One small group of troopers wound or kill almost sixty Indians and horses before they are overrun.

Thirty-two-year-old Corporal Adolph Metzger of the cavalry is armed with a repeating rifle, but he is also the company bugler. The five-foot-eight German-born soldier rides a gray horse named Dapple Dave. He has been in the U.S. Army since coming to America in 1855 and fought in the Civil War, including the Battle of Gettysburg. He has blue eyes, brown hair, and an eighteen-year-old wife named Fredericka, to whom he hopes to return when his three-year enlistment ends in the summer. It was Metzger who blew "charge" as the horsemen raced into battle. Now, his rifle empty, he continues to fight the only way he can. Corporal Metzger stands to face his opponents as they come for him, using his bugle as a club, swinging it with lethal effectiveness. He never once turns his back on the enemy. But in the end, the musical instrument cannot stop the flurry of arrows that ensure that he will never see his beloved Fredericka again.

The wife of cavalry officer Lieutenant George Grummond is in closer proximity to her husband. Frances Grummond, the woman with whom Grummond had an affair during the Civil War, has made the journey west for her husband's posting at Fort Phil Kearny. She waits there now, praying for his return, even as the lieutenant fights for his life. But the pregnant Frances Grummond, due to give birth any day, will pray in vain. Lieutenant Grummond fights bravely, leading his men with honor, even decapitating one warrior with a single slash of his saber. But like his troopers, Grummond is soon overwhelmed, dragged off his horse, and hacked to pieces.

As all of this takes place, Captain William Fetterman is a half mile behind Lieutenant Grummond, in the thick of his own fight. Indians now surround him and his infantry on all sides, rising up out of the valleys and the slopes alongside the trail, on horseback and on foot.

Completely enveloped, Fetterman's chance to "ride through the Sioux nation" has come and gone.

Forever.

※

Crazy Horse weaves his pony deftly through the confused American cavalry, swinging his hatchet with powerful ruthlessness as he splits heads and severs arms. This is war, but it is also a continuing saga of revenge. It was just two years ago, on November 29, 1864, that Colonel John M. Chivington led seven hundred men of the Third Colorado Cavalry on a surprise attack into a Cheyenne and Arapaho camp at a location on the open plains known as Sand Creek. The tribe's warriors were away, so Chivington—a towering fire-and-brimstone Methodist preacher who famously used the saying "Nits make lice" when justifying his brutal actions—eagerly ordered the execution and mutilation of more than one hundred Indian women and children. Scalps were taken, sometimes so vigorously that the single head of a child was sliced away several times. Fetuses were cut from women's wombs. Reproductive organs were cut from female bodies and used to decorate the saddles of the "Bloody Third's" horses.

"The massacre lasted six or eight hours," one U.S. officer wrote to a fellow soldier two weeks after the slaughter. "I tell you Ned, it was hard to see little children on their knees have their brains beat out by men professing to be civilized. . . . They were all scalped, and as high as a half a dozen [scalps] taken from one head. They were all horribly mutilated. . . . You could think it impossible for white men to butcher and mutilate human beings as they did there, but every word I have told you is the truth, which they do not deny. . . . I expect we will have a hell of a time with Indians this winter."

The prophecy of Lieutenant Silas Soule, writer of that letter, comes to pass. Crazy Horse was part of an avenging force in two separate battles during 1865. The Battle of Platte Bridge and the Battle of Red Buttes saw the Sioux nation join forces with the Cheyenne and Arapaho in an attempt to regain control of the plains. The approach of the white man, with the escalating advances of the Pony Express mail service, then telegraph lines, and finally the ongoing development of a railroad from one side of the nation to the other, is being met with brute force. The whites have shown themselves capable of great brutality toward the Indians of the Northern Plains. The Americans should expect the same in return.

And that is what the eighty-one men from Fort Phil Kearny are now experiencing.

But death does not stop the desecration. The temperature will fall to twenty degrees below zero tonight, so when the wagons are sent out to retrieve the dead in the morning, each corpse will be frozen as solid as cordwood. Each man will be naked, having been stripped of boots, uniforms, socks, underwear, gun belts, weapons, and items of sentimental value.

But as with the Chivington massacre at Sand Creek, death and nudity will be the least of the debasements these soldiers will endure.

Some atrocities will be committed while the whites are alive. But many of the soldiers commit suicide rather than be captured.

The after-battle report compiled by the American leadership at Fort Phil Kearny will detail the fates of the eighty-one U.S. soldiers: "Eyes torn out and laid on rocks, noses cut off, ears cut off, chins hewn off, teeth chopped out, joints of fingers taken off, brains taken out and placed on rocks with members of the body, entrails taken out and exposed, hands cut off, feet cut off, arms taken out from the socket, private parts severed and indecently placed on the person; eyes, ears, mouths, and arms penetrated with spear heads, sticks and arrows; ribs slashed to separation with knives; skulls severed in any form, from chin to crown; muscles of calves, thighs, stomach, breast, back, arms, and cheeks taken out; punctures of every sensitive part of the body, even to the soles of feet and palms of the hand."

Bugler Adolph Metzger is spared this horror. His bravery so impresses the Indian force that his body is left untouched. Instead, his body is covered in a buffalo robe as a sign of respect.*

❖

Crazy Horse sanctions the horrendous brutality. As he watches the battle, he sees the Cheyenne warrior Big Nose shot from his horse, his earlier acts of bravery ensuring his legacy with the tribe will live on. Big Nose does not die right away and is carried to a small depression in the earth to witness the remainder of the fight.

Crazy Horse is impressed with the courage of the Americans, for not a single soldier turns to flee. But it is also apparent that these men do not know how to fight his warriors, and they are clearly terrified of the circular nature of the Sioux strategy, attacking the soldiers from all directions.

Crazy Horse is determined to not just win the battle but also ensure that not a single American escapes alive.

"Do not even let a dog get away," shouts one Cheyenne warrior.

---

* Corporal Metzger's horse, Dapple Dave, will be the lone American survivor of the Fetterman Battle. The gray will flee the battlefield but will be shot through with so many arrows and bullets that he will be put down upon his discovery by U.S. troops.

There is no attempt at sentiment. A flurry of arrows cripples and kills the fort dog in an instant.

※

It is a warrior named American Horse who surprises Captain Fetterman. The officer's many boasts prior to the fatal fight were the words, "Give me a single company of regulars and I can whip a thousand Indians." But now the captain saves a single bullet in his pistol for himself as his men are overwhelmed, all claims of whipping the Sioux nation a cruel memory.

Captain Fetterman's death, however, is not quick, nor is it by his own hand. Fetterman is jumped by the young warrior American Horse, who clubs the captain over the head, knocking him from his mount. American Horse then leaps from his own steed and uses his scalping knife to slice Fetterman's throat. The Indian spares no effort, wrenching the knife clear through the thick muscles of the captain's neck, all the way to Fetterman's spine.

His hands now dripping with blood, American Horse takes the captain's scalp.

※

This is the best day of Crazy Horse's life. His success as a decoy, and his ability to lead men using ingenuity and guile, now mark him as one of the Sioux nation's future leaders.

Just a dozen warriors have been killed today, but Crazy Horse knows many more will die in the future. The white man will not be deterred. But this thought does not disturb the young Sioux. He will not accept the white man's march into his land.

Ever.

Chapter Fifteen

CHRISTMAS NIGHT, 1866
FORT LARAMIE, WYOMING
11:00 P.M.

The Ghost of Christmas Present is about to appear.

It has been a challenging year for the officers and men stationed at this frontier outpost. Tonight's full-dress Christmas ball offers a rare chance to relax. Outside, the subzero temperatures and driving snow mean almost no chance of an Indian attack. There isn't a pine tree within a hundred miles, so wives and children have decorated the indoor "Christmas tree" by hanging painted egg shells, buttons, lace, and even cigar butts on a small prairie sapling. A blaze roars in the great fireplace here at Old Bedlam, as the post headquarters was nicknamed when it served as bachelor officer quarters and a hub of frontier socializing. Stockings are hung on the mantel. Officers and their ladies glide across the dance floor in their finest attire as the drinks flow freely. The air smells of damp wool, cigars, and spilled whiskey. It is a celebration that has been planned for weeks and is certain to last into the morning.*

---

* The celebration of Christmas was a relatively new phenomenon in America at the time. Following the Revolutionary War, citizens of the United States turned their backs on all traditions associated with Britain, among them Christmas. But the popularity of Charles Dickens's *A Christmas Carol*, first published in 1843, and a growing reconnection with European customs, saw the return of Christmas. However, December 25 did not become a federal holiday until 1870, when President Grant signed it into law.

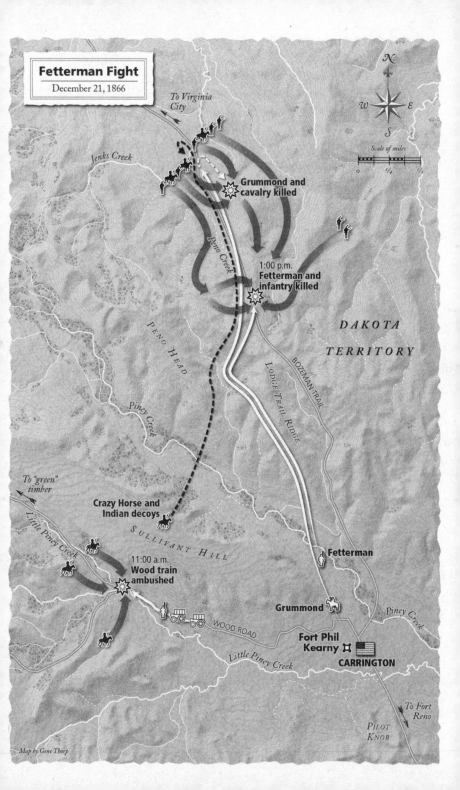

Fetterman Fight
December 21, 1866

To Virginia City

Jenks Creek

Grummond and
cavalry killed

Peno Creek

1:00 p.m.
Fetterman and
infantry killed

DAKOTA

TERRITORY

PENO HEAD

Piney Creek

LODGE TRAIL RIDGE

BOZEMAN TRAIL

To "green" timber

Crazy Horse and
Indian decoys

Little Piney Creek

SULLIVANT HILL

Fetterman

11:00 a.m.
Wood train
ambushed

Grummond

WOOD ROAD

Piney Creek

**Fort Phil
Kearny**

Little Piney Creek

CARRINGTON

*To Fort
Reno*

*PILOT
KNOB*

Map by Gene Thorp

"Everyone appeared superlatively happy, enjoying the dance, notwithstanding the snow was from ten to fifteen inches deep on the level and the thermometer indicated twenty-five degrees below zero," Lieutenant David S. Gordon of the Second Cavalry will write.

Suddenly, the merriment is abruptly interrupted. A hulking figure "dressed in a buffalo overcoat, pants, gauntlets, and cap," steps through the double doors fronting the parade ground. The man's face is completely bearded. It is well known that a caravan of traders arrived today, en route to Nebraska. Their wagons are laden with buffalo, elk, and deer hides. Such men are welcome to overnight at the fort for their own safety, but the intrusion of this unwashed traveler into a private party goes far beyond the bounds of military hospitality.

Aggressively striding into the gathering, the unkempt man is accompanied by an enlisted orderly and urgently requests to speak with the fort commander, Lieutenant Colonel Innis N. Palmer.

The music keeps playing, but all eyes are on the intruder as he and Colonel Palmer step into another room to have a private word. "The dress of the man, and at this hour looking for the commanding officer, made a deep impression upon the officers and others that happened to get a glimpse of him. And consequently, and naturally, too, excited their curiosity as to his mission in this strange garb, dropping into our full dress garrison ball at this unseasonable hour," Lieutenant Gordon will later write about his direct involvement in the moment.

"As we were about to select partners for another dance, word was passed into the ballroom that Colonel Palmer desired to see me. Excusing myself, I reported to the commanding officer, who handed me a dispatch dated Fort Phil Kearny, December 21, 1866, signed by Col. H.B. Carrington, commanding post, that Brevet-Colonel Fetterman, with a detachment . . . had been massacred outside of the post."

A shocked Lieutenant Gordon returns to the ball. He knows Fetterman well. The ballroom is small, and Gordon's departure was noticed. In hushed tones, the lieutenant explains himself to a fellow cavalry officer. Word quickly circulates about the horrific slaughter at Fort Phil Kearny.

The news "created such a gloom over all that the dancing party dispersed early," Colonel Palmer noted. What is to come seems to occupy all the guests. There is no more appetite for gaiety.

❄

The bearer of the mournful news is John Phillips, a thirty-four-year-old miner of Portuguese birth who chooses to winter in Fort Phil Kearny rather than endure the cold of the Montana gold fields. Immediately after Captain Fetterman's death was confirmed, Colonel Carrington paid Phillips the amazing sum of $300 to ride through the night and deliver the news to other Americans on the frontier.* Phillips first stopped at the Horseshoe Station telegraph office so that the message could be wired to Washington, D.C. There it will shock the nation, as the news is soon published in the *New York Times* and *Chicago Tribune*. A period of national mourning will commence, followed by divided reaction in Congress as to the proper level of vengeance against the Sioux. President Andrew Johnson is ordinarily accommodating toward the western Indians—preferring to spend his time reconstructing the South after the Civil War. Thus, it is left mainly to the Senate to determine military action regarding Indian matters.

John Phillips rested for a few hours before riding on through the snow to Fort Laramie, more than two hundred miles south of Fort Phil Kearny. He arrived after four hard days of wind and cold in the saddle, an act of personal courage that will lead some newspaper reporters to compare him to a western Paul Revere.

Phillips is safe now, at last able to relax in the warmth of Fort Laramie. Meanwhile, back at Fort Phil Kearny, the dead are still to be buried.

All building of winter quarters and the new army hospital ceases as carpenters focus all their labors on constructing coffins. "One half of the headquarters building, which was my temporary home, and this part was utilized by carpenters for making pine cases for the dead," Frances Grummond, wife of Lieutenant George Grummond,

---

* Roughly $5,000 in modern money.

will write. "I knew my husband's coffin was being made, and the sound of hammers and the grating of saws was torture to my sensitive nerves."

Enlisted men are to be buried two per casket, while the officers are interred privately. Eighty-one mutilated bodies are reassembled as best as possible, and arrows are removed or simply cut away. The living soldiers and officers alike offer up their spare uniforms so the naked corpses can be dressed and buried with dignity. But the Indians have performed their acts of desecration so well that there is no choice but to bury some of the dead in haunting fashion. Captain Frederick Hallam Brown, the post quartermaster whose frozen body will not thaw, has the misfortune of being buried just as he was discovered on the battlefield. "The privates of Capt. Brown were severed and placed in his mouth," one soldier will recall more than fifty years later. "Considering the nature of the extreme cold weather, they could not be extricated."

Meanwhile, a mass grave is being hacked out of the frozen earth. Measuring fifty feet long, seven feet wide, and seven feet deep, it takes five days to dig. "The cold was so intense that the men work in fifteen minute reliefs, and a guard was constantly on the alert lest the Indians disrupt their service," Frances Grummond will remember.

The men are buried the day after Christmas, just hours after the party at Fort Laramie ends. The ceremony proceeds without pomp or speechifying. The freezing weather means the regimental band's brass instruments cannot be used, so there is no music. Afterward, there is nothing for the residents of Fort Phil Kearny to do for the remainder of the coldest winter anyone can remember but wait for an Indian attack that never comes. Rather than take the chance of allowing women and children to be taken hostage, the plan is for them to take refuge in the powder arsenal at the first sign of attack. Should the fort be overrun, the magazine will be immediately detonated.

Reinforcements arrive from Fort Laramie on January 16, delayed three weeks by the severe weather. Colonel Carrington is then relieved in disgrace and begins the long journey home. Frances Grummond, who will become so close to Carrington that she will one day become his second wife, demands that she be allowed to take her dead husband home with her.

So it is that Lieutenant George W. Grummond is exhumed after just a few weeks of burial, then loaded onto a wagon. It is thirty-eight degrees below zero as the caisson rolls away from Fort Phil Kearny on January 23, 1867. The body of Lieutenant Grummond is bound for Tennessee, his widow winning her quest.

❖

For the Sioux, the change of guard at Fort Phil Kearny goes unobserved.

Crazy Horse and his warriors briefly linger on the battlefield after the Fetterman massacre, tending to their wounded. Those Indians who cannot ride are tied to a travois to be dragged from the battlefield by horse. The dead are stashed behind rocks and in the grass so the white men cannot desecrate them. Their corpses will soon be covered by snow.

Among the severely wounded is Lone Bear, a warrior and lifelong friend of Crazy Horse. Despite the falling snow, Crazy Horse and his fellow leader, High Backbone, remain with Lone Bear, who has been shot in the leg and is now suffering blood poisoning. It is apparent Lone Bear cannot be saved. Crazy Horse cradles his childhood playmate in his arms as the Sioux warrior breathes his last.

Even as the whites in Fort Phil Kearny remain vigilant, waiting for another Indian assault, their Sioux attackers are miles away, celebrating. Soon they will ride to their winter camps on the Little Bighorn River or in the Yellowstone Valley. But for now Crazy Horse and the other warriors gather along the Tongue River to dance and feast. The Indians gather in their lodges to share tales of their exploits, recounting the battle over and over again in great detail. They did not burn the white fort, as they had hoped, and it is certain that reinforcements will soon arrive at Fort Phil Kearny. But thanks to the decoy exploits of Crazy Horse, the Americans have been dealt a cruel blow. The coming spring will bring new chances to strike again.

It was never the Sioux nation's intention to wage war during

A reconstructed stockade wall at Fort Phil Kearny, in what is now Johnson County, Wyoming. The fort, along the Bozeman Trail through the northern Rocky Mountains, was an outpost of the U.S. Army in the late 1860s.

months of heavy snow. After their celebration, Crazy Horse and his band settle into their lodges, enduring the harsh winter. He is now a "shirt wearer," as battlefield commanders are known. The massacre marks Crazy Horse's ascendance to tribal leadership, and despite his preference for solitude and silence, he now freely offers advice and opinion to warriors and chiefs alike who seek his insight.

Crazy Horse and his band make winter camp along the Powder River, their seventy lodges forming a large encampment on the banks. The geese and ducks flew south long ago, but now the elk herds and buffalo also flee for warmer territory. Food becomes scarce as the months pass. Crazy Horse and his fellow warriors hunt for food almost daily but often return to camp empty-handed. The few remaining buffalo who fail to keep up with the migrating herd can be found alone in the snowdrifts, their bodies frozen solid.

Then on February 27, 1867, an impatient Crazy Horse strikes a detachment of American infantry heading toward the Bozeman Trail, killing three soldiers. He quickly retreats, reminding the whites that the Sioux can strike wherever and whenever they want.

It is Sioux tradition that the passage of time is marked by counting winters, with significant events painted on buffalo skins. The tribe's history is spread through such visual reminders, as well as by the many nights of storytelling as warriors gather before a campfire. It is natural that word travels from one Sioux band to another in this oral tradition, particularly when warriors boast about their exploits on the battlefield. The harsh winter of 1866 and the victory at Fort Phil Kearny are no doubt primary topics of conversation in lodges throughout the Wyoming Territory.

History does not record the specific day or time when members of the Hunkpapa Sioux learn of the battlefield exploits of Crazy Horse. The Hunkpapa were too far north to take part in the massacre. So on those occasions when Crazy Horse's Lakota Sioux and the Hunkpapa gather together in their winter lodges, it is the Lakota warriors who can brag with confidence about that fateful day.

Among the Hunkpapa leadership is a revered warrior in his late thirties named Tatanka Iyotake. Translated from the Sioux language, the words mean "Buffalo Bull Who Sits Down." His childhood nicknamed was "Slow," for his unhurried approach to life. As an adult, his wisdom, patience, courage, and grit are already legendary. He fought his first battle at the age of fourteen and still prefers to lead the charge during attacks, refusing to rein in his horse as he approaches the enemy. In September 1864, this warrior was wounded in battle with the white soldiers, enduring a gunshot wound in his left hip. Among his band, he is respected for his generosity, kindness, and abilities as a peacemaker.

The whites call him Sitting Bull.

"The name 'Sitting Bull' was a tepee word for all that was generous and great. The bucks admired him, the squaws respected him highly, and the children loved him," U.S. Army scout Frank Grouard will write. "He would have proved a mighty power among our politicians—a great vote-getter from the people."

Sitting Bull, the Hunkpapa Sioux leader

Sitting Bull is thirty-five years old. He is five foot nine, with a slim build. His face is stoic, belying his fondness for storytelling and laughter.

In time, the battlefield genius of Crazy Horse and the political power of Sitting Bull will unite. Neither is now a chief, but both enjoy the deepest respect from their warriors. Because the white man shows no sign of retreating from their lands, the Sioux nation will require a most unique form of leadership to counter that intrusion.

Sitting Bull and Crazy Horse will provide it.

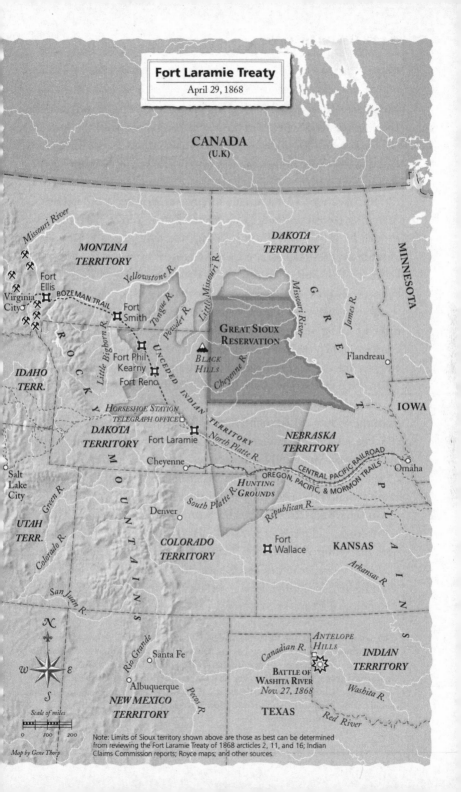

Fort Laramie Treaty
April 29, 1868

CANADA
(U.K)

Missouri River

MONTANA
TERRITORY

DAKOTA
TERRITORY

MINNESOTA

Yellowstone R.

Fort
Ellis

BOZEMAN TRAIL

Virginia
City

Fort
Smith

Tongue R.

Powder R.

Little Missouri R.

Missouri River

G R E A T

James R.

Little Bighorn R.

Fort Phil
Kearny

Fort Reno

UNCEDED INDIAN

GREAT SIOUX
RESERVATION

BLACK
HILLS

Cheyenne R.

Flandreau

ROCKY

IDAHO
TERR.

HORSESHOE STATION
TELEGRAPH OFFICE

TERRITORY

IOWA

DAKOTA
TERRITORY

Fort Laramie

North Platte R.

NEBRASKA
TERRITORY

Cheyenne

P L A I N S

Salt
Lake
City

CENTRAL PACIFIC RAILROAD

Omaha

M O U N T A I N S

HUNTING
GROUNDS

OREGON, PACIFIC, & MORMON TRAILS

UTAH
TERR.

Green R.

Denver

South Platte R.

Republican R.

KANSAS

Colorado R.

COLORADO
TERRITORY

Fort
Wallace

Arkansas R.

San Juan R.

ANTELOPE
HILLS

INDIAN
TERRITORY

N

Rio Grande

Santa Fe

Canadian R.

BATTLE OF
WASHITA RIVER
Nov. 27, 1868

Washita R.

W   E

Albuquerque

Pecos R.

S

NEW MEXICO
TERRITORY

TEXAS

Red River

Scale of miles

0   100   200

Map by Gene Thorp

Note: Limits of Sioux territory shown above are those as best can be determined
from reviewing the Fort Laramie Treaty of 1868 arcticles 2, 11, and 16; Indian
Claims Commission reports; Royce maps; and other sources.

❖

The aftermath of Fort Phil Kearny massacre is felt across America. The country divides between those who wish peace with the Indians and those who seek to destroy them. Finally, after Crazy Horse once again successfully raids near the fort in the summer of 1867, the United States of America seeks peace.

The Treaty of Fort Laramie of 1868 establishes a Sioux nation stretching from the Black Hills of the Dakota Territory all the way west to Montana and south into Nebraska. Whites are forbidden to settle on these lands. The treaty is ratified by the U.S. Senate on February 16, 1869, then signed by President Andrew Johnson on February 24, just one week before leaving office.

During his successful run for the presidency in that same year, General Ulysses S. Grant admits the duplicitous nature of America's relationship with Native Americans, stating, "Our dealings with the Indians properly lay us open to charges of cruelty and swindling." Grant promises to abide by the new treaty and avoid further war on the plains.

The new accord is signed by the U.S. government and leaders from the Sioux and Arapaho nations. In a display of good faith, the U.S. Peace Commissioners add a clause stating that the forts lining the Bozeman Trail will be abandoned. However, Sitting Bull, now a Sioux chief, refuses to sign the treaty, having no faith in the white man's promises. Crazy Horse is not in attendance.*

In the weeks to come, the U.S. Army marches away from a number of forts, including Fort Phil Kearny. Crazy Horse and his warriors then return to the fort. But there is disagreement about what to do with the structure—some warriors believe it should remain standing because it provides the perfect place to endure a hard winter.

---

* The decision to close the forts was made on March 2, 1868, by General Ulysses S. Grant, whose position as General of the Army gave him full authority to withdraw these forces. The decision was pragmatic, based on the belief that the Bozeman Trail was defenseless against the Sioux and that the troops within these forts could be put to better use fighting Indians on the Southern Plains. However, making the closures a tenet of the Treaty of Fort Laramie allowed the Sioux to believe they had won the war for control of their lands.

But Crazy Horse and others disagree, wanting all vestiges of the white man destroyed.

So it is that on August 1, 1868, flames climb into the summer sky as Fort Phil Kearny burns to the ground.

The hellish scene convinces some of the Indians that they have prevailed over the hated white intruders.

But Crazy Horse and Sitting Bull know differently.

Chapter Sixteen

B revet Major General George Armstrong Custer is apprehensive. The newly appointed commander of the U.S. Seventh Cavalry has slept just one hour on this frozen morning. His seven hundred troops have not been allowed to sleep at all. Instead, they spent the night in the saddle, dressed in boots and thick overcoats. Speaking in a voice above a whisper is forbidden. An Indian village has been located along the distant riverbank. Custer does not know the name of the tribe or whether they are peaceful. He does not care. This will be the young general's first engagement with an Indian force, and he aims to use the element of surprise to destroy them. Indeed, Custer has been so vigilant about maintaining silence that he has not allowed his men to pitch tents, light pipes, or even dismount and stamp their feet in search of warmth, believing the noise could alert the nearby tribe.

Custer rises from the buffalo robe laid atop the snow that briefly served as his bed. A thick beard covers his face, his blond hair covered with rime and icicles. The three years since the end of the Civil War have been a time of upheaval for the brevet general, who left the service for a time as he weighed a potential run for Congress and enjoyed the night life of Manhattan. Upon his return to the military in 1866, the nation was confronted by the massacre at Fort Phil Kearny. Railroad companies and stage lines were demanding the army provide better protection for western travelers. Some newspapers even accused soldiers of cowardice for allowing Indians to control the prairie. "As might naturally be expected, a massacre like that at Fort Phil Kearny," Custer will write in his autobiography, ". . . excited discussion and comment throughout the land, and raised inquiry as to who was responsible for this lamentable affair."

The violent actions of the Sioux nation were directly responsible for Custer's posting in Oklahoma. The brilliant battlefield tactics of Crazy Horse and subsequent call to arms by white settlers will lead to his new posting in Kansas as commander of the Seventh.

But Custer's ascent did not come easily, despite his heroics at Gettysburg. He was actually court-martialed four years later, in July 1868. The offense was deserting his post at Fort Wallace in Kansas, to be with his wife, Libbie, a society debutante whom he married in 1864. His sentence was a one-year suspension from the army without pay.

The Custers' relationship is deeply amorous, and the two are fond of writing steamy letters to each other, fraught with innuendo and sexual double entendres. In response to Libbie's written admission that she likes to "ride tomboy," Custer responds: "I'm nearly starved for a ride. But I cannot without much expense and much danger enjoy the luxury of such a ride as that I refer to. I never did enjoy riding strange horses."

Even before their marriage, the correspondence between George Custer and Elizabeth "Libbie" Bacon was so randy that Custer requested she be more careful. Confederate soldiers had intercepted a batch of their letters during the war, and he was aghast at the thought of them being read by the enemy.

So it was little surprise that Custer would make the decision to risk his career for what Libbie would call "one perfect day." This should have been the end of the flamboyant Custer's military aspirations. However, General Phil Sheridan, the nation's leading Indian fighter, interceded. He personally requests that General of the Army U. S. Grant revoke the suspension after just two months, thus allowing Custer to once again rejoin the Seventh Cavalry as commander. Sheridan did so in order that Custer could participate in a winter campaign against the tribes of the Southern Plains.

The main food source for Indians is buffalo, which are being hunted to extinction by roving bands of white sharpshooters. Literally hundreds of buffalo are gunned down each day, then stripped of their hides. In the next four years, some four million buffalo will be shot in this fashion. And despite the fact that these rogue hunters are disallowed by treaty from entering or hunting on Indian land, General Sheridan does nothing to stop the whites from violating the treaty and slaughtering the Indian's main sustenance.

In addition, though the transcontinental railroad is a year away from completion, its slow creep westward means the arrival of train stations at regular intervals, and with them the small towns that spring up to service the rail lines. The loss of the buffalo, coming of the railroad, and encroachment of white civilization onto lands once promised the Indians in perpetuity is pushing the plains tribes such as the Cheyenne, Sioux, Arapaho, and Comanche farther and farther into the fringes of the frontier as they seek to maintain their way of life.

It is Sheridan's ambition to find these tribes in their winter quarters and force them to relocate to government reservations. In the general's mind, even Indians that have agreed to terms of peace and presently live on reservations are acceptable targets of violence. "The only good Indian is a dead Indian," believes Sheridan.*

"I will back you with my full authority," Sheridan's handwritten order to Custer makes clear. "I will say nothing and do nothing to restrain our troops from doing what they deem proper on the spot, and will allow no mere vague general charges of cruelty and inhumanity to tie their hands, but will use all the powers confided to me to the end that these Indians, the enemies of our race and of our civilization, shall not again be able to begin to carry out their barbarous warfare on any kind of pretext they may choose to allege."

---

* Sheridan would forever deny making this statement. Eyewitnesses attested that the general made the claim in 1869, although some say his actual utterance was, "The only good Indians I ever saw were dead."

Elizabeth Clift Custer, American author, public speaker,
and wife of General George Armstrong Custer

Now, as the sun casts its first rays upon the ice-cold waters of the Washita River, Custer prepares to carry out those brutal orders. During a snowstorm four days ago, he and his men marched away from their base camp on the North Canadian River. Custer brings two of his dogs along for company—and warmth, planning on having them sleep alongside him each night. A buffalo robe draped over his shoulders, Custer navigates through the blizzard by compass, ordering his soldiers to ride in tight formation to prevent anyone from getting lost. The path takes the Seventh through Texas and Oklahoma in their search for an Indian camp. Buffalo are hunted along the way so that the men might have meat.

Yesterday afternoon, three days into the search, Custer's scouts located what appears to be a path followed by Indians returning from a hunting expedition. "Early in the night, with my scouts, I struck a hostile trail leading southeast," chief scout Ben Clark will tell the New York *Sun*. "Two of these scouts discovered a campfire. Crawling cautiously toward it, they learned that the Indians had gone toward the river, having joined the war party. Several miles down the river the tinkle of pony bells was faintly heard, and from the summit of a hill the ponies were seen in the valley below, their bodies standing out dark against the snow."

Custer is immediately alerted and rides forth. The night is clear. Stars shine brightly. Tribal dogs bark in the distance. The brevet general lies down atop the snow so his silhouette does not give him away. The scouts point out a series of lodges hidden within the forest.

"When the camp was discovered," Sergeant John Ryan of the Seventh Cavalry's M Company will write, "Custer thought the dogs might alarm the Indians' dogs and arouse the camp, and I understood that Custer had to kill two of his hounds. One dog in my company, of whom the men were very fond, was a little black dog called Bob, and harmless as a kitten. We had to part with him, and one of our men drove a picket pin into Bob's head and left him for dead."

The tribal camp is located in a wooded valley. It is 1:00 a.m. as Custer gathers his officers and asks them to temporarily remove their sabers, believing the weapons might accidentally make a metallic clanking sound that can be heard in the distance. He then lays out a daring plan, which calls for splitting his force and attacking the Indians from four directions at once.

The next five hours are spent carefully moving the separate columns of troops into position. The snow is deep, with a layer of ice on top that makes a crunching sound as the horses walk forward. There is nothing that can be done to silence the animals, but in the end the noise is not a problem. The tribe fears nothing and has posted no guards. All is silent in the Indian encampment, and not even their dogs bark to send the alarm.

At dawn a low fog settles over the valley. "The hour was so still that a man could almost hear his watch tick," one American soldier will long remember.

The calm is shattered when Custer gives the regimental band the order to play "Garry Owen," a triumphal drinking song that has become the Seventh's official anthem. Custer has positioned the band near the river crossing leading to the Indian encampment. Though the cold is so intense that spittle almost instantly freezes within the brass horns, the raucous tune can be heard across the river and into the trees.*

The Seventh Cavalry gallops into the sleeping village with orders to spare no one.

"The Indians were taken completely by surprise and rushed panic-stricken from their lodges, to be shot down almost before sleep had left their eyelids," chief scout Ben Clark will remember.

"The air was full of smoke from gunfire, and it was almost impossible to flee, because bullets were flying everywhere. However, somehow we ran and kept running to find a hiding place," a fourteen-year-old Cheyenne girl will remember. "In the grass we lay flat, our hearts beating, and we were afraid to move."

Wounded Indian ponies moan loudly in pain as they limp off to escape the battle. American soldiers shoot every man, woman, and child they can find in the village—even as many other Indians escape to hide in the freezing river or in the snow and tall grass. Scalps are taken. Bodies are mutilated and stripped.

Soldiers looting the many lodges come across coffee, as well as

---

* The original Irish title was spelled "Garryowen," based on a village near Limerick of the same name. The composer Ludwig von Beethoven wrote his own version of the song. British soldiers during the Peninsular and Crimean Wars made it their regimental march. The song came to America in 1851, when a group of Irish immigrants formed a volunteer regiment and made it their official marching song. The Seventh Cavalry adopted "Garry Owen" as their official "air" in 1867. To this day, the regimental band plays this song.

U.S. Army pots and pans, evidence that this tribe had been given these gifts as signatories of the 1867 Medicine Lodge Treaty and are thus peaceful. Yet the killing does not stop. The corpses of dead Indian men and women are posed by the soldiers in sexually provocative positions. Other dead are hurled into the flames as the entire village is set ablaze. Finally, to ensure that the Indians lack the ability to ever again raid or wage war, Custer gives the order to shoot each and every one of the spotted Indian ponies. Eight hundred horses are quickly shot dead. The skulls of these ponies will litter these lands for decades to come.

"The loss of so many animals of value was a severe blow to the tribe," Custer will write, "as nothing so completely impairs the war-making facilities for the Indians of the Plains as the deprivation or disabling of their ponies."

The village leader is a chief named Black Kettle. He is known as a man of peace and for many years has been eager to establish treaties with the whites to protect his people. It was Black Kettle's Southern Cheyenne tribe who were attacked at Sand Creek on November 29, 1864, even though he had personally flown a white flag of truce and the American Stars and Stripes over his tepee on that day so soldiers would not see him as a threat. Black Kettle survived the infamous slaughter, as did his wife—who suffered nine bullet wounds.

Yet once again, Black Kettle's people are now being attacked without cause, even though he signed a treaty with the U.S. government that promised his tribe "perpetual peace" after their sufferings at Sand Creek. Black Kettle is in his late sixties on the morning Custer and the Seventh Cavalry thunder into his camp, the American soldiers shouting fierce battle cries. Black Kettle panics and mounts a horse with his wife in retreat. Back in the village, the chief's own warriors mock him as he tries to gallop away.

But Black Kettle and his wife do not get far. They are shot in the back by American soldiers, their corpses falling into the Washita River.

"We saw the bodies of Black Kettle and his wife, lying under the water," the Cheyenne teenager named Moving Behind Woman will recount many years later. "It was getting late, and we had to go, so we left the bodies. As we rode along westward, we would come across the bodies of men, women and children strewn about. We would stop and look at the bodies and mention their names."

❄

With more than a hundred Indians dead, George Custer writes his full report shortly after the battle. Messengers travel through the night to deliver news of the great victory to General Sheridan's headquarters. Custer's success is a validation of Sheridan's strategy of taking the battle to the enemy during the winter, when they least expect it.

"The Major General Commanding announces to this Command the defeat, by the Seventh Regiment of Cavalry, of a large force of Cheyenne Indians under the celebrated Chief Black Kettle . . . on the morning of the 27th instant, on the Washita River, near the Antelope Hills, Indian Territory, resulting in a loss to the savages of one hundred and three warriors killed, including Black Kettle."

So reads Major General Phil Sheridan's after-action report about the surprise attack on the Cheyenne at the Washita. The general does not mention that women and children were slaughtered.

"The gallantry and bravery displayed, resulting in signal success, reflect the highest credit upon both the officers and men of the Seventh Cavalry.

"Special congratulations are tendered to their distinguished commander, Brevet Major-General George A. Custer, for the efficient and gallant services rendered."

The history of Washita was initially written by the victors, as is so often the case. But the slaughter sets forth a series of events on the plains that would eventually shock America. Because a nonthreatening tribe had been annihilated, peace and negotiation will become much more difficult between the Indians and the U.S. government.

Payback is coming.

Chapter Seventeen

The new president of the United States, Ulysses S. Grant, seeks peace.

"The proper treatment of the original occupants of this land—the Indians," he states during his inaugural address, is "one deserving of careful study. I will favor any course toward them which tends to their civilization and ultimate citizenship."

The short, bearded, paunchy Grant, whose clothing smells permanently of tobacco smoke from his habit of smoking as many as twenty cigars per day, stands on the East Portico of the U.S. Capitol Building. Supreme Court justice Salmon P. Chase has just delivered the oath of office, making the former Union general the eighteenth president of the United States. Now, as he delivers his fifteen-minute oration, Grant speaks openly about an issue that seems to have no solution: what to do about the Indians.

America has three options: assimilation, isolation, or annihilation.

In the words of Kansas senator Samuel Pomeroy, the Indian warrior must now "take his place among other men and accept the march of civilization, as he must ultimately, or there is nothing except his destiny that awaits him, which is extinction."

In fiscal terms, it makes little sense for Grant to wage war against the Native American population. It costs the United States somewhere between $1 and $2 million per week to maintain a fighting force on a frontier stretching from the Apache lands along the Mexican border to the Lakota and Nez Percé tribes all the way north into Canada. Yet as the nation relies more frequently on overland transportation to reach cities and towns in the west, this fighting force is vital to protect railroads, stagecoaches, wagon trains of settlers, and even the solitary riders on horseback who carry the mail.*

As Grant speaks on this cold Thursday afternoon, the Central Pacific and Union Pacific Railroads are just two months away from driving the final spike into a single length of track linking America's east and west. Once that occurs, the transportation of passengers and freight will instantly become quicker and more affordable. This transcontinental railroad line is the most dramatic intrusion yet of white civilization into the Indian realm.†

Many in America argue that assimilation is possible, yet an equal number believe the two races will never live in harmony. Both sides, however, believe in placing Indians on separate and supervised reservations. However, this is also a financial drain on the federal government. A typical treaty consigning tribes to a reservation includes the stipulation that Indians adopt an agrarian lifestyle. But until the tribes learn to be self-sustaining through planting crops and raising livestock, the American government must feed the Indians. For example, one key provision of the Treaty of Fort Laramie Treaty is that the government promises to give each member of the Lakota nation a regular ration of a pound of meat and pound of flour for four years. That is part of the $100 million dollars a year the Indian pacification is costing.

But not all that money is being spent on Native Americans.

---

* The most famous of these was the Pony Express, which saw service between St. Joseph, Missouri, and Sacramento, California, from April 1860 to October 1861. The telegraph brought the demise of the Pony Express, but mail riders were still passing through Apache territory in New Mexico and Arizona well into the late 1860s.

† The first passengers to make the journey arrived in San Francisco on September 6, 1869.

Political appointees who care little about the tribes run the U.S. government's Indian Bureau, first founded in 1824. "No branch of the federal government is so spotted with fraud, so tainted with corruption," a congressman will state on the floor of the House. Reservation Indians often go hungry and without shelter or blankets, due to embezzlement, theft, and misappropriation of funds. Grant plans to completely overhaul this system, removing political appointees and replacing them with representatives from protestant religious groups. It is felt that their inherent honesty and determination to civilize the Indians through introducing the white religion will be transformative.

For the nomadic tribes of the plains, whose warriors believe farming is women's work and who worship their own spirit world, such an agrarian adaptation is difficult—if not impossible. Thus, even after tribes sign a treaty and begin life on the reservation, they often wander off to hunt in their traditional fashion, leading to incidents like General Custer's attack on Black Kettle's band.

An exception to this practice is the tribal lands bequeathed to the Sioux in the Dakota and Wyoming territories. This grant was ratified by the Senate in mid-February and signed by former president Andrew Johnson as one of his last acts in office.

The Sioux reservation is so vast, and the game so plentiful, that there is no need for warriors to consider a future tilling the earth. In theory, there is also no need for them to worry about conflict with whites, because the Treaty of Fort Laramie promises the Sioux "absolute and undisturbed use and occupation" of their vast new reservation, "completely off limits to whites."

President Grant campaigned on the platform of "Let us have peace" and has no intention of breaking any treaty with the Indians. Quite the contrary—his stated ambition is to offer citizenship to the tribes. That would be the most revolutionary act ever by an American president regarding Native Americans.

The new president well knows that last week, on February 26, 1869, just two days after Andrew Johnson signed the Treaty of Fort Laramie, Congress voted to approve a new amendment to the U.S. Constitution. While coincidental, the timing could not be better for Grant. The new Fifteenth Amendment promises the vote to all

American males, regardless of "race, color, or previous condition of servitude."

Ostensibly, that would include Indians. But the issue becomes complicated.

Ulysses Grant is now forty-six years old. He is an introverted man whose quiet bearing is mistaken by some as a lack of intellect. He is bad with money, making many financial mistakes, and often trusts the wrong people. The president has "a puzzled pathos, as of a man with a problem before him of which he does not understand the terms," the poet and diplomat James Russell Lowell will write of his meeting with Grant.

But that quiet façade can be misleading. The president is an idealist, willing to take a stand on those things in which he deeply believes. During the Civil War, he switched party alliances from the Democrats, whose pro–slave owner policies remained close to the beliefs of Andrew Jackson, to the new Republican Party, led by anti-slavery president Abraham Lincoln.

Ironically, Grant was once a slave owner himself, making him the last president of the United States to possess a human being as personal property. In 1859, U. S. Grant set free his lone slave, at a time when he sorely needed the money selling the man could have garnered. Grant's newfound belief in equality was reinforced during the Civil War, as he watched black troops fight and die with professionalism and courage.

The change of heart would prove vital to Grant's election as president. His Democratic opponent, Horatio Seymour, campaigned on a pro-white platform—blaming blacks for the nation's ongoing postwar division. "This is white man's country; let white men rule," read one Democratic campaign button. The Democrats further went on to claim that the Republicans fostered "military despotism and black supremacy" in the South. Indeed, the words "black supremacy" were written into the Democrats' official platform statement of 1868. Pro-Democrat newspapers predicted that a Republican victory would allow black men to openly rape white women. This absurdity actually stoked fears on the western frontier that if Republicans were elected, captured white females would be raped by Indian warriors.

Ulysses S. Grant with the U.S. Capitol in the background

Grant and the Republicans, while taking great care to not be openly solicitous of blacks for fear of losing the white electorate entirely, had been in favor of black suffrage and equality throughout the Reconstruction process. It is Grant's plan to continue this "Radical Reconstruction" during his presidency.

In the end, Ulysses S. Grant received a minority of the white votes on Election Day, 1868. Of the 5.7 million voters who went to the polls, Grant won by just 306,000 votes. The deciding factor was the 500,000 black ballots cast in his favor.

President Grant's views on race stand in marked contrast to those of his predecessor, Andrew Johnson. As governor of Tennessee, Johnson publicly stated that every American should own a slave and sided with the interests of white southerners throughout Reconstruction. Grant slowly distanced himself from the coarse Johnson after the Civil War, even while serving as General of the Army. The divide grew so deep that by 1869 the two men no longer speak. Grant would not even allow Johnson to make the traditional ride of incumbent and president-elect to the inauguration in his personal carriage this morning. Now, even as Grant speaks about not just Native American rights but also rebuilding the nation, Andrew Johnson remains at the White House he inherited upon the assassination of Abraham Lincoln.*

Grant is about to finish his address as he stares out at the crowd, which includes eight full divisions of the U.S. Army, standing in formation as they prepare to march in review past the presidential box.

"In conclusion, I ask patient forbearance one toward another throughout the land, and a determined effort on the part of every citizen to do his share toward cementing a happy union."

✳

But the "happy union" will not be easily achieved. Four years after the Civil War, Mississippi, Virginia, Georgia, and Texas still resist efforts to return to the United States and are occupied by federal troops

---

* Abraham Lincoln chose Andrew Johnson as his running mate in 1864, casting aside Hannibal Hamlin, the vice president from his first term. Johnson was a Democrat and Lincoln a Republican. The decision was made in pursuit of national unity and because Lincoln admired Johnson's effort to keep the southern state in the Union while governor of Tennessee. Lincoln even set aside his Republican affiliation for this election, preferring that the two men run on the ticket of the National Union Party. As the authors wrote in *Killing Lincoln*, the first signs of trouble between Lincoln and Johnson began when the governor showed up quite drunk at their 1865 inauguration.

and a military governor. Eventually, those states will capitulate to Washington's demands and rejoin the Union in 1870.

Other than uniting the nation, the Indian conflict is perhaps the greatest obstacle facing the presidency of Ulysses S. Grant. White farmers continue to flood onto the prairie lands of the Sioux, Cheyenne, and Crow, encouraged by the prospect of cheap acres promised by the Homestead Act of 1862. "Barbed wire" is emerging as a means of dividing western lands and keeping cattle from straying. And "cow boys," a new breed of individual whose primary role is guiding large herds of longhorn cattle from their grazing lands in Texas to railheads in Kansas, routinely travel through Comanche territory at great risk.*

But in the end, it will not be the farmers or the cow boys who will put President Grant's Indian policy to its greatest test.

No, it will be the discovery of a sparkling mineral in the land of the Sioux: gold.

---

* Congress passed the Homestead Act of 1862 in an effort to settle the plains. Citizens were given 160 acres of land if they settled on the spot for five years and improved the property. About one-third of those who filed an application to homestead failed, but more than 400,000 families were successful.

Chapter Eighteen

President Grant wants to meet the fierce Apache chief, Cochise, face-to-face.

And it may happen.

Readers of this morning's *Weekly Arizona Miner* are startled to see that the elusive Chiricahua leader has recently met with the U.S. Army to discuss a peaceful settlement of the Apache wars, now entering their eighth year. The fact that Cochise has actually been seen in person is just as shocking. His name has become synonymous with terror and stealth, for he continues to raid with impunity, seldom seen by his victims and confounding all attempts by the U.S. Army to locate him. There are now fourteen military outposts in Arizona, occupied by a collective force of more than two thousand soldiers. But none have been able to find Cochise—and none have been able to stop his aggression. It is estimated the Apaches have killed almost a thousand people since the early 1860s.

Unlike all the other Native American opponents the United States has faced, Cochise has never surrendered, preferring to withdraw from the field of battle when the tide turns against his band rather than laying down his arms. So it is that miners, stagecoach passengers, ranchers, and anyone else foolish enough to inhabit the Apache lands live in fear of a fatal attack by Cochise's warriors.

"Cacheis [Cochise] is about six feet three inches high, strongly muscled, with mild prominent features, hooked nose, and looks to be a man who means what he says," reports the *Miner*. "Age is just beginning to tell on him."

In his fashion, Cochise dictates the terms of the meeting. Ever since the 1861 "tent cutting" act of duplicity in Apache Pass, and the subsequent hanging deaths of his relatives, the chief has despised American soldiers. But the ongoing war with the United States has killed many of his warriors, leaving Cochise with a tribe consisting largely of women and children. The chief is almost sixty now, and growing weary of fighting. His face is harshly lined from years of sun and wind, and his black hair is streaked with silver. His beloved refuge at Apache Pass is now home to a large American fort, thus off-limits to Cochise and his tribe. His father-in-law and fellow chief, the towering Mangas Coloradas, was murdered by soldiers seven years ago after he entered Fort McLane in southwestern New Mexico under a flag of truce.

On February 5, a force of sixty-one American soldiers marched into Dragoon Pass, Cochise's new stronghold in southern Arizona. But as the *Miner* is reporting, instead of allowing himself to be hunted, Cochise sent a messenger stating he would meet with the Americans on the morning of February 6.

"His camp was six miles off, up in the mountains," the *Miner* reports. "He came down the next day with some of his men and met the [Captain] and escort. All hands were soon talking and smoking. The following is the conversation that ensued."*

COCHISE: What are you doing out here, Captain?

CAPTAIN FRANK W. PERRY: Come to see you and prospect the country generally.

COCHISE: You mean you came to kill me or any of my tribe; that is what

---

* It is believed that the conversation took place in Spanish, the common language between the Americans and the Apache. It is further believed that Cochise's translator was a young warrior named Geronimo, who would go on to great renown.

all your visits mean to me. I tried the Americans once and they broke the treaty first, the officers I mean, this was at the Pass. . . . I lost nearly 100 of my people in the last year, principally from sickness. The Americans killed a good many. I have not 100 Indians now. Ten years ago I had 1,000. The Americans are everywhere, and we must live in bad places to shun them. . . . My Indians will do no harm until I come in, which I may do inside two months.

PERRY: I heard you were wounded often. . . .

COCHISE: I was wounded twice. First near Santa Cruz, in the leg 12 years ago. I had a bad leg for some time afterwards. Next near Fronteras, two years ago, in the neck.

❈

The conversation continues, but in the end Cochise refuses to accompany Captain Perry the one hundred miles north to his headquarters at Fort Goodwin. However, he requests and receives gifts of blankets, bread, and tobacco from the soldiers. The chief and his followers then depart the meeting site, disappearing back into the Dragoon Mountains to their secret campsite. No attempt is made to stop them.

"Why he and the others were let off . . . beats my understanding," writes the *Miner*'s reporter, a man whose byline reads only "Occasional."

The reporter concludes: "I expect the mail to be jumped soon."

"Occasional" is correct, as Apache attacks on the U.S. mail service are stepped up.

Upset by Cochise's desire not to "come in"—vernacular for agreeing to life on a reservation—the U.S. Army begins a policy of total war on the Apache people.

Cochise will respond in kind.

❈

The date is October 5, 1869. Apache scouts have spotted a mail coach traveling through Sulphur Springs, just a dozen miles from the mountain fortress commonly referred to as Cochise's "eastern stronghold." Night is falling. Four American soldiers ride as escorts.

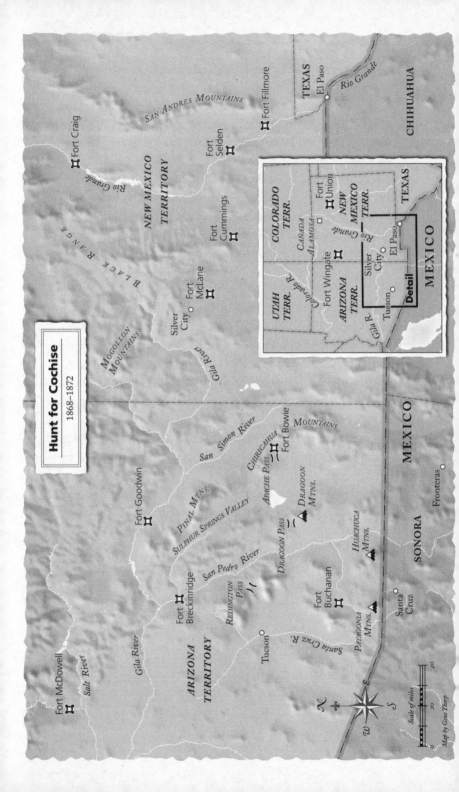

Hunt for Cochise
1868–1872

Map by Gene Thorp

ARIZONA TERRITORY

NEW MEXICO TERRITORY

SONORA

MEXICO

CHIHUAHUA

TEXAS

Fort McDowell

Salt River

Gila River

Tucson

Fort Breckinridge

Fort Goodwin

Silver City

Fort McLane

Fort Cummings

Fort Selden

Fort Fillmore

Fort Craig

Rio Grande

San Andres Mountains

Black Range

Mogollon Mountains

Gila River

San Simon River

Fort Bowie

Chiricahua Mountains

Apache Pass

Pinal Mtns.

Sulphur Springs Valley

Dragoon Mtns.

Dragoon Pass

San Pedro River

Redington Pass

Fort Buchanan

Huachuca Mtns.

Patagonia Mtns.

Santa Cruz R.

Santa Cruz

Fronteras

El Paso

Rio Grande

Scale of miles
0 20 40

N
E
S
W

Detail

UTAH TERR.

COLORADO TERR.

Colorado R.

Canada Alamosa

Fort Union

NEW MEXICO TERR.

ARIZONA TERR.

Fort Wingate

Silver City

Tucson

Gila R.

El Paso

Rio Grande

TEXAS

MEXICO

The driver and a portly, bearded man ride side by side in the buckboard's seat.

Cochise positions his warriors for an ambush, instructing them to hide in a small wash next to the road, then conceal their bodies with grass and dry brush. As the coach draws near, the Apache open fire, killing the driver and three soldiers immediately with arrows and rifle fire. The bearded man, a local named John Finkle Stone, who has desecrated Apache Pass by opening a mine within Cochise's favorite domain, grabs the reins and guides the panicked horses off the road. The nameless remaining soldier gallops after him.

Within seconds, both men come face-to-face with Cochise and other members of his band, who sit on their horses to block any chance of escape. The whites have no chance—they are executed on the spot.

In the two weeks that follow, the U.S. Army hunts Cochise, engaging him in battle on several occasions. Each time, it is the Apache who emerge victorious, leading American commander Captain Reuben F. Bernard to marvel that Cochise was "one of the most intelligent hostile Indians on the continent."

However, the reality is that more than two dozen Apache warriors are killed in these skirmishes. The loss of even a single warrior impacts the tribe. Such brave men cannot be replaced. But the Americans will always have fresh blood arriving to reinforce army units.

It may take another decade, but it is only a matter of time and bullets before Cochise and the Chiricahua Apache are completely exterminated.

❄

Three bloody years later, Cochise once again seeks peace.

The date is March 19, 1872. Mexican soldiers now routinely raid north into Arizona, crossing the American border with the sole intent of killing Cochise and other Apache. At the same time, five companies of U.S. Army cavalry under the command of General George Crook, whom the Apache have named Gray Wolf, relentlessly scour the same region, determined to take Cochise, dead or alive. So the Apache are caught in a classic pincer movement.

The chief is weary of fighting. The decade of war has slowly whittled away at his band, killing many and making it difficult to remain in one place for any length of time.

He has now led his followers to a remote corner of New Mexico Territory known as Canada Alamosa to meet with U.S. officials. Colonel Gordon Granger has ridden for six hours from his post at Fort Craig in a carriage drawn by six mules. He brings with him several other officials, two medical professionals, and an armed cavalry escort. Among the whites is the director of Indian Affairs for the region, Nathaniel Pope, to whom President Grant has personally given the task of conducting Cochise to Washington so the two leaders might meet in person.

To a man, the American group is eager to get a glimpse of Cochise. And yet, "when we reached the place of the conference, there were no Indians to be seen, so we dismounted and seated ourselves under the shade of a cottonwood tree to await developments," assistant surgeon Henry Stuart Turrill will recall. "Soon from over the hill . . . Cochise approached. We all looked with much curiosity, as we believed ourselves the first white men that had seen him face-to-face and lived to tell of it. . . . He was rather tall, over six feet, with broad shoulders, and impressed me as a wonderfully strong man, of much endurance, accustomed to command and to expect instant and implicit obedience. . . . He seemed to me in this first meeting the greatest Indian I had ever seen."

Cochise wears a buckskin hunting shirt, belt, leggings, moccasins, and Mexican poncho, "draped about him with a careless grace," in the words of Dr. Turrill.

Colonel Granger begins the negotiations in a straightforward manner. The terms are simple: "The Great Father in Washington wants to live at peace with his red children. He is anxious to do what is right in the matter, but peace he must have. If he does not get it one way, he will have it in another."

The fifty-year-old Granger, a balding and bearded veteran of the Mexican and Civil Wars, goes on to state that the U.S. gov-

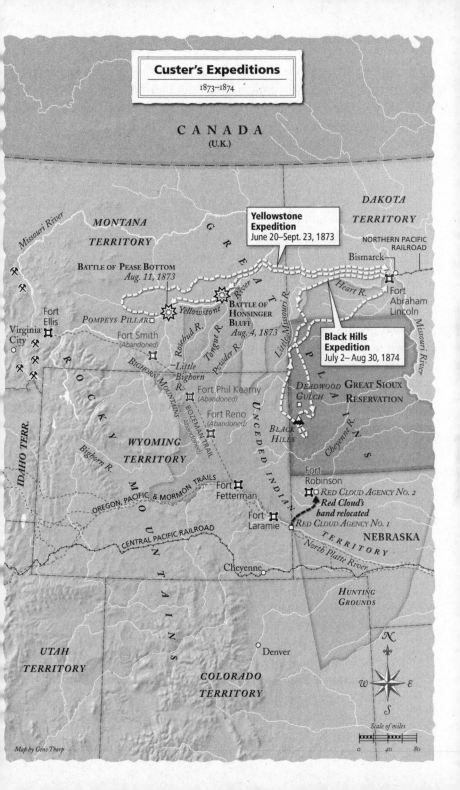

Custer's Expeditions
1873–1874

CANADA
(U.K.)

DAKOTA
TERRITORY

MONTANA
TERRITORY

NORTHERN PACIFIC
RAILROAD

Bismarck

**Yellowstone
Expedition**
June 20–Sept. 23, 1873

Missouri River

BATTLE OF PEASE BOTTOM
Aug. 11, 1873

Fort
Abraham
Lincoln

Heart R.

Fort
Ellis

POMPEYS PILLAR

Yellowstone

BATTLE OF
HONSINGER
BLUFF
Aug. 4, 1873

Virginia
City

Rosebud R.

Tongue R.

Powder R.

Little Missouri R.

Fort Smith
(Abandoned)

**Black Hills
Expedition**
July 2– Aug 30, 1874

*Little
Bighorn
R.*

BIGHORN MOUNTAINS

Fort Phil Kearny
(Abandoned)

BOZEMAN TRAIL

Fort Reno
(Abandoned)

DEADWOOD
GULCH

GREAT SIOUX
RESERVATION

Cheyenne R.

Bighorn R.

WYOMING
TERRITORY

UNCEDED INDIAN

BLACK
HILLS

IDAHO TERR.

ROCKY

OREGON, PACIFIC, & MORMON TRAILS

Fort
Fetterman

Fort
Robinson

RED CLOUD AGENCY NO. 2

*Red Cloud's
band relocated*

RED CLOUD AGENCY NO. 1

Fort
Laramie

TERRITORY

NEBRASKA

CENTRAL PACIFIC RAILROAD

North Platte River

MOUNTAINS

Cheyenne

HUNTING
GROUNDS

UTAH
TERRITORY

Denver

COLORADO
TERRITORY

N

W   E

S

Scale of miles

0   40   80

Map by Gene Thorp

ernment will give the valleys and mountains to Cochise as a reservation, "a home for him and his children for all time," where "they should be fed for several years until they learned to work for themselves."

The conditions are stark: if Cochise accepts these terms and makes peace, he can no longer raid away from the reservation or permit his warriors to leave its borders.

When Colonel Granger finishes speaking, the Apache contingent leaves for an hour to discuss the American offer. When they return, Cochise remains standing as the Indians take their place sitting in the circle on the ground with the whites.

The chief is urged by the Americans to go to Washington to meet with President Grant. He demurs. Cochise still feels the betrayal of the Bascom incident, and the hanging of his relatives that began this war. He tells the soldiers that he does not like the white men's ways. In a passing reference to the food the army promises to provide for his tribe should they settle on the reservation, Cochise tells the soldiers that he does not care to "eat little fishes out of metal boxes."

It is obvious to the Americans that Cochise is a man of great physical strength, and his tactical genius on the battlefield is beyond dispute. Less known is the chief's ability to inspire his band through the use of the spoken word. Now, addressing the assembled circle of whites and Apache, he delivers an astounding summation of current relations between his people and the Americans.

"The sun has been very hot on my head and made me as in a fire," Cochise begins, speaking the Apache language. "My blood was on fire but now I have come into this valley and drunk of these waters and they have cooled me. Now that I am cool I have come with my hands open to you to live in peace with you. I speak straight and do not wish to deceive or be deceived."

In his long military career, from which he will one day emerge a general, Dr. Turrill will spend years among the Indians. He will encounter not just the Apache, but also the great tribes of the plains, such the Cheyenne and Sioux. He will take part in many a council between whites and Indians and listen to speeches from both sides.

But he will describe today's impassioned speech by Cochise as "the finest bit of Indian oratory that I ever listened to."

Cochise continues speaking: "I want a good, strong, and lasting peace. When God made the world he gave one part to the white man and another to the Apache. Why was it? Why did they come together?"

Cochise lapses from Apache into Spanish, simultaneously using his hands to add sign language. "Now that I am to speak, the sun, the moon, the earth, the air, the waters, the birds and beasts shall, even the children unborn shall rejoice at my words. The white people have looked for me long. I am here! What do they want? They have looked for me long—why am I worth so much? If I am worth so much why not mark where I set my foot and look when I spit? The coyotes go about at night to rob and kill. I cannot see them. I am not God. I am no longer chief of all Apaches. I am no longer rich. I am but a poor man. The world was not always this way. God made us not as you. We were born like the animals, in the dry grass, not on beds like you.

"This is why we do as the animals, go about at night to rob and steal. If I had things such as you have, I would not do as I do, for then I would not need to do so. There are Indians who go about killing and robbing. I do not command them. If I did, they would not do so. My warriors have been killed in Sonora. I came in here because God told me to do so. He said it was good to be at peace—so I came. I was going around the world with my clouds, and the air, when God spoke to my thoughts and told me to come in here and be at peace with all. He said the world was for us all. How was it . . . ?

"I have no father or mother. I am alone in the world. No one cares for Cochise. That is why I do not care to live, and wish the rocks to fall on me and cover me up. If I had a father and mother like you, I would be with them and they with me. When I was going around the world, all were asking for Cochise. Now he is here. You see him and hear him. Are you glad? If so, say so. Speak, Americans and Mexicans. I do not wish to hide anything from you nor have you hide anything from me. I will not lie to you. Do not lie to me."

❋

Cochise agrees to peace but balks when the Americans attempt to dictate the location of the Chiricahua Reservation. Colonel Granger wishes the tribe to relocate to the Mogollon Mountains, here in New Mexico. Cochise insists that his people be allowed to return to his homeland at Apache Pass, there to be left alone by the whites.

Granger reluctantly agrees.

Eight months later, the Great Father in Washington makes it official. Despite having signed into law the Indian Appropriations Act of 1871, which ceased the practice of recognizing tribes as sovereign nations and brokering treaties with Native Americans to settle disputes, the president acknowledges the new treaty between the Chiricahua and the United States.

President Grant orders that a tract of land approximately one hundred miles square be granted to the Apache as a sanctuary.

Cochise, it seems, has won the negotiation.

❋

The Apache, however, are still at war with Mexico. Thus, raids south of the border continue with unabated ferocity. "About the 15th of January," the *New York Times* reports in its March 8 edition, "Apaches killed Don Leopoldo Valencia, a member of the Supreme Court of Sonora ... about the same time a train was attacked near there, two men killed, and the mules all taken. About the same time, they stole a lot of fine horses from the Pozos ranch. A few men followed the Apaches two days and nights, but being poorly armed compared with their foes, and so many less in number, they gave up the chase while the trail was leading directly into the Huachuca Mountains not far from the Cochise reserve."

Cochise himself does not take part in these raids. He now prefers a quiet life on his reservation, spending his days relaxing and drinking tiswin, a mild alcohol made by fermenting corn provided to the Indians by the United States. Cochise refuses to eat food rations provided by the Americans, believing they may be poisoned. Instead, he prefers the taste of fresh deer and antelope young warriors hunt in the wild. But his distaste for tinned American beef and his growing dependence upon tiswin belie a darker truth about Cochise: the great chief is dying. Those close to him know that stomach cancer now makes it hard for him to digest meat.

But while he does not accompany his young warriors on their raids into Mexico, Cochise sanctions the incursions. Though in his early sixties and dying, Cochise can never forget that it was the Mexicans who killed his father. Also, his warriors are restless, unwilling to adopt the sedentary lifestyle of reservation living. The raids keep these young men fit and prosperous because of the many horses they steal. Cochise revels in the full knowledge that the terms of his peace treaty mean there is nothing the U.S. Army can do to halt the aggression.

"The Mexican troops do not feel at liberty to direct troops to operate in the United States, and according to the terms of the peace with Cochise, his tribes are not to be interfered with by United States troops," the *Times* article explains. "The 'peace' made with Cochise bids fair to be the most costly yet indulged in on the part of the government . . . Mexico cannot endure it and General Crook has no authority to stop it on behalf of the United States."

But Crook is not as passive as the *Times* suggests. The veteran Indian fighter is determined to confine the Chiricahua to their reservation and put an end to their murderous raids south. Throughout his career, General Crook has displayed a flair for ingenuity—defeating Indian opponents in the Pacific Northwest and now Arizona. Crook prefers to attack during winter, when least expected, and pays Native Americans from other tribes to serve as scouts to track and find his enemies. In the case of Cochise and the raids into Mexico, Crook does not put pressure on Cochise, over whom he has little authority. Instead, the general makes life very difficult for Tom Jeffords, the white man handpicked by Cochise to serve as the liaison between the Apache and the Americans. The red-haired, bearded Jeffords is widely considered to be the only white man Cochise has ever trusted. Five years ago, when Jeffords managed a mail concession through Cochise's lands, the Chiricahua would routinely attack his carriers. Fed up with the loss of the mail and his men, Jeffords boldly risked his life by marching into Cochise's camp to demand that the Apache leave his riders alone. A stunned Cochise was so impressed by Jeffords's brazen courage that he agreed. In time, Jeffords becomes Cochise's most trusted adviser.

Now, in his role as "reservation agent," Tom Jeffords is pressured into counseling Cochise to end the Mexican raids. General Crook is prepared to violate the treaty with Cochise by putting his soldiers directly on the Apache reservation. Each warrior will be expected to report each morning for a daily roll call to ensure they have not gone off the reservation. Furthermore, Jeffords is warned that the Chiricahua may also be removed entirely from Apache Pass and relocated to New Mexico, far from the temptation of raiding into Sonora.

Upon the advice of Tom Jeffords, Cochise agrees to end the raids. Shortly afterward, Cochise anoints his son Taza as his successor.

With the death of Cochise imminent, the Chiricahua Apache have a new leader.

※

The date is June 7, 1874. Cochise has been in and out of consciousness for the last six weeks. Apache Pass resounds with singing and drumming as the Apache medicine men try to drive out the demons bewitching their leader. The noise continues day and night as the Apache war chiefs drum on beef hides stretched over sticks. Cochise believes that a fellow Apache with whom he has had a disagreement has cast a spell on him.

It is Sunday evening when Tom Jeffords comes to pay his final respects. Cochise rests facing east, atop a high bluff, "and commanded a view of the surrounding mountain valley as far as the Chiricahua Mountains to the east and as far as the eye could reach to the north and south," writes an American who accompanies Jeffords.

"The old chief was suffering greatly."

Cochise asks Jeffords to take care of the remaining 375 members of the Chiricahua band and continue providing advice to Taza, the new chief. When Jeffords expresses doubt that the new leadership will listen to him, Cochise responds: "We will fix that."

Immediately, Taza and the other tribal leaders are summoned and instructed to heed Jeffords's opinions.

"Do you think you will ever see me alive again?" Cochise asks Jeffords after the group is dismissed.

"I do not know," Jeffords responds. "I think by tomorrow night you will be dead."

Cochise nods. "Do you think we will ever meet again?"

"I don't know," replies Jeffords. "What do you think of it?"

"I have been giving it a good deal of thought since I have been sick here," says Cochise. He points to the sky. "I think we will . . . somewhere up yonder. Good friends will meet again."

❊

As Tom Jeffords predicts, Cochise dies the next morning, June 8, 1874. His wife, Dos-teh-seh, begins the burial preparation by bathing his body. Cochise's illness has robbed him of his athletic appearance, so his corpse is skeletal as she carefully washes the dirt from his skin. She combs and braids the hair that Cochise always kept meticulously groomed. His face is painted, as if he is off to war. His body is wrapped in new deerskin, then placed in a thick red wool blanket into which his name has been woven.

Finally, in a manner eerily reminiscent of burial rituals of the Ancient Egyptian pharaohs and Norse Vikings, Cochise is equipped for his journey to the afterlife. The chief is armed with a gun belt containing a hunting knife and revolver. A loaded Springfield rifle is slipped under his left arm. Cochise is then placed in a litter, to be dragged to the grave site by his favorite horse.

Two riderless horses also make the journey. One is shot two miles from the grave site, the other just one mile distant. In this way, Cochise will always have a horse when he needs one in the afterlife.

In the words of Tom Jeffords, the horse pulling Cochise "was guided to a rough and lonely place among the rocks and chasms in the stronghold, where there was a deep fissure in the cliff. The horse was killed and dropped into the depths. Also [killed], Cochise's favorite dog. His gun and other arms were thrown in [to the crevice].

And last, Cochise was lowered with lariats into the rocky sepulcher, deep in the gorge."

Mesquite branches are laid upon the body, then the grave filled in. Horses are ridden over the site to tamp down the earth, then cactus planted to disguise the spot.

So it is that the location of Cochise's burial site becomes a secret known only to the handful of Chiricahua present for the ceremony, and to Tom Jeffords, who was not present but told of the funeral afterward.

That secret has never been told. To this day, the burial site of the great Chiricahua Apache chief Cochise remains a mystery.

Chapter Nineteen

The ferocious Comanche tribe is in trouble. Tribal leader Quanah, the son of the white kidnapping victim Cynthia Parker and Comanche chief Peta Nocona, is now himself the supreme Comanche warlord. The passionate and focused twenty-six-year-old sits astride his pony on a bluff just south of the Canadian River. The first morning light illuminates the darkened prairie, and the air smells of dew and sweet green grass. Quanah is tall and muscular, like his father, but has his mother's straight nose, rounded chin, and high cheekbones. His hair is dark black, his eyes gray. Though a time will come when Quanah will adopt Cynthia Parker's last name, the war chief currently has no interest in flaunting his white blood.

The sun rises behind the Comanche, illuminating a sod-roofed saloon, corral, blacksmith shop, and two general stores on the grassy plain below. The buildings' walls are made of adobe, giving the settlement its name. This small trading post exists solely to shelter the hated buffalo hunters now destroying the Comanche way of life. Utilizing their new Sharps "Big Fifty" long-range rifles, these aggressive men kill hundreds of animals a day. Whites have long been shooting buffalo for sport and to feed the laborers building the transcontinental railroad, but the decimation of the buffalo has now become a lucrative business.

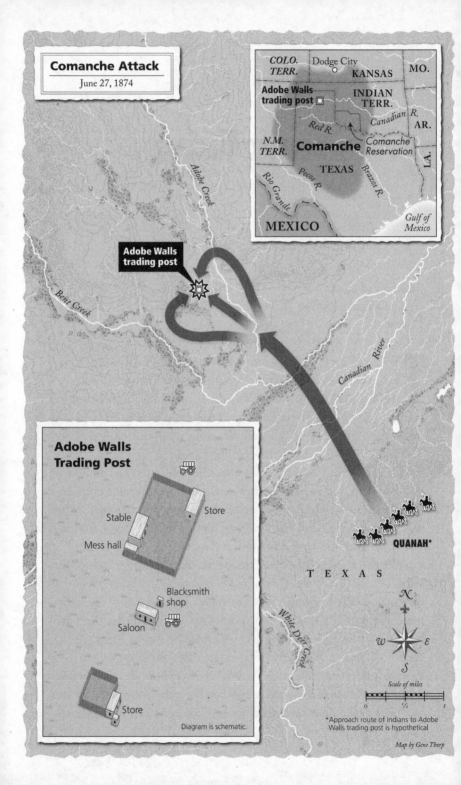

Comanche Attack
June 27, 1874

COLO. TERR. | Dodge City | KANSAS | MO.
Adobe Walls trading post | INDIAN TERR. | Canadian R. | AR.
N.M. TERR. | Red R. | Comanche Reservation | LA.
Comanche
Pecos R. | **TEXAS** | Brazos R.
Rio Grande
MEXICO | Gulf of Mexico

Adobe Creek

Adobe Walls trading post

Bent Creek

Canadian River

QUANAH*

T E X A S

Adobe Walls Trading Post

Stable | Store
Mess hall
Blacksmith shop
Saloon
Store

Diagram is schematic.

White Deer Creek

N
W — *E*
S

Scale of miles
0 | 1/2 | 1

*Approach route of Indians to Adobe Walls trading post is hypothetical

Map by Gene Thorp

New technology developed in 1870 allows hides to be processed into fine leather, feeding a growing European demand for buffalo robes. Additionally, the buffalo tongue has become a delicacy, served in America's finest restaurants—seven million pounds of this coarse meat was shipped east from Dodge City, Kansas, in 1872 alone.

A single buffalo hide fetches $3.75. Multiply this by dozens of hides per day, and the only limits on a hunter's ability to make money are locating a herd, skinning the animals, and transporting hides safely to market. The buffalo is an unusual beast, unwilling to run or stampede so long as there is no visual threat. Even if the animal next to it in the herd topples over dead, a buffalo will simply remain in the same place, as if nothing has happened. For this reason, the killers conceal themselves in blinds or under buffalo robes, taking steady aim and shooting from hundreds of yards away with the Sharps's 600-grain bullet. The grisly task of slicing hides off the carcass is a small price the hunters pay for growing extremely wealthy.*

This slaughter outrages Quanah. The Medicine Lodge Treaty of 1867 specifically forbids whites from hunting on lands between the Arkansas and Canadian Rivers. This is Comanche territory. Yet these hunters break the treaty every day, and the U.S. Army willfully allows the violations, knowing that killing buffalo destroys the Indians' traditional way of life. Thus, the Comanche people, whose primary dietary staple is buffalo meat, go hungry.

Which is why Quanah plans to drive these hunters from Comanche land, now and forever—shooting a few of these barbarians himself, should he be so lucky.

The warlord commands seven hundred Comanche, Cheyenne, and Kiowa warriors who now spread out atop the bluff on both sides of him, their bodies and horses painted red, yellow, and blue. Human scalps dangle from their bridle reins. Many wear bonnets festooned

---

* The 1872 price of $3.75 per hide is slightly more than $82 in 2019 money. The legendary hunter Brick Bond shot more than six thousand buffalo over a sixty-day span in 1874, utilizing a team of five wagons and fifteen skinners to bring back hides from Comanche lands in the Texas Panhandle. Unfortunately for the twenty-five-year-old Bond, the repetitive firing of his .50-caliber Sharps took his hearing. He lived to be eighty-eight. In a turn of heart, he devoted the final years of his life to advocating for strict laws against the killing of wild game.

with the feathers of a golden eagle, signifying previous courage in battle. Falcon and hawk plumes are tied into the tails of their horses. Four days ago, these warriors gathered north of here to prepare for battle by dancing and singing. The medicine man who led this "Sun Dance" is the renowned Comanche spiritual leader Eeshatai. He adapted the ceremony to inspire the tribe on the eve of battle.

But the time for dancing is done. Quanah raises his lance toward the sky, the signal to attack. All seven hundred warriors prod their ponies forward, descending carefully from the mesa before quirting the animals to prod them into a full gallop.

The warriors are armed with rifles, bows and arrows, tomahawks, and knives. There are just twenty-nine occupants of Adobe Walls. Among them is a twenty-year-old hunter named Bat Masterson, destined to go on to fame as a Dodge City lawman, and a twenty-three-year-old sharpshooter named Billy Dixon, well renowned for his ability to down buffalo from amazing distances. As is the custom on warm summer nights, these two men and the lone female resident of Adobe Walls had planned to sleep outside in the fresh air. But at 2:00 a.m. the sound of a breaking roof beam in the saloon roused almost everyone, forcing the men to rise and work all night repairing the problem. For this reason, the residents of Adobe Walls are awake as hundreds of Indians now ride hard to kill them.

"Twenty-eight men and one woman would have been slaughtered if the ridge pole in Hanrahan's saloon had not cracked like a rifle shot," Dixon will later write in his memoirs.

"There was never a more splendidly barbaric sight. In after years I was glad that I had seen it. Hundreds of warriors, the flower of the fighting men of the southwestern Plains tribes, mounted upon their finest horses, armed with guns and lances, and carrying heavy shields of thick buffalo hide, were coming like the wind."

Dixon will continue: "The bronzed, half-naked bodies of the riders glittered with ornaments of silver and brass. Behind this headlong charging host stretched the Plains, on whose horizon the rising sun was lifting its morning fires. The warriors seemed to emerge from this glowing background."

Quanah Parker, a Comanche chief, 1900

The Indians fan out, letting loose enormous war whoops as they bear down on the town. "War-whooping had a very appreciable effect on the roots of a man's hair," Billy Dixon will long remember.

At first, it seems the battle will become yet another bloody plains massacre. Quanah's strategy of traditional Comanche terror is succeeding. The Indians swarm the small town, shooting out windows as the beleaguered residents hunker down inside. The doors have no locks, so hasty barricades of flour and grain sacks are constructed to keep the attackers at bay. Some of the defenders had gone back to bed after working through the night and now fight barefoot in their underwear. Two buffalo hunters asleep in their wagon are shot and scalped. A Newfoundland dog is also shot and scalped. Strangely, the sound of a stolen bugle wafts across the prairie, blown by an Indian mimicking the battle calls of the U.S. Cavalry.

But even as the warriors ride close enough to hammer on the wooden doors, the buffalo hunters let loose a fusillade of bullets: the Sharps .50-caliber can do much more than hunt buffalo. Taking careful aim, they begin firing out the windows, picking off the attackers. At first, the shots are focused on the warriors who have dismounted and surrounded the buildings on foot. When these warriors are dead, the hunters start killing from long range.

"The bugler was killed late in the afternoon of the first day's fighting," Bat Masterson will remember. "[Harry] Armitage shot him through the back with a .50-caliber Sharp's rifle."

The battle soon becomes a siege. The hunters have plenty of ammunition and kill Indians and their horses with precision. Quanah himself is wounded and carried from the battlefield, where he directs the action from afar.

Eventually, the shooting stops. But the Comanche and their allies remain, unwilling to retreat. The stalemate lasts into the night and through the next two days. Fearing the accuracy and range of the Sharps rifle, the Indians are reluctant to attack again at close range. Already, dozens of warriors have been killed. The medicine man Eeshatai, who encouraged the battle and predicted victory, is disgraced. His authority gone, several warriors take turns beating him.

On the third day, with the Indians so far out of range that killing them seems impossible, Billy Dixon casually takes aim at a warrior one mile away. He fires. The Indian topples from his horse, never having heard the crack of rifle fire that killed him.

Most of the buffalo hunters survive. In time, they and others will kill millions of buffalo, so many that there will no longer be any to shoot. When that day comes, the hunters will make their living collecting the sun-bleached buffalo skulls that litter the prairie, to be sold as fertilizer.

The Comanche will disappear along with the buffalo. As Quanah oversees the battle, he does not yet realize that the attack at Adobe Walls will so infuriate the Great Father in Washington that Ulysses S. Grant will change the rules of engagement. From this day forward, the president will no longer pursue the "peace policy" he espoused in his inaugural address. President Grant orders that all Indians not on their reservations are to be considered an enemy of the United States of America and treated as such.

Within a year, the U.S. Army will track down Quanah and his band, shoot more than one thousand of their ponies, and finally rid the plains of the dreaded Comanche after their undisputed three-hundred-year reign.

※

So it is that the last Comanche war leader, Quanah, leads his people onto a reservation, ironically located just a few miles from Adobe Walls. There the Comanche will learn white ways and live a white lifestyle. Quanah will never again paint his body for battle or place another golden-eagle feather in his war bonnet. The whites will even anoint him as "chief" of the Comanche, a title not previously used by the tribe.

Eventually, the new chief will live inside a proper white home, dressed in a suit, tie, and bowler hat.*

This is by far the greatest victory the whites have ever known against the Native American tribes who once dominated the North American continent.

Yet the Great Father in Washington is not content.†

---

* In fact, President Theodore Roosevelt became good friends with Quanah Parker. The Comanche leader marched in Roosevelt's 1905 inauguration parade and the two men went wolf hunting later that same year. During their conversations, Parker successfully lobbied the president to reintroduce buffalo to the Southern Plains.

† As far as the authors can find, the president never showed any remorse for reversing his Indian policy.

Chapter Twenty

G eneral George Armstrong Custer is ready to ride.

The Sioux nation calls this time of summer "the moon when the chokeberries are ripe." To Americans, the first week of July is synonymous with their nation's birth. In fact, in just two years the United States will celebrate one hundred years since the Declaration of Independence.

Custer embarks this morning on a two-month trip designed to neutralize the Northern Plains Indians. He will do so by illegally traveling into the Black Hills, a journey specifically denied to whites by the Fort Laramie treaty of 1868, which granted those lands to the Sioux. Publicly, Custer's stated goal is to find a suitable location for a new U.S. Army fort to supervise the Indians. Secretly, the general is doing something much more devious.

Known to the Plains Indians as Paha Sapa, the Black Hills is a mountainous oasis rising from the flat and treeless plains. This idyllic land of meadows, forests, and streams is sacred to the Sioux, Cheyenne, and Arapaho. Deer, elk, and antelope are so abundant that the Indians call this land their "meat locker." The tribes are extremely protective of the Black Hills—few white men venturing into this verdant landscape make it out alive.

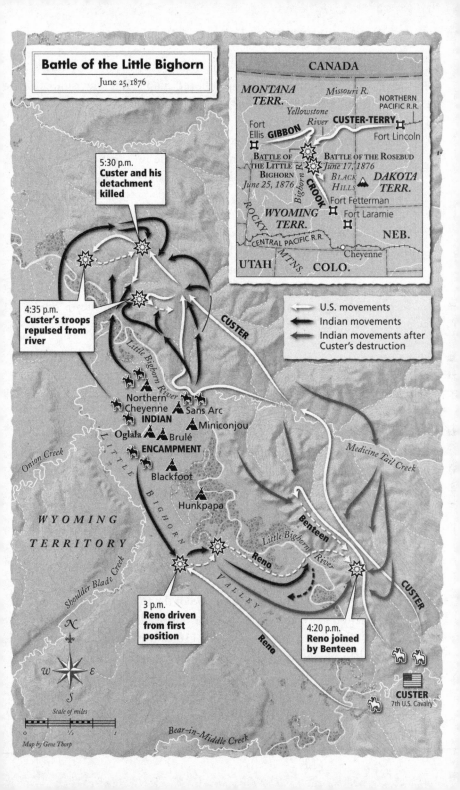

Battle of the Little Bighorn
June 25, 1876

5:30 p.m.
Custer and his detachment killed

4:35 p.m.
Custer's troops repulsed from river

3 p.m.
Reno driven from first position

4:20 p.m.
Reno joined by Benteen

CUSTER

CUSTER

Benteen

Reno

Reno

U.S. movements
Indian movements
Indian movements after Custer's destruction

Little Bighorn River

Northern Cheyenne
Sans Arc
INDIAN
Oglala
Miniconjou
Brulé
ENCAMPMENT
Blackfoot
Hunkpapa

Little Bighorn River

LITTLE BIGHORN VALLEY

Onion Creek

WYOMING TERRITORY

Shoulder Blade Creek

Medicine Tail Creek

CUSTER
7th U.S. Cavalry

Bear-in-Middle Creek

N
W E
S

Scale of miles
0   ½   1

Map by Gene Thorp

Inset map

CANADA

MONTANA TERR.
Missouri R.
NORTHERN PACIFIC R.R.
Yellowstone River
Fort Ellis
GIBBON
CUSTER-TERRY
Fort Lincoln
BATTLE OF THE LITTLE BIGHORN
June 25, 1876
BATTLE OF THE ROSEBUD
June 17, 1876
BLACK HILLS
DAKOTA TERR.
CROCK
Fort Fetterman
WYOMING TERR.
Fort Laramie
NEB.
ROCKY
CENTRAL PACIFIC R.R.
UTAH
MTNS.
COLO.
Cheyenne

Americans once considered Paha Sapa worthless, which is why they had no problem offering it up at Fort Laramie. But now, rumors of gold in these hills have made their way back to Washington. And just as similar discoveries in California, Colorado, Arizona, and Montana dramatically worsened relations between the U.S. government and Indians in those regions, so the prospect of gold in the Black Hills could very well do a similar thing on the Northern Plains.

The Seventh Cavalry's sixteen-piece brass band strikes up "The Girl I Left Behind" as Custer kisses his wife, Libbie, goodbye on the steps of their white frame home. Throughout the fort, officers and their wives do the same. The general had hoped to bring Libbie along, even going to the extreme of preparing a special wagon for her personal travel, but the danger of this journey is too great. That notion has been set aside, sending Libbie into a deep depression.

As Custer mounts his horse, Dandy, the general is clad in buckskin, a suede garment made of deer hide, which will keep away the dense clouds of mosquitoes but is sure to make him sweat throughout the long summer days. Custer doffs his hat one last time before galloping to the front of the waiting cavalry column, showing off the shoulder-length blond mane that has led the Sioux to give him the nickname Pahuska—"Long Hair."

"I expect to visit a region of the country as yet unseen by human eyes, except those of the Indians," he bragged just days ago, penning the final paragraph of what will soon become his bestselling book, *My Life on the Plains*. "Abounding in game of all varieties, rich in scientific interest, and of surpassing beauty in natural scenery."

But there is much more on the mind of the thirty-four-year-old general than science and nature. Custer now leads 995 soldiers and civilians, 60 Native American scouts, 110 canvas-covered wagons being pulled by 660 mules, 700 horses, and a small herd of cattle soon to serve as the nightly meal. Each step of their path will be charted by sextant-toting engineers, the soils tested by a group of scientists, and their exploits written about in great detail by reporters from New York, Chicago, and the local *Bismarck Tribune*. Among Custer's fellow officers are his twenty-seven-year-old brother Tom, who was awarded the Congressional Medal of Honor twice during the Civil War, and Lieutenant Colonel Frederick Grant, the racist son of the president.* Custer's youngest brother, twenty-five years old, has been declared medically unfit for military life due to tuberculosis, but the general has arranged for him to join the expedition as a civilian contractor in charge of foraging. Two individuals whose specialty is finding gold round out the party. All these travelers are men, save a black woman named Sarah Campbell, who serves as Custer's personal cook, and a hard-drinking, lice-ridden twenty-two-year-old woman nicknamed Calamity Jane, who will do the soldiers' laundry and provide sexual services in exchange for whiskey and food.

The general's hope about what lies ahead is not bluster, for he is genuinely curious. At a time in history when headlines are rife with tales of Victorian explorers charting the unknowns of Africa and the Far East, Custer has chosen to name this armed treaty violation an "expedition," expecting to soak up similar glory. Like the most remote corners of Africa, the Black Hills are mythic to settlers of the frontier, the subject of legends and tall tales. It is Custer's mission to see whether or not these stories are true.

The Seventh Cavalry's first day on the trail is short, just fifteen miles. Wagons get stuck in the Little Heart River two hours into the journey. The day ends with Custer riding ahead to scout the next morning's route. The men call him "hard ass" for his ability to ride hour after hour in the saddle. Dinner is served at 10:00 p.m., with reveille scheduled for 2:45 a.m. Custer will sleep those few hours on a buffalo-skin robe. The caravan will feed the horses, strike their tents, and breakfast promptly at 4:00 a.m. "Boots and Saddles,"

---

* While a cadet at West Point, Frederick Grant was responsible for the brutal hazing of James Webster Smith, the academy's first black student. During a meeting with his father at the White House, in which President Grant requested that his son tone down the abuse, Frederick Grant's reply was, "No damned nigger will ever graduate from West Point." Smith, who was born a slave, was termed "deficient" in his studies at the end of his junior year and expelled. Smith was posthumously awarded a commission in the U.S. Army in 1997.

the bugle call signaling that all troops mount their horses and take their place in line, sounds at 5:00 a.m. The soldiers under Custer's command chafe at the early start but know better than to complain aloud. Not so the civilians. Very often the grumbling happens as Custer stands incognito within earshot. "His campaigning dress was so like that of an enlisted man, and his insignia of rank so unnoticeable, that the tongues ran on, indifferent to his presence," Libbie Custer will write, basing her words on her husband's lengthy letters. "The civilians accused him of having something on his conscience, and declared that, not being able to sleep himself, he woke everyone else to an unearthly reveille. At this he choked with laughter, and to his dismay they discovered who he was."

The distance from Fort Abraham Lincoln to the Black Hills is a little more than three hundred miles. Ideally, Custer will be able to prove that area's great forests are large enough to provide lumber for plains families seeking to build their new homes from wood instead of sod. The general would also like to report back that the rumored vast meadows are perfect forage to graze cattle and are full of game.

However, none of that will matter if Custer can't find gold. Rumors about enormous wealth hidden in these secret lands have inflamed frontier settlers. America has been rocked by a massive economic downturn. Hard times and a growing number of white people populating the plains means that anger toward the Treaty of Fort Laramie is reaching a crescendo, as settlers seek Indian land in order to prosper.

"What shall be done with these Indian dogs in our manger?" writes the Yankton *Press and Dakotan*. "They will not dig the gold, or let others do it. . . . They are too lazy and too much like mere animals to cultivate the fertile soil, mine the coal, develop the salt mines, bore the petroleum wells, or wash the gold. Having all these things in their hands, they prefer to live as paupers, thieves, and beggars; fighting, torturing, hunting, gorging, yelling, and dancing all night to the beating of old tin kettles.

"Anyone who knows how utterly they depend on the government for subsistence will see that if they have to be supported at all, they might far better occupy small reservations and be within military reach, than to have the exclusive control of a tract of country as large as the whole State of Pennsylvania or New York, which they can neither improve or utilize," the brutal editorial concludes.

Despite opposition to the Fort Laramie treaty, the U.S. Army has been steadfast in upholding it. Miners attempting to travel into the Black Hills are stopped and threatened with arrest. However, a new railway line known as the Northern Pacific may change that circumstance. It begins at Lake Superior and is supposed to extend all the way to the Puget Sound on the Pacific Coast. Track has been laid westward from the Missouri River to Bismarck in the Dakota Territory, and also a short distance eastward from Tacoma, Washington. But the vast land in between—a distance of almost one thousand miles—is Indian Territory. The new railway is considered so vital to America's growth that Custer and the Seventh Cavalry were relocated to the Dakota Territory one year ago to provide a military escort for railway surveyors searching for the best route to lay track. But there can be no railroad unless there is peace with the tribes who hold the land.

Adding to the confusion, the Northern Pacific went bust ten months ago, its financiers overextended and out of money. President Grant publicly backs the sanctity of the Fort Laramie treaty but also needs that railroad to succeed. Thus, he authorized Custer's expedition into the Black Hills at a White House meeting not long after the bankruptcy.

Grant orders General Philip Sheridan to move Custer quickly into Indian Territory in search of gold. But Custer is not to make that public.

President Grant has many problems, among them a staggering economic crisis known as the Panic of 1873. As Americans rich and poor struggle to stay financially solvent, the onus falls upon Grant to find a solution—and quickly. And though the president has had more than his share of personal financial emergencies and hardly qualifies as a monetary genius, he believes the answer to the panic and the moribund Northern Pacific can be found in the Black Hills—that is, if Custer can find vast amounts of gold.

So it is that President Ulysses S. Grant, the great Sioux leaders Sitting Bull and Crazy Horse, and General George Armstrong Custer are now on a collision course for total war.

❉

The roots of the upcoming conflict really begin on July 26, 1861, after the Civil War's Battle of Bull Run—coincidentally, the first military engagement of young George Custer's career. The Union loses the battle, seen by hundreds of spectators who drove their horses and buggies twenty-five miles south of Washington to witness the fighting as popular entertainment—only to find themselves stunned and horrified as men on both sides actually fall dead and dismembered.

The U.S. Treasury has slightly less than $2 million in monetary reserves as Bull Run ignites the Civil War. No one believes the conflict will continue for more than three months, but as the fighting soon consumes more than $1 million per day in spending, the federal government in Washington must either find a new source of money or concede defeat to the Confederates.

For the first time in its brief history, the United States is forced to admit the failure of its monetary policy. The nation does not have any debt but issues only coins as legal currency. Individual states print paper money, but the paper is not accepted in other states. This changes when Abraham Lincoln signs the Legal Tender Act of 1862, which introduces a national paper currency that quickly earns the nickname "greenbacks," for the color of ink on one side. But printing too much cash to pay for the war would be ruinous, as the Confederate states will soon learn. Their "blueback" paper money is so worthless by war's end that a shoebox full of cash is not enough to purchase a loaf of bread.

President Lincoln sees the solution to America's war funding in Treasury notes. These "war bonds" are essentially a loan to the government from banks and private citizens, purchased and repaid in gold. By the end of the Civil War, $6.2 billion of war bonds have been traded, with one-fourth sold by a single man, Jay Cooke, a banker and devout Christian born in 1821. Named after former Supreme Court justice John Jay, Cooke has an unsurpassed skill at selling war bonds to Americans. By March 7, 1862, President Abraham Lincoln places Cooke in control of all U.S. bond sales. The financier opens banks in New York, Philadelphia, and Washington bearing his name. By war's end commissions and fees have allowed Cooke to amass a fortune of more than $10 million.* He has become America's most powerful financial figure.

On April 14, 1865, Abraham Lincoln is assassinated. At that time, the United States has paid off all but $2.5 billion of its war debt. However, eight years later, despite the introduction of income, excise, and estate taxes, the country's financial obligation remains just about the same. Seeking a new source of revenue, Jay Cooke has turned his moneymaking efforts to selling bonds to support construction of the Northern Pacific railroad.

Among Cooke's many influential friends is President Ulysses S. Grant. With the completion of the Northern Pacific deemed vital to America's economic growth, the president authorizes the U.S. Cavalry as armed escorts for Cooke's surveying crews. Between June 20 and September 23, 1873, a contingent of more than fifteen hundred infantry soldiers and the Seventh Cavalry watches over 353 civilians attempting to link Tacoma and Bismarck by train tracks running directly through Indian Territory in Montana and Wyoming.

General George Custer is among the officers in charge. This journey into Indian Territory is Custer's first significant foray into Montana and Wyoming. The general has long been at home on the plains and revels in the long days and short nights in the saddle. The route takes him past rivers with names like the Powder, Tongue, and Little Bighorn. His men camp for one night at a spot known as Pompey's Pillar on the Yellowstone River, a giant sandstone rock where the explorer William Clark carved his initials on July 25, 1806, during the legendary Lewis and Clark Expedition.

The *New York Times* has been following the story of the Yellowstone railroad survey from its beginning, receiving detailed reports from the War Department in Washington. On Saturday, August 16, the paper declares the project an unqualified success, stating that "the

---

* This figure is equivalent to $220 million in 2019.

new and final route across Western Dakota, from Missouri to the Yellowstone River, is entirely practicable and satisfactory," thus raising Jay Cooke's hopes of selling more bonds to finance construction.

But George Custer will dash those hopes. Writing in the shadow of Pompey's Pillar, on a plain beside the Yellowstone River, the general pens the after-action report that will doom Jay Cooke's bond sales—and much more.

On August 15, 1873, the general writes a detailed report of two recent skirmishes with Sioux warriors. "The Indians outnumbering us almost five to one were enabled to envelop us completely between their lines," Custer writes in his official version of events, detailing a three-hour battle on August 4. "Until the Indians were made to taste freely of our lead they displayed unusual boldness, frequently charging up to our line and firing with great deliberation and accuracy."

Then, noting the presence of Crazy Horse leading the Sioux into battle, Custer adds: "Among the Indians who fought us on this occasion were some of the identical warriors who committed the massacre at Fort Phil Kearny, and they no doubt intended a similar program when they sent the six warriors to dash up and attempt to decoy us into a pursuit past the timber in which the savages hoped to ambush us."

✷

One week later, on August 11, it is Sitting Bull whose warriors ambush Custer. Again, the Seventh Cavalry escapes annihilation. Despite the deaths of eleven U.S. soldiers during the Yellowstone journey, Custer and his men are battered but not defeated. He sends the report to Fort Laramie. From there it travels by telegraph to Washington.

In August 1873, Custer's "Official Report of the Engagements with Indians on the 4th and 11th" is leaked to the press.

The general is fond of the limelight and is no stranger to self-aggrandizement. He cannot possibly imagine the effect his words will soon have upon the nation.

"The truth is, we have now struck upon the last and bravest of the old Indian races of the plain," the *New York Times* reports after reading Custer's accounts. "The Sioux beyond the Missouri is a very different Indian from the stupid, peaceful vagabond creatures who haunt the neighborhood of white settlement in the north-west, or who are learning agriculture on reservations. . . . If several thousand of our best soldiers, with all of the arms of the service, under some of our most dashing officers, can only hold the ground on their narrow line of march for 150 or 200 miles west of the Upper Missouri, [what] will peaceful bodies of railroad workmen be able to do, or what can emigrants accomplish in such a dangerous region?

"The . . . [Sioux] must be taught a lesson by force. They must learn to submit," the newspaper opines.

Public reaction is swift. Investor confidence in the Northern Pacific railroad plummets. The stock market dips. Jay Cooke & Company, America's largest banking house, soon runs low on cash. President Grant has dinner at Cooke's fifty-three-room mansion north of Philadelphia on September 15, with the Northern Pacific and a panicked Wall Street as the main topics of discussion. Europe is facing similar economic problems. But after eating well, both Grant and Cooke agree that the crisis will soon pass.

They are wrong.

On Thursday, September 18, at 11:00 a.m., Jay Cooke is notified of a run on his bank. Investors have lost faith in the Northern Pacific, thanks to General Custer and the *New York Times*. Average citizens are racing to withdraw their life savings. Cooke's banks cannot possible pay out all the money. The financier immediately orders the doors closed and locked. But Cooke is too late.

America's premier financial institution, Jay Cooke & Company, collapses, and its demise has catastrophic effects on the nation. In a domino effect, other banks begin closing. The New York Stock Exchange closes for ten days. Bank after bank fails. The price of Treasury bonds plummets. Thousands of Americans lose their jobs as factories go out of business. The nation will soon see a wave of impoverishment, as the newly unemployed cannot find work. By sheer coincidence, America is further punished by a yellow fever epidemic breaking out in the Mississippi Valley from Illinois down to New Orleans. In addition, grasshoppers blacken the skies over Nebraska and Kansas in a plague of biblical proportions, descending only to feast on the crops of local farmers.

In America, bad news is everywhere.

This is the Panic of 1873.

❖

Nine months later, as General George Armstrong Custer leads nearly a thousand soldiers into the Black Hills, it might be said that the fate of the national economy rests on his shoulders. Simply put, Custer needs to find enough gold so the federal government can begin selling lucrative Treasury bonds again. With that potential revenue stream, the nation might emerge from its yearlong depression. So it is no surprise that journalists are allowed to join Custer's expedition. If there is gold in the hills, this news needs to find its way to the general public as soon as possible in order to bolster confidence. America's destiny can no longer be stymied by the Treaty of Fort Laramie or the spiritual concerns of the Plains Indians.

President Grant eagerly awaits Custer's findings.

❖

It is August 3, 1874, almost one year after George Custer wrote the ruinous report that damned the Northern Pacific railroad. Custer's 883-mile Black Hills Expedition still has one more month before its conclusion, but he has completed a new report, this one spreading far more positive news. The information is so promising that Custer sends delivery rider Charley Reynolds to Fort Laramie so the document can be immediately transmitted by telegraph to the East Coast.

"Gold was obtained in numerous localities in what are termed gulches," Custer writes. "No large nuggets were found. The examination, however, showed that a very even, if not a very rich distribution of gold is to be found throughout the entire valleys."

The correspondent from the Chicago *Inter Ocean* is much more sensationalist: "From the grass roots down it was pay dirt."

Custer and his expedition soon ride for home. Both he and

Libbie are glad she has been allowed to remain at Fort Abraham Lincoln in his absence.

"When the day of their return came, I was simply wild with joy," Libbie Custer will write of their reunion one month later. Her husband is sunburned and heavily bearded, his clothing torn and patched. "I hid behind the door as the command rode into the garrison, ashamed to be seen crying and laughing and dancing up and down with excitement. I tried to remain there and receive the general, screened from the eyes of outsiders. It was impossible. I was down the steps and beside my husband without being conscious of how I got there."

General Custer's gift to his wife is a keg of clear stream water, a novelty at Fort Abraham Lincoln, where a muddy drink is the norm. The couple race to their home, then quickly up the steps, shutting the door behind them. In the distance, Libbie will always remember hearing the wonderful sound of a brass band after two months of silence.

So it is that the Custers are at peace on the Northern Plains. The general has once again succeeded in his command and pleased President Grant. The nation sees George Custer as a hero.

But in the Black Hills, there is another point of view. The Sioux and other tribes are not naive. They know George Custer has now put their lands in danger.

And they know this is something they will not accept.

Chapter Twenty-One

JUNE 9, 1875
WHITE HOUSE
DAY

Chief Red Cloud is on a mission.

The fifty-four-year-old Sioux leader has traveled by train from his northwestern Nebraska reservation to meet with the Great White Father. There is talk that the government wants to purchase the Black Hills, but there are many other issues present on Red Cloud's mind that must be discussed first. The Sioux chief is two years older than President Grant but is physically far more conditioned than the potbellied, chain-smoking former general. At two hundred pounds and six feet tall, the chief towers over the diminutive Grant.

Except for the lone eagle feather in his hair, Red Cloud wears white man's clothing: a button-down shirt, black vest and pants, hard leather shoes. The president wears his usual three-piece business suit with a bow tie. This is Red Cloud's second visit to Washington. In his lifetime, the chief will make twenty-one such journeys to lobby on behalf of his people, but none will be as important as today's.

Five years ago, Red Cloud stood defiant before Grant. The warrior chief had successfully driven the U.S. Army off his tribal lands, defeating them in battle time after time. Red Cloud signed the Fort

Laramie Treaty reluctantly, and only as a means of protecting his tribe from another generation of war. The chief brought his people onto the reservation under his own free will, believing in the white promises of food and protection in exchange for peace. On that day in 1870, when Red Cloud last visited the White House, he and Grant met as equals.

That meeting led to the establishment of a reservation bearing Red Cloud's name on the North Platte River in 1871. But as time passed, the Great White Father lost interest in Red Cloud's fate. In 1874, the government relocated Red Cloud's band one hundred miles north, to the border of Nebraska and the Dakota Territory. The reservation still bore Red Cloud's name, but the U.S. Army also opened a military installation on the premises, pointedly giving it the name Fort Robinson, after a young officer killed by Indians. The peace Red Cloud once sought from the president has diminished with each passing year, replaced by a growing contempt from the white man toward the Sioux. In fact, the once-proud chief is now often treated as a beggar.

So Red Cloud has returned to Washington to air his grievances. With him are several other chiefs and tribal leaders, including Spotted Tail and American Horse, the warrior who personally slit the throat of Captain Fetterman almost a decade ago. Red Cloud tells President Grant that the white agent assigned to his reservation is corrupt. The chief is also angered by the fact that his people have no blankets to keep them warm and by the poor quality of their rations, which often include rotten bacon. This is when they are fed at all. Instead of an issue of rations every week, as promised, a month or more can go by without food. In those times, Red Cloud's tribe must slaughter their own ponies to sate their hunger.

But the Great White Father has no interest in the quality of life on Red Cloud's reservation, and he cares even less for the chief's griping. Since summoning Red Cloud and a host of other Sioux leaders from the Oglala, Miniconjou, and Brulé bands to Washington in late May, the president has been elusive, pawning them off on his subordinates.

But the time has now come to let these Indians know that the relationship between Washington and the tribes of the Northern Plains is about to drastically change.

For the worse.

❉

The president's "peace policy," which defined relations with America's Indians during his first six years in office, is now a myth. There is no peace. In fact, the worst fighting between the U.S. Army and America's Indian population has taken place since Grant's first inauguration. And if the point of these battles has been to subjugate the tribes and confine them to reservations, that aspect of Grant's peace policy has also failed. Some tribes choose to live on a reservation, while many do not. The Sioux nation is almost evenly divided between those who choose to "come in" and those determined to fight for their freedom. But even then, the distinction is fluid. Reservation Indians routinely pack up and ride off for months at a time to hunt, and even wage war on the Americans or other tribes, then return to the reservation when it is convenient.

President Grant's top frontier commander, General Phil Sheridan, has noted that "if a white man commits murder or robs, we hang him or send him to the penitentiary; if an Indian does the same, we have been in the habit of giving him more blankets."

But the failure of the reservations to contain the Native American population does not rest entirely with the tribes. Money and food guaranteed to the Indians by treaty is often stolen by the agents responsible for safeguarding tribal life. The problem is so bad that Grant's entire Board of Indian Commissioners was forced to resign in 1874 amid charges of corruption and scandal.

But without a doubt, President Grant's greatest headache is the Black Hills problem. Thousands of miners are now flooding into these sacred Indian lands, following the "Thieves' Road," as General Custer's exploratory route is known to the Sioux. As the *New-York Tribune* has noted, "If there is gold in the Black Hills, no army on earth can keep the adventurous men of the west out of them." This assessment has already proven correct.

"Black Hills fever" is sweeping the nation. Despite a spring that saw sixty-seven consecutive days of rain in the Black Hills—and snow on June 2—many Americans now unemployed by the Panic of 1873 rush west to make their fortune. Lugging their tents, belongings, and food supplies in overstuffed carryalls, they travel by the Union Pacific Railroad to Cheyenne, Wyoming, 175 miles south of the gold fields. Also, they travel by the Northern Pacific to Bismarck, 300 miles away from the Black Hills.

There is little the U.S. Army can do to stop them. The Black Hills span eight thousand square miles—and almost none of the rugged terrain is conducive to military maneuvering.

Just two months ago, on April 7, 1875, the army managed to evict a small contingent of prospectors. But they soon snuck back, giving lie to the president's promise to protect Indian land.

In fact, Grant is under increasing pressure to annex the Black Hills and forcibly relocate the Sioux and other plains tribes. Many in his administration are pushing the president to move them all to Oklahoma, there to reside with the Creek, Cheyenne, Comanche, and other tribes already under strict U.S. supervision. And even as Grant now meets with Red Cloud here in the White House, yet another group of soldiers and scientists are marching into the Black Hills not only to confirm the gold claims of General Custer but also to map the entire region.

This, of course, infuriates the Indians.

Red Cloud puts it directly to President Grant: "I have two mountains in [my] country—the Black Hills and the Big Horn Mountain. I want the Great Father to make no roads through them."

But that is exactly what is now occurring.

Thus, as the American presence on Sioux land grows quickly, U. S. Grant becomes aggressive in confronting Red Cloud and the Sioux. The Great White Father wants to renege on the Fort Laramie treaty, even if that means extortion. Grant informs Red Cloud during their White House meeting that the rations his tribe were promised in exchange for moving onto the reservation were a gift of the White Father's "that could be taken from them at any time." The president adds that "white people now outnumber the Indians 200 to one." Grant then demands that Red Cloud cede the Black Hills to the United States or his rations will be withheld. In addition, the president requests that the Sioux move to Oklahoma.

In what is a colossal insult, Grant offers to pay the Sioux the paltry sum of $25,000.

It is not the great orator Red Cloud who offers the Sioux response. Instead, it is his friend Spotted Tail of the Brulé band: "You speak of another country, but it is not my country; it does not concern me, and I want nothing to do with it. I was not born there," says Spotted Tail.

"If it is such a good country, you ought to send the white men now in our country there and let us alone."

But Spotted Tail does not have the final word. As the Indian delegation leaves Washington for a return to the reservation, Red Cloud and the other chiefs reluctantly agree that selling the Black Hills is the best plan of action for the Sioux nation. But that sale cannot take place without the approval of the Hunkpapa and Oglala bands.

And that means the approval of Sitting Bull and Crazy Horse.

※

Now in his prime, Crazy Horse is a lean and quick-thinking man of just thirty-four. His leadership is beyond question, and his calm, collected behavior on the battlefield is legendary.

A visible reminder of Crazy Horse's warlike ways is the creased flesh wound disfiguring his face, the result of a pistol shot that very nearly killed him. However, the accident did not occur in battle but when Crazy Horse stole the wife of a fellow tribe member. The lady in question is named Black Buffalo Woman. Crazy Horse courted her before she married and considers the woman to be the love of his life. So it was a triumph when he convinced her to run away with him. But when the vengeful husband, a warrior named No Water, found the lovers, he took aim and fired from point-blank range. Amazingly, Crazy Horse escaped with his life. However, a shaken Black Buffalo Woman returned to her husband in order to end the hostilities.

Crazy Horse has since married, to a woman named Black Shawl. Their daughter, They Are Afraid of Her, recently died of cholera. She was just three years old.

Crazy Horse and his good friend He Dog have been ordered by tribal elders to closely monitor the comings and goings of miners and soldiers in the Black Hills. They are mandated to guard the Indian food supply. It has been a year of famine for the Sioux bands of the Northern Plains. The two warriors, both the same age and lifelong brothers in battle, stand watch. A small band of younger Indians works for them, spying on the whites and reporting back with any news.

One bit of information arrives from the north. The army officer "Long Hair" has returned to Fort Abraham Lincoln. In addition to overseeing last year's violation of Sioux rights by leading the Seventh Cavalry into Indian land, George Custer is well known among the Sioux for his massacre of Black Kettle's Cheyenne band on the Southern Plains six years ago. Crazy Horse does not know why Long Hair left Fort Abraham Lincoln last autumn, or where the white general traveled. He only knows that this enemy of the Sioux nation has now returned.

Despite the dwindling number of buffalo, Crazy Horse has chosen not to live on a reservation and receive free food from the U.S. government. He has heard many tales of the feuding and petty arguments on the reservation, in addition to the obvious lack of daily freedom. If Crazy Horse needs further proof of malevolence, he need only look at Red Cloud. The once-proud chief now takes orders from the white man.

Crazy Horse was asked to accompany Red Cloud on the journey to see the Great White Father, and even gave the matter some thought. But in the end, he turned down the invitation. When messengers were sent to Crazy Horse from the reservation asking why he chose not to make the journey, the warrior's response was brusque. He had "concluded to remain behind to guard the Black Hills."

Crazy Horse knows that Red Cloud and many other Sioux living on the reservation are seriously considering the Great White Chief's offer to purchase the Black Hills. But the Oglala war chief does not see the logic: "One does not sell the earth on which people walk."

In truth, Crazy Horse knows that the coming of the white people into the Black Hills cannot be stopped. And he is also well aware that there may come a day when his people are forced onto the reservation. But for now he is encouraged by the actions and words of his friend, the charismatic chief Sitting Bull.

"We want no white men here." Sitting Bull has made it clear. "The Black Hills belong to me. If the whites try to take them, I will fight."

The supreme Sioux chief is now forty-seven years old. Time has not diminished his superior skills as a warrior and charismatic leader. His courage on the battlefield was proven two years ago when General George Custer and his expedition traveled up the Yellowstone River. Sioux legend has it not only that warriors under Sitting Bull confronted the American soldiers but that he boldly walked the battlefield during a short firefight, indifferent to the bullets flying all around him. This bravery, plus Sitting Bull's defiant refusal to accept any help from the whites or entertain offers of settling people on a reservation, has emboldened the Sioux tribe. Of all the great chiefs in America, Sitting Bull holds an unparalleled level of power and influence.

Now, as Crazy Horse stealthily observes the influx of miners into the sacred lands, Sitting Bull is assembling a coalition of tribes far to the north on the Rosebud River. In addition to Hunkpapa and Oglala Sioux, Sitting Bull has asked the Northern Cheyenne to take part. Clearly, the time has come to respond in force to the white man's incursion into the Black Hills.

✳

Preparing for war, Sitting Bull is in a trance.

The chief is nearly naked as he dances before the seven hundred assembled warriors, elders, and families, wearing just a breechcloth and war bonnet. His body is painted bright yellow to show the spirits working within him, with black bands painted on his face, chest, shoulders, and ankles. Sitting Bull's coal-black war pony, walking slowly behind him, is also painted down its hindquarters and right leg in white clay depicting holy wakan imagery. Dots painted on the animal's neck depict hail.*

---

* Wakan Tanka is variously translated as the "Great Spirit" and "Great Mystery"—a god influencing and empowering the Lakota people through both animate and inanimate objects.

The Sun Dance lodge is packed, and Sitting Bull dances from the center pole all the way to the back of the crowd, then once more back to the center. His stocky figure limps slightly from a long-ago bullet wound. Hunkpapa, Oglala, and Miniconjou Sioux share the tent with the Northern Cheyenne led by Little Wolf and the holy man known as Ice.

In the past, the Hunkpapa under Sitting Bull have kept their distance from the Cheyenne. But now, the Sioux will need the Cheyenne in order to wage effective war. To that end, Sitting Bull will not perform the traditional Sun Dance, with its acts of self-torture and fasting. That is for another time. Instead, he will knit the fate of tribes together by seeing the future.

"I wish my friends to fill one pipe and I wish my people to fill one pipe," Sitting Bull shouts, demanding a display of unity. Taking the pipes, one in each hand, the chief continues his dance, leading his horse the whole while and bringing the ceremony to a crescendo.

"We have them!" Sitting Bull roars, raising his clenched fists to the sky. "Wakan Tanka has given our enemies into our power," he tells the crowd. "We are to wipe them out."

The Indians roar! Cries of "how, how" echo across the Northern Plains. At a time of despair and confusion, with members of their own tribe traveling to Washington to sell their lands to the Great White Father, these words of victory are a source of supreme joy.

The groups closest to Sitting Bull are the tribal elders. Then warriors. And in the back, women and children. The identity of their enemies is not clear. But Sitting Bull has brought the crowd together to reignite the power of the Sioux and reinforce their long-standing alliance with the Northern Cheyenne.

The Indians well know the hunger that comes from the decimation of buffalo herds and the increasing scarcity of game. Sitting Bull now talks about the one place on earth specifically set aside for the Sioux so that they will never go hungry: the Black Hills.

Energy hums through the tent as unity fills the crowd. But as the dance comes to an end, and the people return to their tepees, one thing remains uncertain about Sitting Bull's remarkable act of diplomacy.

Exactly who will the Indians destroy?

The answer will arrive soon.

❄

It is September 4, 1875. President Grant is redoubling his efforts to purchase the Black Hills. More gold has recently been found in an area known as Deadwood Gulch, and miners have begun felling lodgepole pines to build winter cabins and sluices to filter gold from gravel. Even as the army continues to try to prevent the influx of miners, the practice of staking personal ownership to claims along riverbanks is happening so quickly that every creek and stream in the Black Hills will soon be occupied.

So it is that the five-man Commission Appointed to Treat with the Sioux Indians for the Relinquishment of the Black Hills has traveled to Nebraska to sit down with Red Cloud and other Sioux leaders to negotiate the land purchase. William B. Allison, leader of the delegation on behalf of President Grant, proposes to the tribes that in lieu of an outright purchase, the United States will lease the mineral rights of the Black Hills. The money would be paid to the Sioux people over the course of the next seven generations. In addition, the commission proposes to also buy outright the Big Horn Territory in Wyoming in order to take ownership of the lands the government still hopes to utilize in building a Northern Pacific railroad.

Hoping to avoid war, Red Cloud agrees. The Arapaho and Cheyenne tribes, who are also affected by the agreement, approve as well.

Neither Crazy Horse nor Sitting Bull is in attendance. The delegation from Washington knows that these leaders are opposed to the deal. So the government increases the offer—$400,000 per year to lease the Black Hills, or $6 million to purchase the lands outright. A messenger is sent to Sitting Bull, who listens for a moment before bending down to pick up a pinch of dirt from the ground.

"I do not want to sell or lease any land to the government—not even as much as this," Sitting Bull says, letting the dirt fall from his fingertips.

Crazy Horse prefers to seek guidance on the matter through a vision quest. He marches alone into the wilderness to pray and fast. He then returns to his encampment two days later and purifies himself in a sweat lodge. In his dreams, he has seen a vision of the buffalo leaving the hunting grounds forever, and his people starving to death on a reservation. This confirms to Crazy Horse that the lands must not be sold and that he must do whatever he can to protect his people. Crazy Horse travels once again into the Black Hills to see the intrusion for himself. After more than a year of doing nothing to stop miners from entering the Black Hills, the war chief finally receives approval from his tribal council of elders to attack wagon trains and individual miners.

But it is too late. Already, there are fifteen hundred miners in the Black Hills. By winter's end, with no deal in sight, that number will rise to fifteen thousand. There is no summer or winter to the gold-mining world; these men work in all seasons. The little mining camp in Deadwood Gulch soon becomes a town, complete with saloons and whorehouses where the miners can pay for services by handing over a pinch of gold instead of cash.

It is clear the Black Hills will never be the same, yet Crazy Horse and Sitting Bull refuse to sell.

The commission from Washington concludes their business on September 29, 1875. In his final report, Senator William B. Allison of Iowa, who is also chairman of the Senate Committee on Indian Affairs, writes that the commission agreed to offer "a much larger sum than they believed the hills to be worth. This offer, regarded by the commission as ample and liberal, met with derisive laughter from the Indians assembled."

Senator Allison goes on to conclude: "We do not believe their temper or spirit can or will be changed until they are made to feel the power as well as the magnanimity of the Government.... If the Government will interpose its power and authority, they are not in the condition to resist. . . . They never can be civilized except by the mild exercise, at least, of force."*

✳

President Grant spends the month of October ruminating over the situation. It is his belief that chiefs like Red Cloud who are in favor of the Black Hills sale are being intimidated by Crazy Horse and Sitting Bull.

On November 3, in Washington, Grant convenes a meeting to solve the Sioux problem. This is no mere gathering of officials. Instead, it is a secret cabinet gathering to discuss undeclared war.†

On December 3, the Bureau of Indian Affairs orders that Sitting Bull, Crazy Horse, and other bands have until January 31, 1876, to report to a reservation.

The tribes failing to do so will be labeled as "hostile" and considered enemies of the United States of America.

On February 8, 1876, General Phil Sheridan orders U.S. Army forces in Montana and the Dakota Territory to find and punish the tribes of Sitting Bull and Crazy Horse.

But the landscape of the Northern Plains is vast, and finding the defiant tribes will be a monumental feat. Not until spring of 1876, as the ponies of the Sioux grow fat and strong on new spring grass, are the "hostiles" finally located.

Better for the U.S. Army had they not been found.

---

* Senator Allison actually hated the Indians, calling them "idlers" and "vagabonds" in his report, demanding that the U.S. government use "such powers as necessary to enforce education in English, in manual labor, and other industrial pursuits upon the youths of the tribes"—completely invalidating the traditional tribal way of life.

† President Grant was keeping things quiet because a strong peace movement on the East Coast sought to protect the Indians and their land. The politically astute Grant felt this might become an issue in the upcoming presidential election.

Chapter Twenty-Two

Crazy Horse is uneasy.

A vast Indian campsite echoes with the joyful sounds of song and dance, but the evening feels ominous to the war chief. Dry lightning crackles along a nearby ridge, followed by the boom of prairie thunder. Crazy Horse enjoys a feast of pronghorn antelope with several other tribal leaders. Nearby, a thin ribbon of tall green cottonwood trees marks the steep and winding banks of the Little Bighorn River. In the distance, a lonely Sitting Bull chants to the Wakan Tanka for help in assuring victory in battle. Sitting Bull recently received one hundred small knife cuts on his arms as part of a Sun Dance ritual. He also danced while staring into the sun for hours. Now, the chief is partially blinded and still weak from loss of blood. Knowing he is unfit to wage war because of his wounds, Sitting Bull, as the chief and spiritual leader of the entire Sioux nation, walks alone into the hills to pray aloud.

Crazy Horse ponders what tomorrow morning will bring. This is the largest tribal reunion anyone can remember. Many Indian nations fill the Montana valley. Each band has been assigned a specific campsite and has arranged their tepees in tribal circles. They have come at the behest of Sitting Bull. "It is war," decreed an invitation several months ago to all Indians living on the reservations. The message was carried by couriers on horseback and transmitted verbally to the Northern Plains tribes. By the thousands, Indians left the government lands to join with their brethren from the Northern Bands of Oglala and Hunkpapa Sioux. The Cheyenne are also here, as are a few Arapaho warriors.

Crazy Horse knows the unity cannot last forever. It is here, surrounding the Little Bighorn, that the last great buffalo herds now reside. But there is not enough game to support the enormous tribal gathering for very long. Soon the tribes will disperse into smaller bands. On this night, they celebrate, if only because it feels so powerful to be together.

The great Red Cloud has not made the journey, but his eighteen-year-old son Jack Red Cloud is here, armed with the Winchester rifle President Grant, the Great White Father, gifted to his father last year. The weapon saw action one week ago, when an Indian force under Crazy Horse nearly overran an invading column of U.S. soldiers under the command of General George Crook.

The Battle of the Rosebud, as it became known, was the U.S. Army's first major strike into Indian lands since the "hostile" designation was applied to nonreservation bands five months ago. The campaign led by Crook featured a fighting force of more than a thousand soldiers, miners, and journalists and 250 Indian scouts from the Crow and Shoshone bands. Their aim was to catch or kill Crazy Horse, Sitting Bull, and their warriors. Crook has long specialized in waging war against Native Americans, having successfully engaged tribes in the Pacific Northwest and in Arizona. With his expertise and the massive fighting force, General Crook's success seemed all but assured.

But one week ago, on June 17, Crazy Horse boldly moved to stop the incursion. After leading a thousand warriors on a nighttime ride, the war chief launched a surprise dawn attack on Crook's campsite. The general's men were exhausted, having marched thirty-five grueling miles the day before. Were it not for the vigilance of Crook's Indian scouts, the entire column of U.S. soldiers would have been slaughtered. Instead, in a battle stretching from early morning into the afternoon, Crazy Horse and Crook engaged in a tactical chess match. Unable to utilize decoy riders to lure the whites into difficult terrain, Crazy Horse executed a series of feints, strikes, and well-timed retreats to confuse the soldiers. The growing number of Indians fighting with Winchester repeating rifles allowed the warriors to fire from their horses without the need to reload after every shot. That greatly enhanced their ability to kill U.S. soldiers.

The Battle of the Rosebud ended in a draw. Crazy Horse retreated with the loss of a few dozen warriors. General Crook's casualties were roughly the same. And although the general claimed victory, he soon turned and marched his bloodied army one hundred miles back toward their home fort in Wyoming. The garrison is named for the late Captain William Fetterman.

Crazy Horse knows this was just the beginning. More whites are coming. Scouts rode into camp earlier this afternoon, telling of a large armed force approaching from the east. The whites were last seen at the site where Sitting Bull performed his Sun Dance before an audience of thousands two weeks ago. The soldiers' march will inevitably lead them right into the encampment where Crazy Horse currently sits.

The Indian tepees number more than one thousand, stretched along a two-mile plain. The Little Bighorn River provides water for eight thousand Indians and twenty thousand ponies. Finding the tribes will be easy, for the bands have taken no precaution about concealing their whereabouts. In the morning, the cook fires from so many campsites will give them away, choking the blue sky with smoke, pointing precisely to their location. Crazy Horse is certain that if the whites ride hard through the night, they will own the element of surprise at dawn.

So the legendary warrior goes tepee to tepee, speaking with the leaders of each band, warning that the whites are coming. Yet great fighters like Gall, Crow King, Fast Eagle, and Little Horse do not share his concern. The whites will not come tomorrow, they assure Crazy Horse, but the day after. Now is the time for feasting and long talks before the campfire.

Horses wading in the Little Bighorn River, next to a Crow encampment, circa 1908

Savoring a bite of the freshly cooked antelope, Crazy Horse hears the revelry taking place in the various tribal circles, with singing and dancing so loud that the whites might possibly hear the tribes long before they can see them. It has been years since these tribes have felt so free and independent. Crazy Horse well knows that many young warriors will be up all night and in no condition to fight come morning.

At the age of fourteen, Crazy Horse had a vision that told him he must always take care of his people. In return, no bullet or arrow would ever pierce his flesh. Never before has that prophecy informed the behavior of Crazy Horse as it does tonight. The precise moment when the whites will arrive is unknown, but Crazy Horse knows they are coming.

So it is that Crazy Horse descends deep into thought. He needs to know what the Americans are doing. Avoiding all revelry, he orders scouts to ride out into the night to find the soldiers.

✳

General George Custer is his usual confident self.

Almost twenty miles away from the Indian camp, he gives the order to move out. The general is dressed in a blue flannel shirt, buckskin jacket, and pants tucked into knee-high Wellington boots made of soft calfskin leather.* His wide-brimmed slouch hat is pale white. A hunting knife is strapped to his hip, along with his two pistols.

The hour is 12:30 a.m. There is no moon, and the band does not sound the traditional "Boots and Saddles" because the general has left the band at home. Custer's exhausted men marched twenty-seven miles yesterday and only made camp four hours ago. Many still have whiskey on their breath from imbibing after getting off the trail, but there can be no delay in Custer's pursuit of the Indians. A night march is dangerous, particularly in total blackness: "You cannot define any particular object, not even your horse's head. You hear the steady, perpetual tramp, tramp, tramp of the iron-hoofed cavalry," *Chicago Times* correspondent John Finerty writes, describing a night ride with General Crook just one month ago. "The jingle of carbines and sling-belts, and the snorting of the horses as they grope their way through the eternal dust [are the only sounds heard]."

Custer believes the danger is necessary. The location of the Sioux encampment is still unknown, but Custer's Crow Indian scouts tell him it is definitely near. Just before dusk they found tracks of hoof-prints and footsteps a mile wide leading toward the Little Bighorn River.

Such a large trail suggests the Indian encampment is well populated, but Custer is sure his Seventh Cavalry matches up well with

---

* First made popular by the Duke of Wellington, the British commander who defeated Napoleon at the Battle of Waterloo in 1815, Wellington boots—or "Wellies," as they are nicknamed—were transformed into a rubber rain boot during World War I because leather rotted in the muddy trenches. Wellington boots are still popular around the world as wet-weather gear.

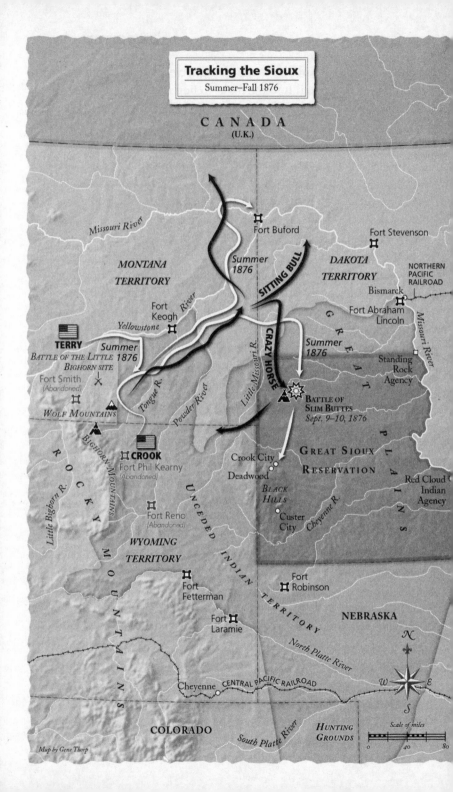

Tracking the Sioux

Summer–Fall 1876

CANADA
(U.K.)

Missouri River

MONTANA
TERRITORY

Fort Buford

Summer
1876

SITTING BULL

Fort Stevenson

DAKOTA
TERRITORY

NORTHERN
PACIFIC
RAILROAD

Bismarck

Fort Keogh

Yellowstone River

TERRY

Summer 1876

BATTLE OF THE LITTLE
BIGHORN site

Fort Smith
(Abandoned)

WOLF MOUNTAINS

CRAZY HORSE

Fort Abraham
Lincoln

Summer
1876

Standing
Rock
Agency

G
R
E
A
T

Missouri River

Tongue R.

Powder River

Little Missouri R.

BATTLE OF
SLIM BUTTES
Sept. 9–10, 1876

GREAT SIOUX
RESERVATION

R
O
C
K
Y

BIGHORN MOUNTAINS

CROOK
Fort Phil Kearny
(Abandoned)

Crook City

Deadwood

BLACK
HILLS

Custer
City

Cheyenne R.

P
L
A
I
N
S

Red Cloud
Indian
Agency

Little Bighorn R.

Fort Reno
(Abandoned)

WYOMING
TERRITORY

M
O
U
N
T
A
I
N
S

Fort
Fetterman

Fort
Laramie

U
N
C
E
D
E
D

I
N
D
I
A
N

T
E
R
R
I
T
O
R
Y

Fort
Robinson

NEBRASKA

North Platte River

N

W   E

S

Cheyenne

CENTRAL PACIFIC RAILROAD

COLORADO

South Platte River

HUNTING
GROUNDS

Scale of miles

0   40   80

Map by Gene Thorp

the enemy. He has claimed on more than one occasion that his men could whip any tribe in battle. The general's force now numbers twenty-seven officers, nearly six hundred enlisted men, forty-three Indian scouts, and various civilian contractors. The mule train carrying ammunition and fifteen days of supplies numbers 175 animals. Mixed-race Lakota-French scout Mitch Boyer leads the scout caravan. He is considered one of the best scouts in the territory—so good that Sitting Bull has allegedly offered a reward of one hundred horses for his capture.

Custer's brothers Tom and Boston are among the group, as is his nephew, Harry Armstrong Reed. The eighteen-year-old works in the pack train as a herder, and not only shares the same middle name as his uncle but also goes by the nickname "Autie."

In addition to leaving behind the regimental band, Custer has not brought along his beloved dogs. The general knows that such a big procession of men and horses will leave a large and dusty trail, and he wants to avoid unnecessary noise such as music or barking that will inform the Indians of their location. In addition, the general has banned all campfires and the use of lanterns at night during the manhunt.

Custer and his men have been aggressively chasing the Indians for the last two days, often stopping for hours at deserted campsites so his scouts can assess the trail. It is the general's great fear that these tribes will disperse into small bands rather than stay together long enough for him to annihilate them. Custer does not wish to wage war in several skirmishes but to defeat the hostiles in one great battle.

It is 3:00 a.m. when the general orders a halt. His troopers gratefully fall out of the saddle. There is little grass to feed the animals, and a small creek is too alkaline to drink. So, clutching the reins of their horses, the men stretch out on the ground to catch what sleep they can. Meanwhile, the general's Indian scouts press on, still tracking the Sioux band. Custer uses the time to discuss strategy with his commanders. He does not sleep.

Dawn comes at 4:45. Shortly afterward, the Crow scouts send word to Custer that they can see campfire smoke in the distance.

Custer is skeptical. The scouts take him to an overlook in the Wolf Mountains known as the Crow's Nest. The general squints into the west, the rising sun at his back. He claims not to see anything. Borrowing a cheap spyglass, Custer looks once more. A slight breeze blows across the prairie and the morning is overcast.

Custer still cannot see the Indian camp. Smoke from the campfires conceals the tribes. The scouts ask him to look once again, this time specifically seeking out "worms" in the grass. By this, the scouts mean the twenty thousand–strong herd of ponies grazing on a bluff overlooking the encampment.

Custer remains doubtful but knows he must trust his scouts. Soon, fresh pony tracks are found near the cavalry's bivouac area. And Tom Custer reports to his brother that a group of Indians was fired upon while ransacking goods from the mule train.

Returning to the campsite, Custer informs his officers: "The largest Indian camp on the North American continent is ahead and I am going to attack it."

Shortly after that, Mitch Boyer, the scout so feared by Sitting Bull, warns Custer: "General, I have been with these Indians for thirty years and this is the largest village I have ever heard of."

Custer's favorite scout, a Hunkpapa Sioux named Bloody Knife who accompanied the general on his two previous trips into Indian land, also warns the general in sign language that there are enough Indians in the village to fight for two to three days.

Custer, however, seems unconcerned. The reports given to him by his superiors about Indian strength in this region suggest he has little to fear. Custer's strategy is to focus on capturing the women and children to use as hostages, then take possession of the Indian ponies. In this way, the warriors will lose their mobility and have no choice but to capitulate.

Custer gives the order to saddle up. It is mid-morning by now, and excitement sweeps through the ranks as the men sense battle. The long line of horsemen ride four abreast, kicking up a large cloud of dust as they descend into the valley through which the Little Bighorn River runs.

It is shortly after noon when Custer calls a halt. The cool morning has given way to an uncomfortably hot afternoon. He removes his buckskin jacket and ties it to his saddle. The men water their horses in a small creek.

Surveying the landscape, Custer decides to split his force into three separate columns. The general will lead 215 men from Companies C, E, F, I, and L. He will soon bear right, riding onto a low line of hills.

Captain Frederick Benteen will command H, D, and K Companies. He will travel south in search of tribes camped in that direction, then turn back and rejoin Custer. Benteen's force comprises 125 men. Custer and Benteen are longtime adversaries, and it chafes the captain that his commanding officer is five years younger than himself.

Frederick Benteen is a forty-two-year-old Virginian who attended military school before joining the Union army in 1861, over the vehement objections of his secessionist father. Benteen fought in eight major Civil War battles, rising from the rank of lieutenant to that of lieutenant colonel. Remaining in the army after the war, he was demoted in rank, like many other officers, due to a reduction in the size of America's fighting force. Benteen served with Custer at the Washita battle in which the Cheyenne under Black Kettle were massacred. As part of the fracas, a cavalry officer who foolishly chased a group of Cheyenne after the battle was later found dead and mutilated. Benteen blamed Custer for the officer's death and wrote a critical account of the general's behavior to a friend. The missive was passed on to the *St. Louis Democrat*, where it was published without Benteen's name. Custer suspected Benteen as the author but chose to let the matter pass. However, despite their nine years of service together, the impasse was never quite settled. The wavy-haired Benteen, whose eyes have the appearance of bulging out of his skull, believes Custer to be reckless.

The other commander, Major Marcus Reno, will take 150 officers and enlisted men of Companies A, G, and M straight into the valley, attacking the heart of the Indian encampment. Bloody Knife, Custer's favorite scout, will travel at Reno's side to show the way. Marcus Reno is a bitter man, having recently lost his wife to

*Colonel Frederick Benteen, American military officer
during the Civil War and the Black Hills War*

illness. The thickset, black-haired Reno often takes to drink and is not popular among the other officers or with General Custer. But Reno is not as defiant as Benteen, who now openly challenges Custer's strategy: "Hadn't we better keep the regiment together, General?"

Custer coolly looks at his subordinate and arrogantly replies, "You have your orders."

These are the last words the two officers will ever speak to each other.

Custer then orders Major Reno to take the lead and charge into the Indian camp.

The time is 2:43 p.m.

At 2:53 p.m., Major Reno crosses with his men to the left bank of the Little Bighorn River. There they water their horses and cinch saddle girth straps tighter. But before they can do anything else, they are startled to see Sioux warriors bearing down hard on them.

Almost immediately, Reno orders a courier to gallop to Custer and deliver a simple message: the Indians are in front of Reno's position "in full force."

At 3:03 p.m., Major Reno orders his men to increase their horses' pace from a slow trot to an all-out gallop. Riding hard at more than twenty miles per hour, rifles drawn, the soldiers of the U.S. Seventh Cavalry charge forth to meet the hostiles.

Not once in the entire history of the United States has the sight of 140 heavily armed U.S. soldiers and their horses bearing down on an Indian village ever failed to make Native Americans cut and run for their lives.

But not this time.

Seven hundred yards from the village, Major Reno is astonished to see hundreds of Sioux and Cheyenne warriors. They are not running away. Instead, they gallop their horses directly toward his men. Quickly realizing that his troopers are outnumbered by at least five to one, Reno cries an alarmed "Halt!" Above the thunder of hooves, he orders his soldiers to dismount. One in every four men is tasked with the role of horse holder, grabbing reins and pulling equines off the battlefield to be used later when needed. The other ninety men kneel or lie down. Utilizing the mounds of dirt comprising a prairie dog town for cover, Reno's forces anchor their line on the right in a stand of cottonwoods. They are armed with Colt revolver pistols and big-bore, breech-loading Springfield Model 1873 carbines. Each .45/55 caliber copper cartridge round is almost two inches long, but the Springfield trapdoor carbine can only fire one shot at a time before the need to reload.

In the months leading up to the cavalry's search for the "hostile" bands, Major Reno has been in charge of training these men. Yet he has not scheduled a single target practice to improve basic accuracy with firearms or to learn the most optimal method of loading the Springfield, thus ensuring the firing of a maximum number of shots per minute.

What's done is done.

The soldiers open fire.

❊

Crazy Horse's intuition was wrong.

The whites did not attack at first light. Indeed, it is hours past noon and there is no sign of them near the village. Thus, warriors, women, and children go about their day without a care: young boys and girls swim naked in the cold but shallow river, women gather prairie turnips, and, as Crazy Horse predicted, some warriors are still sleeping off their night of revelry. The primary movement in the Indian camp is herds of ponies walking across the valley to secure a cool drink in the river on this stifling hot afternoon. Nevertheless, Crazy Horse remains vigilant.

Shortly before the middle of the afternoon, riders gallop into camp, yelling that the whites are coming. The entire village descends into chaos. Women frantically search for their children as warriors race to find their ponies. Some warriors hastily saddle whatever pony is available and immediately gallop toward the intruders. Sitting Bull defiantly directs the action, ordering the fighting men to race toward the soldiers. Cowards, he says pointedly, should remain in the rear. Teenage boys who have not yet reached warrior status tie sage to the tails of their ponies and gallop back and forth on the edge of the village to create a dust cloud that will hide the tribes from enemy sharpshooters.

Crazy Horse steps into his tepee to grab his bridle and Winchester rifle. Gunshots can now be heard coming from the far side of camp, near the tribal circle of Sitting Bull's Hunkpapa Sioux. As warriors from other bands gallop out to confront the soldiers, the whites are waiting. The soldiers lie prone in the swale created by the dirt mounds, separated from one another by five-yard intervals in what is known as "skirmish formation," then open fire as the warriors swarm their position. They shoot in volley fashion, having to reload after every round.

In what will become a tense afternoon of fighting, Privates George Smith and James Turley soon become the battle's first U.S. casualties. Unable to halt their panicked horses and dismount, the out-of-control troopers gallop helplessly into the Indian campsite. Warriors shoot the men dead, pull them to the ground, and then slice their heads from their bodies. Tribal women will soon mount those heads on poles for all to see.

In the cottonwood trees along the river, Custer's Indian scouts extract their own bloody casualties, surprising a group of women and children, then shooting them dead. The Sioux warrior Gall loses both his wives and all three of his children.

Meanwhile, Crazy Horse cannot find his pony. "Take any horse," snaps his brother-in-law, Red Feather. Hundreds of Oglala warriors look on, waiting for Crazy Horse's commands. The snap of gunshots and war whoops just a few hundred yards away tells them that the battle is growing more intense. The youngest of the braves struggle to contain their impatience as the chance for taking scalps slips away. But no warrior dares contradict the war chief.

Crazy Horse is not in a hurry. Despite the urgent pleas of the young warriors gathered at his tepee, the war chief waits for his horses to be brought to him. Crazy Horse knows that his band is not needed right now and that the Cheyenne and Hunkpapa Sioux are already attacking the American soldiers in force. So he uses the time to prepare properly for what promises to be a major battle. Dressed in just a breechcloth and moccasins, Crazy Horse paints his face and body yellow. White dots are then painted on his skin. The warrior buckles a cartridge belt around his waist and adds a stone war club to his arsenal. He smokes a pipe. Finally, his horses are brought to him. Crazy Horse thinks carefully before choosing a white-faced pinto from among his personal herd. The pony is also painted for battle, with lines drawn down his flanks. Crazy Horse slips the bridle over its head, then leaps onto the animal's bare back.

As the warriors also mount their ponies, Crazy Horse calmly gives last-minute instructions. Cradling his rifle in his left hand, he reminds the fighters to be patient and to follow his lead. "Do your best, and let us kill them all off today, that they may not trouble us anymore," Crazy Horse admonishes. His tone is calm and direct.

"Hoka-he! It's a good day to die," he concludes.

✳

Major Marcus Reno is in trouble.

Reno's charge into the village failed. Not only did the Indians not run away but they have counterattacked in force. The major has never seen so many warriors in battle, nor has he ever seen a charge of such ferocity. Unlike the Americans, the Indians are trained not to listen to a single commander once the battle has begun. Their lifetime of tactical training and discipline allows the warriors not only to follow orders but also to think for themselves. In this way, the American soldiers' belief that the Indians are an inferior fighting force of lazy savages is quickly dispelled. They ride better, shoot better, and now outnumber the U.S. Cavalry.

✳

George Custer is nowhere to be seen. The Indians now surround Reno's position. A hail of rifle fire and arrows comes not just from the warriors attacking from the rear but also from the bluffs overlooking the river. Reno retreats, ordering his men to fall back to the right, into the protective cover of the cottonwoods along the riverbank.

Reno and his men mount their horses and ride hard for the timber, hoping to make a stand until Custer arrives. The major calls out to Bloody Knife, but before the scout can respond he is shot through the head—his brains and blood splatter all over Reno's face.

The soldiers make it to the cottonwoods, only to find Crazy Horse and his band of Oglala warriors waiting for them. A panicked Reno orders his hundred men to dismount, then immediately tells them to remount. Crazy Horse smashes through the brush on his horse, killing a trooper with his stone war club, pushing another soldier from his horse and stealing the animal within a matter of seconds. As other warriors swarm his lines, Major Reno has had enough.

He orders his men to flee across the Little Bighorn River.

But there's a problem. The bank is a sheer drop of several feet into the fast-moving current. The troopers are exposed and vulnerable as they guide their reluctant mounts down the treacherous slope. Crazy Horse and his warriors kill with calm and cool precision, looping their bowstrings around the necks of soldiers, then yanking hard to pull them from the saddle. Other fleeing troopers are simply clubbed with stone hammers, then shot as they scramble and crawl unhorsed in the waist-deep water. The river runs red with blood.

A now frantic and terrified Reno finally crosses to the right bank. He does not know how many of his men are alive, only that he needs to get away from the battlefield as fast as he can. He spurs his horse hard, desperately urging his mount up a steep grassy hill. The escaping troopers take heavy fire, but there is no attempt by them to shoot back at their enemy. The rout is complete.

By 4:10 p.m., less than an hour after his initial charge into the Indian village, Major Reno and his troopers have clawed to the top of a high bluff overlooking the river. Approximately forty men are dead, and another fifty are badly wounded. Reno quickly re-forms the men who can still fight into a skirmish line—but the Indians have not given chase.

So for the moment the troopers are safe on this ridgeline. From their vantage point three hundred feet above the river, they can see the entire battlefield below. Dead troopers are being scalped and mutilated before their eyes, women young and old crushing skulls with rocks. As always, all the bodies will be stripped.

Reno's scouts report to him that General Custer's men have already departed from the ridge—presumably in the hopes of attacking the village from another direction. But Reno doesn't know where Custer is. He only knows that his force remains in severe jeopardy.

Ten minutes after mounting atop the summit, Reno and his men are joined by Captain Benteen and his command, which has not seen any fighting.

"Where's Custer?" Benteen demands. He holds an order from the general in his pocket, telling him to race forward with more ammunition.

Reno says he does not know.

Then, five miles to the north, comes the unmistakable sound of gunfire.

⁂

In fact, George Custer witnessed Reno's initial charge into the village. Custer now knows how strong the Indian force is and orders a courier to ride back to Captain Benteen with orders to bring more ammo. "Tell him to come quick," Custer adds.

About a mile away from Major Reno, at a gully known as Cedar Coulee, an impatient Custer sees no sign of Benteen's column. The general knows Reno's force has taken heavy casualties, but he cannot rescue Reno until he is resupplied with ammunition.

So, Custer dispatches a second courier, this time instructing him to make the urgency of their present situation clear. Lieutenant William W. Cooke hands the messenger a scribbled note to reinforce Custer's order. "Benteen. Come on. Big Village. Be quick. Bring Packs."

Custer waits until he can wait no more. Knowing that the warriors are focused completely on Reno, he now has the opportunity to attack from the opposite end of the village, capturing the women and children and hoping the warriors will surrender in order to protect them from death.

But Custer has a problem. With Reno retreating away from the village, he does not have the force to drive directly into it. So Custer compromises. He once again splits his men. One element, comprised of Companies E and F, will charge down and take control of the river crossing two miles north of Reno. The remainder of the force, Custer included, will watch the proceedings from a high vantage point and wait for Benteen and the ammunition.

The time is 4:20 p.m.

At this very moment, Captain Benteen is talking to Major Reno—holding in his pocket orders telling him to rush ammunition to Custer as quickly as possible. In addition to the 125 men under Benteen's command, Reno has 100 soldiers available. They now own the high ground, giving them a tactical superiority that makes up for their smaller fighting force when compared with the Indians.

Captain Benteen knows what needs to be done. As a career officer, he understands what will happen to him if he does not resupply General Custer. He will most likely be court-martialed for disobeying an order, which will most likely end Benteen's military career.

Captain Frederick Benteen does not care.

He and his men will go no further.

Custer and his troopers are on their own.

Chapter Twenty-Three

June 25, 1876
Little Bighorn battlefield, Montana
4:20 p.m.

Crazy Horse is engaged.

Just one hour into the battle, the war chief rides back through the village amid a throng of fleeing Indians. No one can ever remember a fight like today, nor the sight of so many dead and dying men and horses. Some women begin dismantling tepees in the hopes of fleeing as soon as possible, while others run with their children toward new hiding places far from the shooting. Sitting Bull also rides his horse through the commotion, urging calm. He directs the fleeing women and children to follow him to a place of safety.

Arriving back to their tepees, Crazy Horse and his Oglala warriors exchange their ponies for fresh mounts. The war chief dons a white buckskin shirt and leggings to protect his bare flesh from thorns and brush. The battle is shifting north, to where Custer's soldiers are now attempting to ride down the hillside, cross the Little Bighorn River, and attack the village from a different direction. But Sioux and Cheyenne warriors currently line those riverbanks, raining lead on the white soldiers approaching the creek from the other side.

Seeing that Sitting Bull is herding hundreds of women, children, and elderly toward the river crossing, Crazy Horse positions his warriors between these helpless dependents and the attacking cavalry.

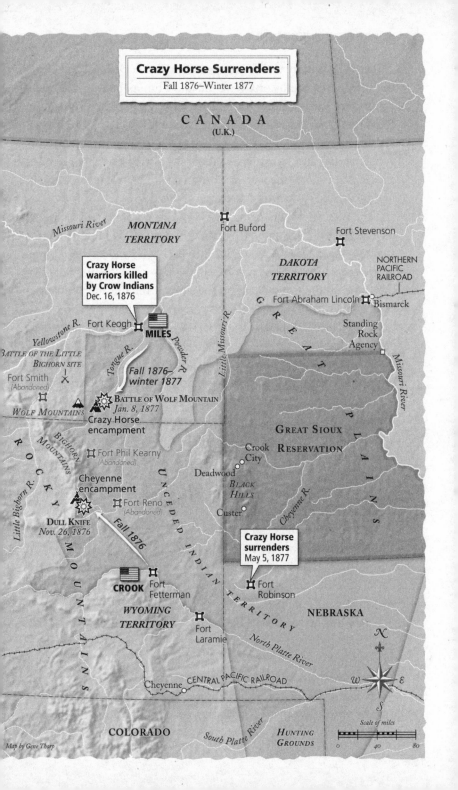

At 4:35 p.m., Custer's troops are driven back from the Little Bighorn River. Bands of Cheyenne and Hunkpapa warriors under a war chief named Crow King follow in hot pursuit, riding hard to catch the Americans as the soldiers race up the grassy hills.

Crazy Horse is not among them. Observing the commotion, gunshots, and dust of battle, he calmly sits astride his pony and takes charge. He exhorts the assembled warriors to be relentless in pressing the attack. No whites must survive this day.

The war chief then gallops his Oglala band a mile north, where he charges his force across the river, then up a low bluff through a spot known as Deep Ravine. But they do not ascend to the very top where the whites will be able to see them. Instead, the warriors hug the gullies and narrow draws on the sides of the hill, keeping out of sight as they slowly work their way around the slope.

Crazy Horse orders his warriors to dismount. They walk their horses as the war chief assesses the battlefield. Rifle in his left hand, he crawls on his belly until he is up and out of the ravine, concealing himself in the tall grass. In the distance to the south, Crazy Horse sees several white soldiers sitting tall in the saddle, so focused on the action that they are unaware that a major Indian force has crept behind them. Crazy Horse takes careful aim.

"He shot them as fast as he could load his gun," a warrior named Flying Hawk will remember. Tasked with holding the reins of Crazy Horse's pony while he fired, Flying Hawk has a unique close-up look at the war chief's prowess.

"They fell off their horses as fast as he could shoot."

Without the whites even knowing it, the combined forces of Crow King attacking from the south and Crazy Horse from the north have the U.S. soldiers completely blocked. The Indian forces are separated by almost a mile.

Now it is up to Crazy Horse to close the trap.

✳

General George Custer is under siege.

A few moments ago, his youngest brother, Boston, galloped to his side with news that Captain Benteen and the ammunition were

U.S. Cavalry troopers being pursued across a river during the Battle of the Little Bighorn, as depicted by noted Oglala Lakota artist Amos Bad Heart Bull

getting close. But forty-five minutes later, there is still no sign of Benteen. Custer cannot wait any longer if he is to capture the village. He orders his men forward, hoping Benteen will catch up.

Though history does not record his thoughts during the last hour of his life, and the actual movements of his troopers are still open to debate almost 150 years after the Battle of the Little Bighorn, it is known that the general's attention is squarely focused on the hundreds of women, children, and old people in the valley below, fleeing the Indian encampment under Sitting Bull's direction.

Custer is frustrated that his plan to capture the entire Sioux encampment might slip away. The smart maneuver seems to be a retreat, galloping his men four miles back along the ridgeline to where other army forces may be setting up defensive positions. By clustering the entire remnant of the Seventh Cavalry in that location, knowing that Captain Benteen and the ammunition must eventually arrive, Custer might still achieve his victory.

But Custer has no plans to retreat. There is still a chance for immediate victory. The five companies under his command are now clustered atop a low summit with a sweeping view of the Little Bighorn River, roughly a quarter mile below. The grassy slopes leading up to their position are not steep, but several ravines and dry creek beds would give cover to an approaching enemy. In addition to George's brothers Tom and Boston and nephew Autie Reed, a fourth member of the extended Custer family sits astride his horse on this magnificent viewpoint. Thirty-year-old Lieutenant James Calhoun is Custer's brother-in-law. Known as the "Adonis of the Seventh" for his good looks, Calhoun is married to General Custer's sister Margaret.

General Custer once again decides to split his command. He orders three companies to remain atop the hill while he and two other companies move forward along the ridgeline to try to flank the Indians. He will then charge down off the ridge to capture the women and children.

Custer dispatches an Indian scout named Curley to seek out help from General Alfred Terry, who is on his way to assist in the fight with Crazy Horse. Terry commands the remainder of the Seventh Cavalry, a force that numbers several hundred men. History will long question whether Custer was supposed to link up with Terry before the battle so that the Americans could enter the village with a greater fighting force or whether Terry gave Custer the order to proceed without him. But none of that matters to Custer now, because he believes victory is before him.

The soldiers Custer has ordered to stay behind are the men of Companies C, I, and L. Their goal is to protect the general's rear. The unit farthest to the south, sure to be the first to bear the brunt of an Indian assault, is Company L, commanded by Lieutenant James Calhoun.

As Curley rides off, Calhoun and his men dismount, setting up defensive skirmish formations. The men arrange themselves in a semicircle five yards apart. Per military guidelines, one in four men is pulled off the line to hold the horses. The "horse holders" believe the Indians cannot see them. They are wrong.

Soon enough, Indian rifle fire zeroes in on their position.

✳

Meanwhile, Crazy Horse waits. He watches the American soldiers from a hidden position in a ravine. All around him, warriors in the grass fire long-distance rifle shots at the soldiers, with little effect. Indian marksmanship is best from close range. But Crazy Horse knows that an ill-timed attack could harm the Indian advantage, and he patiently watches for a weakness to exploit. He believes the men of Company L are the key to this battle. If he defeats them, Custer will be completely cut off. Not only will "Long Hair" be unable to retreat; he will not even succeed in sending a messenger back to Major Reno requesting help.

A warrior named White Bull grows impatient. He is tired of waiting. He tells Crazy Horse he wants to attack.

Crazy Horse orders White Bull to stand down.

✳

George Custer finally gives up on Captain Benteen.

Unable to wait any longer for ammunition, he maneuvers his two companies down toward the village. The general has successfully flanked the enemy by traveling north along the ridgeline, and he can now move carefully down the hillside to cross the Little Bighorn River in force. Because of Custer's patient examination of the battle-field terrain, his movements are carefully screened from the Indian village by the slope of the hill.

One of his companies, E, is led by Lieutenant Algernon Smith. His soldiers all ride gray horses. Custer orders them to stand firm in reserve, while he and the men of Company F lead the way downhill. *Bismarck Tribune* correspondent Mark Kellogg rides with Custer, eager to record this moment for posterity. The river is just a few hundred yards away, as are the women and children, huddled for safety in a tributary known as Squaw Creek. Custer can see them clearly.

Then shots ring out from the riverbank. Kellogg, the journalist, is killed instantly. The gunfire comes from willows along the banks, where elderly warriors have been stationed as a last line of defense against the bluecoats.

Custer cautiously orders Company F to retreat momentarily, just far enough to get out of rifle range.

But scores of Indian fighters still remaining in the village are alerted by the shots. These Cheyenne and Hunkpapa Sioux now attack Custer's men in force. Company E holds the line, protecting Custer's left flank.

George Custer decides to counterattack, arranging the four dozen men of Company F in a V-formation on the hillside, ready to pour fire down on the approaching warriors. The frightened women and children are still on the riverbank. The general has been in many a battle and knows that a single bold action can quickly swing momentum.

Victory is still within Custer's grasp.

Or so he thinks.

⁂

The soldiers holding the horses are killed first.

A wave of Indians led by Chief Gall flows up and over the hill into the positions held by Company L. The troopers fire their single-shot Springfields, but as they pause to reload the Indians are upon them. The fighting becomes hand to hand, soldiers swinging rifle butts as the warriors wield war clubs.

Within moments, bands of warriors open fire from hiding places in gullies and brush. Snapping red blankets, they scare the horses, driving away many animals. Company L pulls back atop the ridge-line. More and more warriors who recently arrived from the village silently crawl up through the grass. They wait for their leaders to give the signal. Some Indians are fewer than fifty yards from Company L's position.

Company C, also atop the summit, refuses to assume a defensive position. Instead, the roughly fifty soldiers on horseback charge the Indians, causing panic as the warriors run for their lives. For a brief moment, the army has regained momentum.

But a Cheyenne chief named Lame White Man changes all that. He does not run in the face of the approaching whites. Instead, he stands his ground, screaming at the fleeing warriors to hold fast and fight. Even as Company C dismounts so they can open fire more accurately with their big-bore carbines, Lame White Man barks orders.

The warriors stop running.

Hundreds of Cheyenne and Sioux open fire on Company C. Once again, brightly colored blankets are snapped to frighten the horses.

✵

Crazy Horse challenges the impatient White Bull to stop complaining and show his courage. Together, the two men mount up and gallop their horses across the battlefield, completely exposed to American rifle fire. Both men taunt the white soldiers. The warriors ride low, hugging the necks of their horses.

Yet, as Crazy Horse's vision quest once prophesied, not a single bullet strikes the war chief. Nor is White Bull hit. Returning safely to the Indian lines, Crazy Horse and White Bull decide to repeat their courageous run. This time, other warriors choose to ride with them even as Indians on the ground rise up from their prone firing positions and attack—rifles in one hand and war clubs in the other.

The charging soldiers, many of whom have lost their horses, quickly run back up the hillside to their brothers in Company L. Upon reaching the summit, all the Americans start to retreat further.

Many soldiers flee in panic. The few who still have mounts get away more quickly, leaving behind those on foot. Carbines and bullets are tossed aside by the panicked soldiers and quickly snatched up by the pursuing warriors.

The men under Custer's command are now in disarray. Indians are everywhere, using war clubs and guns to kill each man they set upon. Hand-to-hand fighting is fierce. Lieutenant James Calhoun dies on the hill that will one day be renamed in his honor.

Just 20 soldiers out of more than 120 escape, running hard to the north toward their commander, George Custer.

✵

But Custer has also retreated.

Following the gray horses of Company E, Custer has pulled back toward the top of the ridge. A group of Cheyenne and Sioux warriors calling themselves the "Suicide Boys" are waging guerrilla warfare, sowing confusion in the lines. From ravines and ridges, Indian arrows and rifle fire pour into the American position. Some white soldiers become confused, even as others form into small fighting positions.

General Custer and his remaining men are atop a high grassy knoll. Those soldiers who can't reach them are butchered. "They were making their arms go as though they were running, but they were only walking," the young boy Black Elk will remember.

There are no trees or rocks to offer protection, so Custer and his men shoot the remaining thirty-nine horses, putting a single bullet in each of their heads. The corpses provide protection from Indian fire. There are roughly fifty American soldiers still alive.

Custer knows the time for desperate measures has come.

Suddenly, Tom Custer falls at his brother's side.

Seeing that, Boston Custer and Autie Reed make a run for it and are quickly shot dead.

Then, a single bullet strikes George Custer in the chest but does not kill him. He drops his Remington rifle, now using only his pistols. Dust is everywhere, as the confused screams and cries of the dying fill the air.

Crazy Horse gallops in a circle around the American position, blowing a whistle made of eagle bone to encourage the Indians to advance closer to the trapped Americans.

The war chief's signal finally brings the battle to a bitter end, as hundreds of warriors overrun Custer's position. It is 5:30 p.m. The final few moments of the fighting are a hectic cacophony of pistol shots, scalping, hand-to-hand fighting, and skulls shattering as heads are clubbed. The war whoops of the Indians punctuate their victory, marking the end of Custer's Last Stand.

Soon, there is silence.

❈

The body of General George Custer will be found naked, his thigh cut, an arrow shot through his penis, his scalp and famous mane still attached to his head. "He did not wear his long hair as he used to wear it," Sitting Bull will observe. "It was short, but the color of the grass when the frost comes . . . where the last stand was made, Long Hair stood like a sheaf of corn with all the ears fallen around him."

Before the whites can come and bury Custer's body, two Indian women will pierce his ears with sharp implements so that he might hear better in the afterworld—since he clearly did not hear the warnings in this lifetime to stay off Indian lands.

General George Custer is thirty-six at the time of his death. His battlefield opponent, Crazy Horse, is the same age. The American loss on this day is 268 dead and 55 wounded, but every man in Custer's direct command dies—all 210 of them.

The Indian numbers are not known, but in later years Sitting Bull stated that 138 Native Americans were killed or wounded. However, some historians estimate that as many as 300 warriors perished.*

※

Custer's men do not all die at once, or even all together. Some soldiers are killed hundreds of yards away as they try to escape. A number of troopers shoot themselves, their bodies later found with a single bullet hole in the skull. Among these is George Custer, though it is unlikely he committed suicide, for the general was right-handed and the bullet wound was in the left side of his skull.

A few soldiers were not killed in the battle. "These soldiers became foolish," the warrior Red Horse later recalls, "many throwing away their guns and raising their hands, saying 'Sioux, pity us. Take us prisoners.' The Sioux did not take a single soldier prisoner, but killed them all. None of them were alive for even a few minutes."

The bodies of George Custer and his brother Tom are found close together. Their younger brother, Boston, and nephew Autie Reed are one hundred yards away. Tom Custer's corpse, in particular, is so completely ravaged that he is almost unrecognizable. One year ago, he allegedly arrested a reservation warrior named Rain-in-

---

* The authors of this book believe they have accurately represented the battle known as Custer's Last Stand. However, scholars differ on some of the battlefield locations and the times at which events took place, and that should be noted.

the-Face for murder. Many believe the Indian got his revenge on this day. Tom Custer's skull is bashed in, his eyes are gouged from his skull, and his tongue is cut out. If not for a telltale tattoo of the Goddess of Liberty on his arm, Tom Custer's body would have gone unidentified.

Curley, the Crow scout, will never find General Alfred Terry or his advancing column. Instead, he will race to the confluence of the Yellowstone and Rosebud Rivers, where he will use sign language to share news of the massacre with the crew of the army supply steamship, *Far West*. After traveling upriver to load wounded survivors of the fight General Reno supervised, the steamship races back to Fort Abraham Lincoln—traveling 710 miles in just fifty-four hours to report the annihilation of Custer and his Seventh Cavalry.

❖

The news of Crazy Horse's great victory finally reaches Washington by telegraph on July 4, 1876—the centennial anniversary of America's Declaration of Independence. It was President Ulysses S. Grant's decision to crush the Sioux nation once and for all, but even as a devastated Libbie Custer grieves over the shocking loss of her husband, Grant wastes little time in placing blame.

"I regard Custer's massacre as a sacrifice of troops, brought on by Custer himself, that was wholly unnecessary," the president states publicly. "Wholly unnecessary."*

❖

Captain Frederick Benteen personally identifies the soldiers' remains on the Little Bighorn battlefield in the days after the

---

* President Grant's animosity toward Custer began in March 1875, when the general was ordered to come to Washington to testify in a federal corruption case involving Grant's brother, Orvil. Custer had spoken out publicly about Orvil Grant, a government contractor, overcharging soldiers at U.S. Army forts in the west. The general even wrote anonymous articles for the *New-York Herald* detailing the graft. President Grant took all this personally, removing Custer from command of the Seventh Cavalry. However, that action made headlines in the New York press, embarrassing Grant. He was forced to reinstate Custer to command. Had he not done so, Custer would not have been killed at the Battle of the Little Bighorn.

*Custer Hill markers where Seventh Cavalry bodies were found,
Little Bighorn battlefield, Montana.*

fight. He later testifies on behalf of Major Marcus Reno before
an army court of inquiry. Both men are cleared of all charges of
incompetence.

Captain Benteen writes home to his wife: "Custer disobeyed
orders, and thereby lost his life."

Benteen omits that he had also refused to obey orders.*

By July 4—which proves to be the first true moment since the

---

* Captain Benteen was not held responsible for Custer's defeat at the Little Bighorn and went on to fight in the Nez Percé War of 1877. He was promoted to
major but in 1887 was suspended from the army for drunk and disorderly conduct. Benteen retired the following year, then died in Atlanta on June 22, 1898, at
the age of sixty-three. Major Marcus Reno was dismissed from the army after the
Battle of the Little Bighorn. However, he requested a formal court of inquiry,
which successfully restored him to active-duty military status. Unlike the tee-
totaling George Custer, Reno's impulsivity was often due to drink. This would
be his undoing. Shortly year after returning to the service, Reno faced charges of
drunkenness. He was dismissed from the army on April 1, 1880. Major Marcus
Reno died in 1889 of tongue cancer. In 1967, Reno's remains were reinterred
at the Custer National Cemetery on the Little Bighorn Battlefield National
Monument.

Civil War that citizens from the North and South unite to celebrate the founding of America—Crazy Horse, Sitting Bull, and the Indian tribes have completely scattered. The great encampment along the Little Bighorn River is no more. The tribes packed up and left just one day after the massacre.

But even though Crazy Horse and Sitting Bull go their separate ways, the chiefs both know one thing: the whites will be back with a vengeance.

Chapter Twenty-Four

Less than two months after George Custer is killed, 230 miles southeast of the Little Bighorn, a man with just a minute to live is playing cards.

Wild Bill Hickok entered the Saloon No. 10 at noon. A scale to weigh out gold dust rests atop the far end of the bar. Painted wainscoting lines the walls, and four chandeliers hang from the ceiling. A game of draw poker is in progress at a low table in the center of the room, ringed by four chairs—three of them occupied by intense men who make card playing their business. The open seat is positioned with its back to the tavern's rear door. Hickok does not like that, knowing he has enemies everywhere. But the other three players refuse to let him sit in a more secure seat, so he reluctantly places himself in a vulnerable position.

In the two short years since George Custer found gold in the Black Hills, Deadwood has sprung into being. What was once a small gulch is now a prosperous, seedy boomtown. It is the sort of place where miners drink themselves to death after striking it rich. The town is lined with well-appointed saloons, whorehouses, a muddy Main Street, and even a new luxury palace aptly named the Gen'l Custer Hotel.

Like most men who have chosen to make Deadwood their home since the Custer expedition of 1874, the six-foot-tall Hickok says he is here for the gold. But in reality, he is among those hustlers who does not work the mines or stand in a cold stream panning silt. Instead, Wild Bill is a card sharp who follows the money around the American frontier, whether it be gold or buffalo hunting or driving cattle. Wherever there is wealth, there are stupid men willing to part with it through drink and cards. James Butler Hickok knows this fact all too well, having witnessed the "opening" of the American frontier for two decades as a gunfighter and lawman. Along the way, Bill Hickok has kept the peace in towns stretching from Abilene, Kansas, all the way north to Cheyenne, Wyoming.

With the Indians on the run, Deadwood and other new Black Hills towns like Custer City and Crook City are perfectly situated for business owners to enrich themselves fortifying and resupplying the hordes of miners. Crazy Horse and Sitting Bull are furious over the denuding of the landscape. As miners seek deep deposits of gold in the streams, the lodgepole pines that once covered the nearby hills are disappearing as newcomers chop them down to build homes and businesses. Even as Wild Bill sits down for an afternoon of cards, a group of Pony Express riders are racing through the Black Hills from Fort Laramie, two hundred miles south. Again, not fearing Indian interference at all, the local government has launched a contest wherein the fastest riders will get a contract to deliver the mail.

If ever there was a sign that the Native Americans have lost the Black Hills, it is Deadwood. The debauchery and decadence stand in vivid contrast to the once-sacred Sioux lands.

The wood-framed Saloon No. 10 is named for a gold claim. The building is just twenty feet wide, its depth extending back sixty feet from the street entrance. The bar is on the right as Hickok enters.

"Wild Bill" is a name the gunman gave himself, rather than live with the dubious moniker "Duck Bill," once bestowed upon him for his large lips and nose. He has long, wavy hair and an unkempt mustache spreading wide over his cheeks, and is losing his vision to glaucoma at age thirty-nine. The camp follower Calamity Jane, well known among the Seventh Cavalry for her "skills" and penchant for whiskey, likes to claim she is Hickok's wife, even though Wild Bill is married to another woman. Despite her fondness for Hickok, Calamity Jane is not above taking work from a local madam when she is short of cash and in need of a drink.

Hickok won big at the table last night, taking a bag of gold from a drunken and unlucky miner. But the amount of dusty golden flakes in the sack was not enough to cover the man's losses. So Hickok demanded that the miner make it up to him by producing more gold—which the miner did. However, when Wild Bill realized that the man had given him his last cent, the gunfighter returned a small portion so that the miner might buy himself breakfast. The man in question claims that his name is Bill Sutherland, but in fact he is Jack McCall, a twenty-three-year-old former buffalo hunter from Kentucky.

Still angry from losing so heavily the night before, McCall enters the Saloon No. 10. The time is 3:00 p.m. as bartender Harry Young steps out from behind the bar to deliver $50 in chips to Hickok, who has been losing steadily for the past three hours. Hickok observes McCall but does not perceive him as a threat. As always, Wild Bill drinks and draws cards with his left hand, leaving his right hand free to pull his Smith & Wesson five-shot pistol, now holstered snugly against his left hip. The butt faces out, per Wild Bill's preference for a "cavalry draw."

McCall walks the length of the bar, toward the saloon's rear entrance. Hickok's focus is on the hand he was just dealt, two black aces and two black eights. The hole card is still a matter of debate, but it is not enough to win the hand. "The old duffer," Hickok says of riverboat captain William Massie, "he broke me."

By now, Jack McCall has moved directly behind Hickok, who cannot see him. McCall pulls a long-barreled Colt Model 1873 army revolver and shoots the legendary lawman in the back of the head.

Wild Bill dies instantly.*

---

* Wild Bill Hickok is laid to rest in Deadwood. A quarter century later, at her own insistence, Calamity Jane is buried at Wild Bill's side, where she remains to this day. Poker players still consider a hand containing two black aces and two black eights a "dead man's hand," based on Wild Bill's murder.

Jack McCall runs but is soon caught. The jury for his first trial is a group of sympathetic miners. Incredibly, he is found not guilty.

In the United States of America, a citizen cannot be tried twice for the same crime. But Deadwood is *not* in the United States—it is still Indian Territory. So the first trial is invalid. When McCall makes the mistake of bragging about the murder, believing he cannot be tried again, authorities arrest him and transport him four hundred miles east to Yankton, capital of the Dakota Territory, which *is* part of the United States.

This time Jack McCall is found guilty. Six months after he murdered Hickok, McCall is hanged by the neck until dead. McCall is buried with the noose still tight around his throat.

Chapter Twenty-Five

SEPTEMBER 9, 1876
SLIM BUTTES, DAKOTA TERRITORY
4:45 P.M.

The man with less than a year to live is on the run.

Marauding soldiers under the command of General George Crook pillage a small Sioux village looking for Crazy Horse, who humiliated Crook at the Battle of the Rosebud. Crook is now obsessed with the war chief and is pushing his two-thousand-man force to its limit, practicing scorched-earth tactics on any Sioux band he finds. The result is that General Crook's men are now themselves starving—the force so low on food they have been reduced to eating their horses and mules. They are traveling south to Deadwood in search of supplies but have stumbled upon the thirty-seven lodges of a band led by American Horse, the same Indian who personally killed Captain William Fetterman ten years ago.

After Crook's attack, American Horse is dead, his entrails hanging out the front of his torso as soldiers mutilate him. However, most of his band escapes, leaving behind food stockpiled for the freezing winter months soon to come. Now, as pounds of dried meat and nuts are being greedily consumed by the famished soldiers, the troops are stunned to find the Seventh Cavalry's Company I battle flag affixed to the side of one tepee, along with $11,000 in cash and the leather riding gloves of Captain Myles Keogh—all confiscated after the Little Bighorn massacre.*

※

The hunt for Crazy Horse and Sitting Bull has turned into a disaster for the army. Hardened soldiers actually break into tears after hours slogging through thick mud, overcome by the hardship and the overwhelming hunger they have experienced. But General Crook will not be deterred. Crazy Horse embarrassed him and then annihilated Custer. The U.S. Army has not won a battle against the Sioux all summer, a situation Crook intends to change.

Today's fighting was over by early morning, and as the day stretches into afternoon there is no hurry to press on for Deadwood since food has been discovered. By 4:45 p.m. two soldiers killed in the action are buried and the men have settled down to warm themselves by campfires, set to stay the night in the shadow of the stony outcroppings inspiring the location's name of Slim Buttes.

A few miles away, Crazy Horse is not resting. Warriors from the fight with Crook traveled quickly to give the war chief the news. Others from American Horse's tribe flee farther north to Sitting Bull's encampment. Both chiefs now assemble warriors to counterattack, but it is Crazy Horse who strikes first. Ringing Crook's encampment, knowing that the setting sun will soon be in the soldiers' eyes, the Indians open fire. The bluecoats quickly scramble for their weapons to shoot back.

Crazy Horse and his warriors are outnumbered four to one. Riding about the battlefield on his white charger, the war chief directs the action. When it is clear that the army encampment cannot be overrun, he orders his fighters to fall back.

The next morning, watched from a distance by Crazy Horse and Sitting Bull, General Crook orders the captured Indian tepees

---

* Keogh's horse, Comanche, survived the Battle of the Little Bighorn, despite several bullet wounds. He was never ridden again, living out his days on army posts. Comanche died in 1891, but visitors to the Natural History Museum at the University of Kansas can still view Comanche's stuffed remains on display in a climate-controlled glass case.

burned. Then the soldiers resume their march to Deadwood. Along the way, the Indians harass them in small skirmishes, attacking from places of concealment in a driving rain, giving the appearance that they are everywhere at once.

✵

Meanwhile, as the season changes to autumn, and the month known by the Sioux as the Moon of Falling Leaves has arrived, a group of chiefs led by Red Cloud is forced to sign over the Black Hills to the U.S. government. Under threats of destruction, the Indians also give away the Unceded Territories, which the tribes of the Northern Plains depend upon so greatly for hunting buffalo and other wild game. Finally, under orders from the U.S. Army, which has taken control of all reservation activities since the death of Custer, Sioux and Cheyenne warriors currently living on the reservation are stripped of their guns and ponies. Adding to the insult, the army chooses to give these confiscated horses to the Pawnee tribe—a major enemy of the Sioux—which has aligned with the United States.

Crazy Horse and Sitting Bull are angered by Red Cloud's capitulation and refuse to go to the reservation. They decide to winter far to the north, as they have throughout their lifetimes. At the end of September, Sitting Bull leads almost five hundred warriors and their families toward Canada. He will spend the winter going back and forth across the border into "Grandmother's Country," as the Sioux call the land controlled by Great Britain's Queen Victoria.

The band led by Crazy Horse now has fewer than three hundred lodges, and heads west, toward the Little Bighorn. By early November, Crazy Horse has imposed Sioux dominance over the region by raiding a Crow village and taking many scalps from the tribe's long-time enemy. Among the dead is a woman whose husband swears revenge.

Adding to Crazy Horse's troubles is the terrible news that the U.S. Army is building a new fort in this region. Although it is not yet completed, a force of cavalry and infantry under the command of Colonel Nelson Miles has already arrived. The Indians call Miles "Bear Coat," due to his preference for wearing a fur garment on cold days. He has been specifically tasked by the government with hunting down Sitting Bull and Crazy Horse. A second force led by a now resupplied General Crook marches north from Fort Fetterman to join the search for the legendary chiefs.

But while the Sioux are keeping a close watch on the soldiers, they are not overly concerned. It is well known that the Americans have no stomach for winter warfare and will remain sheltered in their stockades until the green grass returns. In this way, the tribes can live off the supplies of buffalo and game they have stored for those hard months, spending the winter in peace after a summer of combat.

Or so they think.

＊

The U.S. Army is relentless. The combined forces of Crook and Miles do not remain in their forts through the heavy snows and subzero temperatures. Instead, they ruthlessly seek out Indian encampments, using reservation warriors from the Oglala, Arapaho, and Cheyenne bands as scouts. Sitting Bull has now fled to the safety of Canada, where Indians are left alone. That allows Miles and Crook to focus their attention on Crazy Horse. The war chief is weary. Game is scarce as winter comes early, and ammunition stores are low after a long summer of warfare. Many of his warriors now talk of leaving for the reservation in order that their families might be fed. On November 19, 1876, a small band of Sioux does just that. Crazy Horse feels betrayed but does not try to stop them.

Almost a week later, General Crook strikes a savage blow. He and his men stumble upon the Cheyenne encampment of Chief Dull Knife in their search for Crazy Horse. The village is burned to the ground, depriving the Cheyenne of food and warmth. Forty Indians die. Seven hundred ponies are captured. But for the survivors, the worst is yet to come. After the soldiers ride away, Dull Knife and his people march through the snow in search of Crazy Horse's village, which represents their only hope of survival. The cold is so intense that ponies are disemboweled each night, so that infants might be stuffed inside the body cavities for warmth. Elderly tribe members then place their feet and hands in the entrails to avoid frostbite. By the time the Cheyenne finally find Crazy Horse eleven days later, frostbite has turned many of their fingers, toes, and noses black. Others have frozen to death. Crazy Horse welcomes Dull Knife and his people, offering them food and warm tepees in which to sleep after so many nights in the open. But the new arrivals place a strain on the war chief's food supplies and are in no condition to move at a moment's notice. With General Crook searching for him from the south, and Colonel Miles approaching from the north, Crazy Horse knows he may have to abandon a campsite instantly.

Sensing but not understanding Crazy Horse's stern demeanor, some Cheyenne privately complain the war chief cares little for their welfare. Other Indians, even those of his own Oglala band, complain Crazy Horse has become paranoid.

It is the hardest time Crazy Horse has ever known. It is too late to go north to Canada, and crossing the Rocky Mountains to the west in winter is impossible. The Sioux know that the Nez Percé tribe is on the other side of the Rockies and remains a potent fighting force. But linking up with them is a fantasy.

※

Sometime in mid-December, Crazy Horse's concerns for his starving band lead him to a bad decision. Crazy Horse rides with a small group of fellow chiefs and warriors to a hilltop overlooking the newly built Fort Keogh. He has chosen not to go onto the reservation but will allow those who wish to leave to do so. As Crazy Horse observes from the overlook, eight chiefs and warriors trot their horses down to the fort. The contingent flies a white flag of truce atop a battle lance.

The gates to Fort Keogh are pulled open. The Sioux halt their ponies and await the arrival of "Bear Coat" so they might parlay. But Colonel Nelson Miles does not appear.

He remains safely inside the fort because his looking glass shows no sign of Crazy Horse, the man Miles wishes to capture more than any other. So instead of riding forth himself, the colonel allows his Crow scouts to confront the Sioux. These warriors still remember Crazy Horse's raid on their village six weeks ago, and without warning they attack the Indians who are flying the white flag.

They kill five of the surrendering Sioux, sending the other three riding hard to escape.

Returning to camp, Crazy Horse orders the immediate movement of the village. It is only a matter of time before the Crow lead the bluecoats to their location. The tribe does as they are told, but wearily. The constant winter movement is grinding on Crazy Horse's band. This is not the peaceful winter of years past but a prolonged series of flights to escape the relentless American pursuit. And even as the Indians endure frostbite and starvation, the Americans return to the hearths and hot meals of their fort between engagements.

On December 25, Christmas Day, thirteen Sioux warriors and their families slip away from Crazy Horse's band, headed to the reservation. But this time, Crazy Horse hunts them down and forces them to return. This change in policy is enacted to maintain some semblance of tribal unity. As punishment for the act of foolishness, Crazy Horse shoots their horses and takes their guns, shattering what little morale his people have left. The following morning, some warriors revolt against the leadership of Crazy Horse. But once again, the war chief deploys warriors loyal to him to end the rebellion.

Crazy Horse knows this cannot continue. The pressure is becoming unbearable. So the war chief turns to his only solution: attack.

※

The Wolf Mountains are well known to Crazy Horse. Six months ago, in the days before killing Custer, he rode through here as part of the massive Indian caravan headed to camp on the Little Bighorn. These are the mountains in which Custer's scouts first spied the massive Indian village on the morning of that great battle. And it is here, on January 8, 1877, that Colonel Nelson Miles and his combined cavalry and infantry force spend the night, in yet another attempt to find Crazy Horse.

At 7:00 a.m., the pale light of a winter dawn finally limning the morning sky, Crazy Horse and a combined band of Sioux and Cheyenne warriors open fire on the troops. But the attack is not a surprise. Army scouts noticed the Cheyenne moving into position thirty minutes ago. So, Colonel Miles has had time to arrange his men and cannon into defensive positions. The American soldiers wear heavy buffalo robes to protect them from the cold, and they move clumsily through the rocky terrain.

Crazy Horse commands the heights, giving him tactical advantage. He sends warriors galloping into the army camp, firing their Winchesters at full ride. Miles responds by opening fire with his cannon, sending shrapnel into warriors and ponies. Crazy Horse himself is not shot, but his horse dies under him, and the great war chief must fight on foot. After a few minutes, he pulls back from the battlefield, joining a group of warriors taking aim on the soldiers from the ridgeline. Snow begins falling. Were it not for the cannon, an Indian victory would be assured. But as things stand four hours into the fight, Crazy Horse and his warriors clearly have the advantage. When the Americans race up the hillside to assault Crazy Horse's position, he leads a counterattack on foot, personally running into the soldiers and fighting hand to hand. Swirling snow envelops the battle, making it hard for either side to see.

By noon the fight ends in a draw. Crazy Horse and his men ride away. Colonel Miles and his troops remain in the mountains for two days, then return to Fort Keogh, confident that they will soon capture the fugitive Sioux leader.

That is paramount, because Miles may soon have another battle farther to the west. The U.S. government is targeting a tribe known as the Nez Percé for submission. The Indians are led by Chief Joseph and at this point are about three hundred miles away. But Miles cannot do anything until the Sioux are pacified.

One week later, on January 15, Sitting Bull and his band ride into the camp of Crazy Horse. The two have been apart for six weeks, and the sight of a thousand assembled warriors is cause for massive celebration among the depleted Sioux.

Now age forty-four, Sitting Bull is the supreme leader of all the Sioux bands. He knows the thirty-five-year-old Crazy Horse is not an inspiring leader off the battlefield. Sitting Bull also knows there is not enough food to support more than a thousand Indians during these winter months. And he cannot attack the whites, for his ammunition is almost nonexistent. After resting and consultation

Sitting Bull decides to return to Canada with the majority of the Sioux tribe.

Crazy Horse decides to stay west of the Black Hills and try to elude capture. His own mother and father are among the elderly tribe members for whom he is responsible. Making matters even worse, his wife, Black Shawl, endures spells of violent coughing that cause her to spit up blood.

On April 27, 1877, Chief Red Cloud, now a longtime citizen of the reservation, is sent by the Americans to meet with Crazy Horse. The war chief is promised a reservation of his own in the Powder River country, as long as he surrenders his weapons and ponies.

Knowing he cannot hold out against the U.S. government much longer, Crazy Horse finally surrenders the Oglala Sioux band at Fort Robinson, Nebraska.

✵

It is late August and the Sioux are mostly pacified, although Sitting Bull remains at large. The U.S. Army turns its attention to the Nez Percé tribe under the charismatic leader Chief Joseph. At the time, there are rumors on the Red Cloud reservation that Crazy Horse is already weary of such a restricted lifestyle. The Sioux war chief is also angry that the army has rescinded an offer to allow Indians to hunt outside the reservation. Instead, army officers ask Crazy Horse if he would be willing to fight with them against Chief Joseph.

At first, Crazy Horse is reluctant. But after reflection, he attempts to strike a deal: if his warriors are allowed to hunt, he will fight until "all the Nez Percé are killed."

But there is a problem. Lieutenant William P. Clark is dependent on an interpreter, a longtime Indian scout named Frank Grouard. Apparently holding a grudge against Crazy Horse, Grouard lies and tells Clark that the war chief is vowing to "fight until not a white man is left."

Clark immediately wires his superiors, telling them Crazy Horse is on the verge of leading his warriors off the reservation, in order to go on the war path.

An alarmed General Crook quickly offers a reward of $300 for any man who kills Crazy Horse. Also, Crook orders two columns of U.S. Cavalry to ride toward the Sioux reservation in order to arrest the war chief. But Crazy Horse is already gone, galloping off to see friends on another reservation with his wife, whose tuberculosis is worsening.

The following day, Crazy Horse returns to Fort Robinson. He does not know soldiers are seeking to arrest him. As he dismounts, he is seized by Indians working for the army. He is then taken to a stockade. Crazy Horse is unsure of where he is going, but at the sight of barred windows, warriors in leg irons, and shackles hanging on the wall, he refuses to enter the jail.

"I won't go in there."

The guards cock their rifles, but Crazy Horse is quicker than they are. Using a wooden doorjamb as leverage, he propels his body backward into his captors. Then he pulls a small knife, but he is overcome by the guards. His arms are pulled tightly behind his back and he is subdued.

"Let me go," shouts the war chief. "Let me go."

As Crazy Horse is being led inside the stockade, he once again breaks free of his captors and runs toward the fort's parade ground.

"Kill the son of a bitch," yells one American officer.

A single jailhouse sentry stands between Crazy Horse and open ground. Private William Gentles, a forty-seven-year-old soldier born in County Tyrone, Ireland, levels his bayonet toward the war chief. His first jab catches on Crazy Horse's shirt, forcing the Indian to spin. Gentles thrusts again, this time into Crazy Horse's back, the blade slicing downward into the bowels and groin. A third jab pierces the war chief's right lung. Crazy Horse falls to the ground.

"Let me go," cries Crazy Horse. "You have got me hurt now."

But it is all over. Within hours, the great war chief is dead.

❈

Sitting Bull alone remains at large. But four years from now, in July 1881, his band just as famished and depleted as that of Crazy Horse, the supreme chief will finally agree to live on the reservation.

Distrusting Sitting Bull, and fearing he will incite unrest, the U.S. Army sends him down the Missouri River by steamboat and holds him in a military garrison for twenty months as a prisoner of war. Sitting Bull is then allowed to return to the Standing Rock Agency in the Dakota Territory in May 1883.

There he will stay until an incredible thing happens: Sitting Bull is recruited by the show-business entrepreneur William Cody, known as Buffalo Bill, to tour the country in a western show. The five-foot-tall sharpshooter Annie Oakley is also on that tour, and becomes so friendly with the supreme chief that he gives her the nickname "Little Sure Shot," which she will use the rest of her career.

By all accounts, Sitting Bull enjoys entertaining the white man, earning $50 per week for his efforts.* After four months of touring, the supreme war chief finally arrives back at Standing Rock Agency in 1885. But tension almost immediately develops between Sitting Bull and the white reservation agent, a forty-three-year-old Canadian-American named James McLaughlin, who chafes at the authority Sioux bands still give Sitting Bull.

This tension will soon lead to violence.

※

Farther west, in a land the Indians call the Wallowa Valley, where buffalo and game still roam, and where the white man is just beginning to settle, the last free Indian tribe is on the run.

The U.S. Government is attempting to force the Nez Percé band under their leader, Chief Joseph, to give up their tribal lands and relocate to a reservation hundreds of miles away. Once again, the United States is violating a long-standing treaty with a Native American tribe by coercing the Nez Percé to give up their freedom.

So it is that just one month after the murder of Crazy Horse, the blue coats are chasing Chief Joseph and his band—who must now face the might of the U.S. Army all by themselves.

---

* Roughly $1,500 in modern currency.

Chapter Twenty-Six

The tribal lands are calm, but not for much longer.

Chief Joseph, the thirty-seven-year-old leader of the Nez Percé tribe, looks down on five of his warriors riding forth to meet a detachment of U.S. soldiers under the white flag of truce. But Joseph knows not to trust the white man, and so he is hiding in the rocks of the canyon along with seventy-five of his warriors.

Joseph's instincts are correct. Without warning, a civilian riding with the soldiers opens fire on the warriors. It is a fatal mistake. Lead and arrows rain down on the Americans. The Battle of White Bird Canyon is over quickly—with thirty-four soldiers lying dead. Not a single Nez Percé is killed.

※

Chief Joseph knows he is in trouble. His entire band numbers fewer than eight hundred—some of whom are undisciplined killers. Just three days ago, without Joseph's approval, a group of young Nez Percé warriors slaughtered eighteen white settlers who had recently begun homesteading. The defenseless settlers were mutilated in a particularly gruesome way because the Indians were furious that they had been ordered to leave their lands. The atrocity gave the white power structure all the credibility it needed to destroy the Nez Percé.

Chief Joseph's tribe is predominantly peaceful, experts at breeding spotted Appaloosa horses, fond of roaming the grasslands and mountains they call home. The Nez Percé first encountered Americans back in 1805, when the Lewis and Clark Expedition traveled through their homeland. They actually welcomed the famished explorers, treating them to a feast of buffalo and salmon. It was French-Canadian fur trappers who labeled the band Nez Percé—"pierced nose"—for reasons that remain unclear. And while that is the name outsiders call the tribe, it still refers to itself as the Nimipu—"the real people."

Chief Joseph has been an effective leader of his tribe. Since the death of his father, Joseph the Elder, six years ago, he has been trying to negotiate with the whites to keep at least a portion of the Nez Percé ancestral lands. But after the massacre of the sixteen settlers, Joseph knew the army would soon come seeking revenge. In fact, his scouts soon reported that more than one hundred bluecoats were already approaching from the north.

The chief knows he cannot fight the white man alone. His force is greatly outnumbered, burdened by the presence of many women and children. In addition, the Nez Percé have very few guns and even less ammunition and must fight mostly with bows and arrows. Desperately seeking peace, but also preparing for war, Chief Joseph hoped that the five warriors flying a white flag could negotiate.

He was wrong.

᛭

It was President Grant who signed an executive order in 1873 granting the Wallowa Valley to the Nez Percé for the "rest of their natural lives." But Grant is now gone, replaced by Rutherford B. Hayes, a man with little sympathy for the Native Americans. President Hayes has allowed the whites to move into the Oregon and Idaho Territories and is forcing all Indians to live on reservations. In order to accomplish that, the army has appointed General O. O. Howard to subjugate Joseph and his tribe.

It will not matter that Chief Joseph and his people sought peace today. Howard knows the Nez Percé have massacred homesteaders, and that cannot be allowed to stand. So Joseph has just one choice: he and his tribe must run.

❖

"Joseph and his band . . . [are] continuing his retreat toward British Columbia," writes General Oliver Otis Howard in a telegram to his superior officer, General William Tecumseh Sherman. Howard is a Civil War veteran and a staunch advocate that Native Americans must live on reservations, separate from white people.

"We believe he is aiming at refuge with Sitting Bull. He is traveling with women and children and wounded at a rate of twenty-five miles per day."

Howard knows Chief Joseph well. The one-armed forty-six-year-old general is a man who has experienced failure. He was humbled by the Confederates at the Battle of Gettysburg, then spent the years following the Civil War trying to bring about racial equality in the South. Even though he was not successful, his efforts would lead to the founding of a university in Washington bearing his name. However, Howard continues on a mission. The evangelical Christian and married father of seven children now seeks redemption and success in the Northwest, trying to bring Chief Joseph's tribe onto the reservation peacefully.

But Howard's negotiations with Chief Joseph have proven tricky. At one time, the general actually believed the Nez Percé had a valid claim to their lands and should not be moved onto the reservation. But all that changed in the aftermath of the Battle of the Little Bighorn. Howard began to treat Chief Joseph with contempt, seeing Native Americans as a threat rather than an ally. Joseph's refusal to move onto the reservation became a personal insult to Howard. In the days after the Battle at White Bird Canyon the general believes he has trapped Chief Joseph on the banks of the Salmon River. But that is not the case, as the Nez Percé taunt him from the opposite shore, then successfully flee east—ironically, in the direction of the Little Bighorn battlefield.

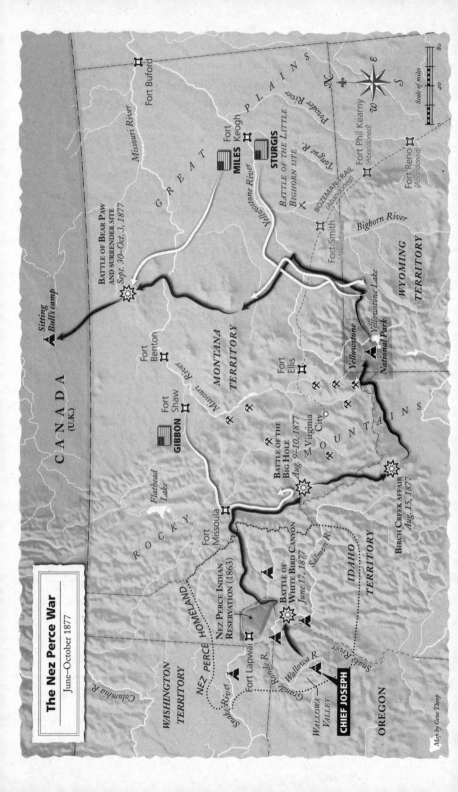

The Nez Perce War
June–October 1877

Map by Gene Thorp

CANADA (U.K.)

Sitting Bull's camp

BATTLE OF BEAR PAW
AND SURRENDER SITE
Sept. 30–Oct. 3, 1877

GREAT PLAINS

Missouri River

Fort Buford

Fort Benton

Fort Shaw

MONTANA TERRITORY

Fort Keogh

MILES

STURGIS

BATTLE OF THE LITTLE
BIGHORN site

Tongue R.

Powder River

Fort Phil Kearny
(Abandoned)

Fort Reno
(Abandoned)

BOZEMAN TRAIL
(Abandoned)

Fort Smith
(Abandoned)

Bighorn River

WYOMING
TERRITORY

GIBBON

Missouri River

Flathead
Lake

ROCKY

Fort Missoula

BATTLE OF THE
BIG HOLE
Aug. 9–10, 1877

MOUNTAINS

Fort Ellis

Virginia
City

Yellowstone River

Yellowstone

Yellowstone
National Park

Yellowstone Lake

BIRCH CREEK affair
Aug. 15, 1877

NEZ PERCE HOMELAND

NEZ PERCE INDIAN
RESERVATION (1863)

Fort Lapwai

BATTLE OF
WHITE BIRD CANYON
June 17, 1877

Salmon R.

IDAHO
TERRITORY

WASHINGTON
TERRITORY

Columbia R.

Snake River

Grande Ronde R.

Wallowa R.

WALLOWA
VALLEY

CHIEF JOSEPH

OREGON

Scale of miles
0   40   80

N E W S

The chase continues on through July and into August. Joseph is proving himself a wily adversary, utilizing complex battlefield tactics to frustrate the Americans time and again. The Nez Percé are not moving forward in an attempt to retake land—rather, they continue to retreat. Eventually, Joseph would like to link up with Sitting Bull in Canada.

In addition to Howard's mounted force, an American unit under the command of Colonel John Gibbon begins tracking Chief Joseph and his people in July. On the morning of August 10, Gibbon's men strike, surprising the Nez Percé in their encampment, killing eighty—mostly women and children. Chief Joseph soon counterattacks—wounding Gibbon and decimating his force. The hunt for Chief Joseph is over for Gibbons and his men. They march home to Fort Shaw in the Montana Territory.

General Howard is furious. With every passing day, his sense of personal humiliation about being bested by his adversary, Chief Joseph, grows. Six days after the battle with Gibbon, that outrage intensifies when the Nez Percé steal all of Howard's horses and pack animals in a surprise raid. It seems impossible, but fewer than three hundred warriors are on the verge of defeating more than two thousand U.S. soldiers under Howard's command.

On August 22, Chief Joseph leads his tribe into a region the United States recently branded Yellowstone National Park. Coincidentally, General William Sherman and some aides are camping there as well on this late-summer day. Joseph has now become national news. In the year since George Custer and his men were massacred, the American public's anger has somewhat abated. With almost every American Indian tribe now on a reservation, the public perceives that the wars are over. However, there is some sympathy for Chief Joseph, whose retreat will eventually be a journey of more than a thousand miles.

From his campsite in Yellowstone, a furious General Sherman orders Colonel Samuel Sturgis and the Seventh Cavalry to get Chief Joseph. Colonel Nelson Miles, so recently responsible for the surrender of Crazy Horse, is also involved, traveling from Fort Keogh to cut off Joseph's retreat into Canada.

By late September a confrontation is near.

Just forty miles short of the Canadian border, Chief Joseph's retreat is undone by bad weather and lack of food to feed his people. His tribe's horses are bony and lame. The Nez Percé have traveled eighteen hundred circuitous miles. They have fought five major battles against the whites, winning three. U.S. casualties number 126 dead, while the Nez Percé have lost 151 warriors.

A now bitter General Howard has given chase for almost a hundred days, but it is Colonel Miles who knows the glory of finally ending Chief Joseph's flight.

In his report to the secretary of war, Miles will write: "The Nez Percés are the boldest men and best marksmen of any Indians I have ever encountered, and Chief Joseph is a man of more sagacity and intelligence than any Indian I have ever met; he counseled against the war, and against the usual cruelties practiced by Indians, and is far more humane than such Indians as Crazy Horse and Sitting Bull."

By the time his flight comes to an end, Joseph's skillful retreat has earned him the nickname "the Red Napoleon" in the American press. Even General Sherman, a master of military strategy in his own right, marvels at the Nez Percé's mastery of the battlefield. "The Indians throughout displayed a courage and skill that elicited universal praise," Sherman noted. "They fought with almost scientific skill, using advance and rear guards, skirmish lines, and field fortifications."

Five weeks after entering Yellowstone, Joseph agrees to meet with Nelson Miles. The Nez Percé are surrounded in a place called Bear Paw but refuse to lay down their arms. As negotiations begin, thirty warriors slip away under cover of darkness. Three days later, they are warmly welcomed by Sitting Bull and his Hunkpapa Sioux band in Canada.

Joseph knows he could also escape. But gaining his personal freedom while abandoning his tribe would forever compromise his leadership. Instead, he allows himself to be considered a prisoner of war. After a five-day negotiation, Chief Joseph agrees to Miles's terms of unconditional surrender.

Chief Joseph surrenders to Generals Miles and Howard, 1877.

"I am tired of fighting," Chief Joseph says. "It is cold and we have no blankets. The little children are freezing to death. My people, some of them, have run away to the hills, and have no blankets, no food; no one knows where they are—perhaps freezing to death. I want to have time to look for my children and see how many of them I can find. Maybe I shall find them among the dead. Hear me, my chiefs: I am tired. My heart is sick and sad.

"From where the sun now stands, I will fight no more forever."

❋

The date the Nez Percé lose their freedom is October 5, 1877.

There are now no more powerful Indian nations roaming free in the United States.

Afterword

Nine years after Chief Joseph surrenders, an Apache warrior named **Geronimo** bolts the reservation in Arizona. In addition to being a great fighter, Geronimo is also considered a medicine man for his spirituality and abilities as a healer. For the past decade, Geronimo has periodically done this, leading warriors on raids into Mexico to plunder and kill.

At first, U.S. authorities looked the other way, but now Geronimo is being pursued by Lieutenant Charles Bare Gatewood, called "Big Nose" by the Indians.

Geronimo is fifty-eight years old. As a younger man, he waged war alongside the great Chiricahua chiefs Cochise and Mangas Coloradas. Geronimo well remembers the glory days of Apache Pass, before the whites intruded and built the garrison known as Fort Bowie atop that sacred land. He respects the treaty Cochise made with the Americans but, like many Apache, Geronimo believes Mexicans are still legitimate targets.

About thirty years ago, in 1858, the Apache medicine man lost a wife and three children when the Mexican Army retaliated against his tribe. For that reason, he still seeks vengeance: "I have killed many Mexicans," he will write in his autobiography. "I do not know how many, for frequently I did not count them."

Geronimo has proved so elusive to U.S. troops that Nelson Miles, who has been promoted from colonel to general, is now in charge of capturing him. Miles has directed Lieutenant Gatewood to stalk the Apache. By August 1886, Geronimo's followers have dwindled to fewer than forty men, women, and children, and he has run out of food and supplies. Like Chief Joseph, Geronimo knows it is futile to keep running. So on September 4, he surrenders to Lieutenant Gatewood.

Fearing Geronimo's charisma among the Apache already on the reservation, the army designates him a prisoner of war and sends him by train to Fort Sam Houston, Texas. From there, he goes to another military prison at Fort Pickens in Pensacola, Florida, then finally to Fort Sill, Oklahoma. All the while, Geronimo enjoys great celebrity throughout the United States and, possibly because of bribes, the military frequently allows him to make personal appearances with Buffalo Bill's Wild West Show. Incredibly, Geronimo even takes part in the inaugural parade of President Teddy Roosevelt in 1905, the same year he writes his autobiography. In February 1909, at age seventy-nine, Geronimo is thrown from a horse while in U.S. custody. He dies shortly afterward. According to his son, his last words were these: "I should never have surrendered. I should have fought until I was the last man alive."

Geronimo is buried at Fort Sill, Oklahoma.

❋

As with Geronimo, **Sitting Bull** was never comfortable on a reservation. Also like the Apache, Sitting Bull toured with Wild Bill Cody and made money doing so.

But upon returning to the reservation in the Dakota Territory, Sitting Bull was confronted with the vengeful reservation agent James McLaughlin. Tension between the two men reaches critical mass when a new religious movement known as the Ghost Dance spreads through the various Indian reservations of the Dakota Territory. The Ghost Dance allows Indians to commune with dead relatives and promises that white settlers would leave tribal lands forever, bringing about a return to Native American superiority.

Sitting Bull does not take part in the Ghost Dance movement, but he openly allows its practitioners to settle near his camp. On December 14, 1890, fearing that Sitting Bull will soon leave the

Standing Rock reservation to spread the Ghost Dance movement, Agent McLaughlin orders tribal police to arrest the supreme chief.

At 5:30 the next morning, thirty-nine Indians working for the U.S. government surround Sitting Bull's home. Word travels around the reservation that he is to be arrested, causing other tribe members to come to his aid. A confrontation ensues—and a Sioux chief named Catch-the-Bear shoots his rifle at a member of the tribal police. Fire is returned, and Sitting Bull is shot in the chest. He dies instantly.

Sitting Bull was initially buried at Fort Yates in North Dakota. In 1953, his body was exhumed by his descendants and relocated to Mobridge, South Dakota. A monument to Sitting Bull now marks his burial spot.

※

Just two weeks after Sitting Bull's death, on December 28, 1890, soldiers of the U.S. Seventh Cavalry—the same mounted regiment once commanded by General George Custer—escort 350 Cheyenne and Sioux warriors with their dependents to a place called Wounded Knee Creek in the Dakota Territory. The Indians are being moved to prevent their participation in the Ghost Dance movement. The Sioux and Cheyenne are restive, not happy about the relocation.

The following morning, more soldiers arrive and surround the Wounded Knee Creek encampment. They are heavily armed. The arsenal includes an M1875 mountain gun artillery cannon. The soldiers enter the camp to disarm the Indians.

As the story goes, a deaf Indian is confused by the disarmament order and fires at the soldiers. Chaos breaks out. Officers in charge lose all control. U.S. soldiers go on a killing rampage that results in the deaths of an estimated three hundred Sioux and Cheyenne.

An eyewitness describes the horror this way: "The women as they were fleeing with their babes were killed together, shot right through. . . . Little boys . . . came out of their places of refuge, and as soon as they came in sight a number of soldiers surrounded them and butchered them there."

The incident is still today lamented by Native Americans all over the country. None of the soldiers were brought up on charges. The Indians were buried at the Wounded Knee site, where a memorial marks the location.

※

On March 2, 1889, **President Grover Cleveland**, who considered Native Americans a nuisance, signs into law the Indian Appropriations Act. That sets the stage for what will become known as the Oklahoma Land Rush. With the stroke of a presidential pen, the prairielands once termed "Indian Territory" are now open to white settlement, with Congress stripping two million acres from Native American tribes. At precisely noon on April 2, 1889, a cannon sounds on the Oklahoma plains, and an estimated fifty thousand men, women, and children rush forth to claim Indian land as their own. Traveling by wagon, by bicycle, by horse, and on foot, whites quickly stake off plots of land and file claims of ownership. The Oklahoma "Sooners" is a nickname given to those who cheat and jump the gun, thereby obtaining by illegal means the most preferred properties. In 1907, Oklahoma is eventually admitted as the forty-sixth state in the Union, ending the term "Indian Territories" forever.

※

The great Sauk leader **Blackhawk** died from illness on October 3, 1838, at age seventy-one. He was buried on the farm of his friend James Jordan on the north bank of the Des Moines River in Davis County. In July 1839, his remains were stolen, leading to years of dislocation. Finally, Blackhawk's sons Nashashuk and Gamesett located the remains and appealed to Governor Robert Lucas of the Iowa Territory, who used his influence to bring the bones to security in his offices in Burlington.

The Chicago Blackhawks of the National Hockey League are named after Blackhawk. The team's first owner, Frederic McLaughlin, was a major with the 86th Infantry Division during World War I—nicknamed the "Black Hawk Division." McLaughlin chose the same name when he became owner of the NHL hockey franchise in 1926.

❈

Quanah Parker, the Comanche chief, dies on February 23, 1911, at age sixty-six. He prospered in the years after the Comanche were ordered to the reservation in Oklahoma. Parker's home still exists just outside the small town of Cache and is listed on the National Register of Historic Places. Quanah was a founder of the Native American Church, which combines Christianity and Native American rituals, among them the use of peyote to see visions. Director John Ford's 1956 Western film *The Searchers* is based on the Comanche abduction of his mother, **Cynthia Parker**. John Wayne's character in the film is based on James W. Parker, the uncle who searched tirelessly to bring Cynthia home. Cynthia Parker is believed to have died in 1871. She was buried in Poynor, Texas.

Like Geronimo, Quanah Parker is buried at Fort Sill, Oklahoma. In 1957, Cynthia Parker's remains are relocated to the Fort Sill Post Cemetery so that she might rest near her son.

❈

Upon his surrender in 1877, **Chief Joseph** had hoped his tribe might return to their lands in Oregon's Wallowa Valley. Instead, they were taken by train to Fort Leavenworth, Kansas, where they were held as prisoners of war for eight months. The Nez Percé were then relocated to the Indian Territory in Oklahoma, where they remained until 1885. Finally, the tribe is allowed to return to the Pacific Northwest, there to settle on a reservation. Chief Joseph becomes an impassioned spokesman for the Native American cause, visiting Washington to speak to several presidents about the welfare of Indians. Joseph dies on September 21, 1904, at the age of sixty-four. He is buried in Nespelem, Washington.

❈

Between the Creek Wars and the closing of the American frontier, twenty U.S. presidents participated in policy decisions concerning Native Americans. However, the actions of **President Ulysses S. Grant** stand above all others, both for his failed "peace policy" and his decision to use overwhelming military force as a means of stealing the Black Hills. Grant left office in 1877, shortly before the murder of Crazy Horse and the flight of Chief Joseph. He then undertook a two-and-a-half-year world tour with his wife, Julia. Upon their return, Grant unsuccessfully seeks the Republican nomination for the presidency in 1880. Never good with money, Grant soon finds himself penniless. In 1884, the lifelong smoker complains of a sore throat, which is diagnosed as cancer. As his health fails, U. S. Grant writes his memoirs with the help of author Mark Twain. He dies on July 23, 1885, just days after completing the book. He and Julia Grant are buried in Grant's Tomb, located in Riverside Park in Upper Manhattan.*

❋

Shortly after the death of **General George Armstrong Custer**, his widow began a vigorous campaign to clear his name from accusations that he was responsible for the Little Bighorn massacre. **Libbie Custer** cooperated in the writing of the first Custer biography, then later writes three bestselling books about her own life. Her literary success leads to affluence. She dies in 1933 at the age of ninety, having never remarried.

General Custer was laid to rest where he fell on the Little Bighorn battlefield, his body wrapped in blankets by a U.S. military burial detail. Animals soon desecrated the grave, scattering his bones. On October 10, 1877, Custer's remains were reinterred with full military honors at the West Point Cemetery in New York. Upon Mrs. Custer's death, she is buried alongside her husband.

❋

In 1927, just fifty years after the U.S. government forced the tribes of the Northern Plains to give up the Black Hills, sculptor Gutzon Borglum begins detonating 450,000 tons of granite from the face of a mountainside in that same region. Borglum then begins to carve

---

* The couple are buried within twin red granite sarcophagi inside the tomb, which is the largest mausoleum in North America.

oversize likenesses of U.S. presidents George Washington, Abraham Lincoln, Theodore Roosevelt, and Thomas Jefferson into the remaining stone. To this day, many Native Americans are offended by what is known as Mount Rushmore, believing it desecrates sacred tribal land while simultaneously honoring the U.S. government, which stole it from the Indians.

Members of the Sioux nation petition Borglum to also carve the profile of **Crazy Horse** alongside the presidents on Mount Rushmore in South Dakota. The sculptor does not respond to the written request. Not to be denied, the Sioux commission a separate structure devoted solely to Crazy Horse. Work begins in 1948. At this point, construction is incomplete.

The actual grave site of **Crazy Horse** remains unclear. The morning after his death in 1877, the war chief's remains were given over to his parents, who placed them on burial scaffolding open to the elements. One month later, the Oglala Sioux were relocated to a new reservation, and once again Crazy Horse's parents took responsibility for his remains. This time, they were removed to a hidden location. Popular legend holds that the war chief's heart and bones are buried at the site of the Wounded Knee Massacre on the Pine Ridge Lakota Reservation in South Dakota.

※

According to the U.S. Census of 1890, the Native American population numbers 248,253. In 1850, Indians were counted at 400,764. After the census of 1890, the superintendent of the survey, Robert Percival Porter, declares the American frontier officially closed. From the Atlantic to the Pacific, American Indian tribes no longer enjoy their traditional ways of life, almost all confined instead to government-run reservations.

With Porter's pronouncement, the "sea to shining sea" mandate first embraced by **President James Monroe** is complete.

SOURCES

The research process for a *Killing* book is largely the same for each addition to the series. The first step is a broad investigation of the subject matter. Next comes the addition of detail through archives, documents, and previous historical works specific to the topic. The focus then shifts to sentence-by-sentence details about the story's finer points, such as the caliber of a weapon or the type of food an individual might eat for breakfast. Facts are checked and cross-checked, searching for historical inconsistencies.

In the case of *Killing Crazy Horse*, however, one aspect of research took on a greater significance than ever before: travel. The central thesis of this book is the struggle for land. Visiting these places in person became even more vital than in any of the previous eight *Killing* books.

Seeing the landscape is always a critical part of historical research. Walking the grounds where an event of significance took place is a great help in describing the scene while writing. Thankfully, many of the locations in *Killing Crazy Horse* are not just open to the public but also protected by the National Park Service and are thus unspoiled by development. Forts, monuments, and memorials are scattered all across the United States, there to be discovered, each telling a story of its own unique role in the conflict between Native Americans and white settlers.

The authors have sought to describe the various historical land-scapes in vivid fashion, but words can only go so far. The reader is highly encouraged to undertake their own road trip to see these marvels. Walking the battlefields at Fort Mims, Apache Pass, the site of the Fetterman massacre, or the Battle of the Little Bighorn, to name a few, unveils a whole new level of emotion to the story, thanks to the beauty of the topography and how military strategy can be understood in its light. The sweep of the landscape is breathtaking, and in the particular case of the Fetterman site, the appreciation for Crazy Horse's daring act of deception becomes much more tangible.

The areas in between are just as vital. To drive the wide-open spaces of Texas, New Mexico, and Arizona offers a much greater appreciation for Comanche horsemanship. The stark plains also offer a glimpse of how isolating life must have felt to members of the U.S. Cavalry posted on the windswept prairies, and a full understanding how a tribal band could leave the reservation and simply disappear into the wilderness.

In addition to archives, newspapers, and various Native American tribal websites, the authors have leaned on previous scholarship, a sampling of which can be found in the following bibliography.

Bibliography

Agonito, Joseph. *Brave Hearts: Indian Women of the Plains.*

Ambrose, Stephen E. *Crazy Horse and Custer: The Parallel Lives of Two American Warriors.*

Babcock, Matthew. *Apache Adaptation to Hispanic Rule.*

Bray, Kingsley M. *Crazy Horse: A Lakota Life.*

Brown, Dee. *The American West.*

———. *Bury My Heart at Wounded Knee: An Indian History of the American West.*

Caughey, John Walton. *McGillivray of the Creeks.*

Confer, Clarissa W. *Daily Life During the Indian Wars.*

Connell, Evan S. *Son of the Morning Star: Custer and the Little Bighorn.*

Custer, Elizabeth Bacon. *Boots and Saddles; or, Life in Dakota with General Custer.*

Dixon, Billy. *Life and Adventures of "Billy" Dixon, of Adobe Walls, Texas Panhandle.*

Donovan, Jim. *Custer and the Little Bighorn: The Man, the Mystery, the Myth.*

Eggleston, George Cary. *Red Eagle and the Wars with the Creek Indians of Alabama.*

Eisenhower, John S. D. *Agent of Destiny: The Life and Times of General Winfield Scott.*

Exley, Jo Ella Powell. *Frontier Blood: The Saga of the Parker Family.*

Fehrenbach, T. R. *Comanches: The History of a People.*

Frankel, Glenn. *The Searchers: The Making of an American Legend.*

Gaines, George Strother. *The Reminiscences of George Strother Gaines: Pioneer and Statesman of Early Alabama and Mississippi, 1805–1843.*

Gray, John S. *Centennial Campaign: The Sioux War of 1876.*

———. *Custer's Last Campaign: Mitch Boyer and the Little Bighorn Reconstructed.*

Gwynne, S. C. *Empire of the Summer Moon: Quanah Parker and the Rise and Fall of the Comanches, the Most Powerful Indian Tribe in American History.*

Hardoff, Richard G. *Washita Memories: Eyewitness Views of Custer's Attack on Black Kettle's Village.*

Hatch, Thom. *The Last Days of George Armstrong Custer: The True Story of the Battle of the Little Bighorn.*

Hutton, Paul Andrew. *The Custer Reader.*

———. *Phil Sheridan and His Army.*

Janin, Hunt, and Ursula Carlson. *Trails of Historic New Mexico: Routes Used by Indian, Spanish and American Travelers Through 1886.*

Johnson, Robert Underwood, and Clarence Clough Buel. *Battles and Leaders of the Civil War*, vol. 3: *The Tide Shifts.*

Journal of the Military Service Institution of the United States, vol. 49 (July–Dec. 1911).

Jung, Patrick J. *The Black Hawk War of 1832.*

Kazanjian, Howard, and Chris Enss. *None Wounded, None Missing, All Dead: The Story of Elizabeth Bacon Custer.*

La Vere, David. *The Texas Indians.*

Lubetkin, M. John. *Jay Cooke's Gamble: The Northern Pacific Railroad, the Sioux, and the Panic of 1873.*

Monnett, John H. *Where a Hundred Soldiers Were Killed: The Struggle for the Powder River Country and the Making of the Fetterman Myth.*

Mort, Terry. *Thieves' Road: The Black Hills Betrayal and Custer's Path to Little Bighorn.*

Parker, Watson. *Deadwood: The Golden Years.*

Parton, James. *Life of Andrew Jackson*.

Perdue, Theda, and Michael D. Green. *The Cherokee Nation and the Trail of Tears*.

Philbrick, Nathaniel. *The Last Stand: Custer, Sitting Bull, and the Battle of the Little Bighorn*.

Rosa, Joseph G. *They Called Him Wild Bill: The Life and Adventures of James Butler Hickok*.

Ross, Jeffrey Ian, ed. *American Indians at Risk*.

Smith, Shannon D. *Give Me Eighty Men: Women and the Myth of the Fetterman Fight*.

Stiles, T. J. *Custer's Trials: A Life on the Frontier of a New America*.

Sweeney, Edwin R. *Cochise: Chiricahua Apache Chief*.

————. *From Cochise to Geronimo: The Chiricahua Apaches, 1874–1886*.

————. *Mangas Coloradas: Chief of the Chiricahua Apaches*.

Trask, Kerry A. *Blackhawk: The Battle for the Heart of America*.

Turner, Thadd. *Wild Bill Hickok: Deadwood City—End of Trail*.

Utley, Robert M. *The Lance and the Shield: The Life and Times of Sitting Bull*.

Vaughn, J. W. *Indian Fights: New Facts on Seven Encounters*.

Wagner, Frederic C., III. *Participants in the Battle of the Little Bighorn: A Biographical Dictionary of Sioux, Cheyenne and United States Military Personnel*.

Walker, Paul D. *The Cavalry Battle That Saved the Union: Custer vs. Stuart at Gettysburg*.

Wallace, Ernest, and E. Adamson Hoebel. *The Comanches: Lords of the South Plains*.

Williams, Albert E. *Black Warriors: Unique Units and Individuals*.

Young, John Russell. *Around the World with General Grant*, vol. 2: *A Narrative of the Visit of General U. S. Grant*.

Acknowledgments

Thanks to Steve Rubin for his vision and encouragement throughout the entire *Killing* series. To Serena Jones for helping the words-to-page process, and to John Sargent for guiding this book to the reader.

—BILL O'REILLY

To Eric Simonoff, Makeda Wubneh, and Bill O'Reilly—thanks so much for your wit, intellect, and insight. To my sons Devin, Connor, and Liam. And to the woman who inspires the work each and every day, my wife, Calene.

—MARTIN DUGARD

Illustration Credits

Maps by Gene Thorp and Kate Thorp

Index

Page numbers in *italics* refer to illustrations.

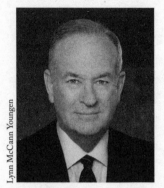

Lynn McCann Youngen

BILL O'REILLY is a trailblazing TV journalist who has experienced unprecedented success on cable news and in writing fifteen nationally bestselling nonfiction books. (There are currently more than seventeen million books in the Killing series in print.) Mr. O'Reilly does a daily podcast on BillOReilly.com. Also, his daily radio program, *The O'Reilly Update*, is heard on hundreds of stations across the country. He lives on Long Island.

Joe Latter

MARTIN DUGARD is the *New York Times* bestselling author of several books of history, among them the World War II epic *Taking Paris*, the Killing series, *Into Africa*, and *The Explorers*. He and his wife, Calene, live in Orange County, California.

READ THE REST OF
BILL O'REILLY'S
KILLING SERIES!

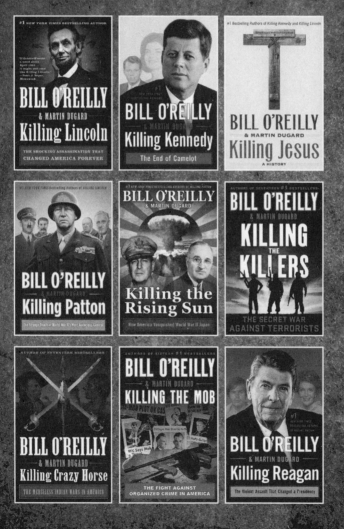